T0316714

Tourism Marketing for Small Businesses

Steven Pike

(G) Goodfellow Publishers Ltd

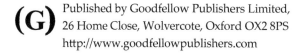

Published by Goodfellow Publishers Limited,
26 Home Close, Wolvercote, Oxford OX2 8PS
http://www.goodfellowpublishers.com

British Library Cataloguing in Publication Data: a catalogue record for this title is available from the British Library.

Library of Congress Catalog Card Number: on file.

ISBN: 978-1-911396-34-5

 Design and typesetting by P.K. McBride, www.macbride.org.uk

Cover design by Cylinder

Printed by Baker & Taylor, www.baker-taylor.com

Contents

Acknowledgements

With thanks to my 'inspirators' …

- my amazing children Jesse and Alexandra … arohanui (big love)…lel
- my father, Don (7/12/27 – 2/12/17)
- my travel gurus Le Cobbler and Fran…anni, amanti e bicchierie di vono non sono da contare
- my surreal collaborator Faye…next welcome, what to do?
- my gym buddies for the fun banter: Nerida, Angelique, Jo, Sean, Leesa, DJ Soji, Denise
- destinations…this book was written between November 2016 and December 2017 at a number of destinations…in order of visitation…Brisbane, Mackay, Madrid, Algarve, Dubai, Burleigh Heads, Paris, Southampton, Bath, Amsterdam, Sydney's Manly Beach, Rotorua, Auckland, London, Brighton.
- my charming editor Sally North

1 Introduction

Chapter outline

The term *tourism* is used in this book as a broad descriptor subsuming an array of activities, including travel, holidays, hospitality, lodging, recreation, events, entertainment and leisure. On the demand-side, the participants of tourism are referred to as travellers, tourists, vacationers, holidaymakers, daytrippers and visitors, and the tourism industry caters to a wide range of market segments and travel situations beyond holidays. Our *industry* represents around 10% of annual global economic activity, the majority in the form of *intangible services*. On the supply-side, around 99% of organisations catering to the needs of travellers are small to medium size businesses. These enterprises have different opportunities, challenges and constraints than the big brands, and operate in competitive markets with scarce resources. This chapter introduces the focus of the book, which is to explore how marketing principles can be applied by small tourism businesses and not-for-profit organisations engaged in *tourism*. A key theme throughout the book is the challenge of *differentiating* tourism services against competitors, offering similar features and benefits, in the minds of target consumers who are spoiled by choice. What is critical is the need for a *marketing orientation*, an outward and forward thinking philosophy dictating that all marketing decisions are made with the target consumer in mind.

Learning aims

To enhance your understanding of:

- the distinguishing characteristics of tourism services
- the challenge of differentiating tourism services
- the importance of a marketing orientation

Key terms

Tourism
Used as a generic descriptor, subsuming the many interrelated activities related to travel, holidays, hospitality, lodging, leisure, events, entertainment and recreation.

Differentiation
Standing out from competitors as being different, in the minds of consumers, on the basis of an attribute or benefit that is meaningful to them in the purchase situation.

Marketing orientation
An outward and forward thinking philosophy that dictates all marketing decision making is made with the interests of target consumers in mind.

A bridge between theory and practice

The aim of this book is to serve as a bridge between academic theory and industry practice, by exploring how marketing principles can be applied in the tourism industry. While academic theories can be used by large and small tourism businesses, this book provides a contemporary approach to formulating, implementing and monitoring marketing plans for small tourism businesses and not-for-profit enterprises (e.g, galleries and museums), which make up over 90% of our industry. The text draws on research from a number of fields, such as psychology, marketing, strategy, management, information technology and tourism, to present the practical relevance of academic theory. As someone who spent 20 years working in the tourism industry, and 20 years as a marketing academic, I appreciate how theory can inform effective industry practice, and vice versa.

The success of a small tourism business requires a hands-on entrepreneurial approach with a skill set not necessarily developed at a university. If you never went to university, and never read an academic journal, would you understand the value of academic research? Often, tourism entrepreneurs are actually implementing theories that they are not aware of, developed through experience or word of mouth advice from those who came before them. The business models commonly used by the management consulting firms, and discussed in business books and blogs, were all derived from theory, whether explicitly acknowledged or not. Therefore, the academic literature plays a major role in this book.

A global perspective has been adopted to highlight the commonality of challenges and opportunities facing small tourism businesses everywhere. Practical examples and cases from many different parts of the world are included. My years in the tourism industry included working as a tour guide, barman, travel agent, sales representative, tour wholesaler, and destination marketer. I was fortunate that these roles took me to many parts of the world. The more I have travelled, the more I have seen how tourism marketers everywhere face a commonality of challenges and opportunities. Much of my research as an academic has explored the practical challenges faced by tourism marketers, and I have published four books on destination marketing (see Pike 2004, 2008, 2010 and 2016). So, I bring to this book biases from my own travel experiences and from working in tourism as a practitioner and researcher for over 40 years. I lay no claim to being an expert, but rather as someone who appreciates both sides of the industry/academic divide, and in particular how marketing theory can be adopted by small tourism businesses and not-for-profit enterprises.

Critical point: A good theory is really practical!

A good theory provides a substantiated explanation of some aspect of our world. This explanation clearly and succinctly defines the key concepts involved, and the relationships between them, in a way that enables us to observe and measure, and make predictions about the outcome of future actions.

Readership

Tourism Marketing for Small Businesses is primarily designed for undergraduate students undertaking a degree or diploma in tourism and/or related disciplines such as travel, hospitality, recreation and leisure. Another audience of interest is students in business schools and creative arts programmes, where tourism is not the degree/diploma major. Given the scale and presence of the global tourism industry, many students heading for careers in public relations, advertising, digital communications, financial services, branding or business consulting are going to engage with tourism clients at some stage. Those students destined for roles with art galleries, museums, parks and gardens, local government, orchestras and events will benefit from an understanding of the nature of tourism marketing. It is also my hope the book will also be a useful reference for those already involved in the management and marketing of small tourism businesses and not-for-profit organisations.

Overall learning goals

The aim of *Tourism Marketing* is to explore how marketing principles can be applied by small businesses and not-for-profit organisations in the tourism industry. The key learning goals are to enhance understanding of:

- the challenge of differentiating tourism services
- a framework for tourism and travel marketing planning
- the role and importance of destination marketing organisations
- factors influencing tourism demand

- characteristics of consumer-traveller behaviour
- the role of marketing research in marketing decision making
- designing tourism services and experiences
- the role of branding
- pricing, packaging and distribution
- integrated marketing communications
- digital and social media opportunities
- visitor relationship management
- public relations and publicity
- marketing performance measurement.

Tourism and the visitor industry

The term *tourism* is used in the book as a broad descriptor of an industry catering to consumers engaged in *travel* from their place of residence to engage in *hospitality, leisure, entertainment* and *recreation* activities. Some historians (see for example Shaffer, 2001:11) have cited the Oxford Dictionary's explanation of the word *tour* originating from the Latin *tornus*, for a tool describing a circle. This is representative of a circular journey from home to a site, and returning home. Shaffer proposed *tour* first appeared in the English language in the 17th century. The term *vacation* also emanates from Latin, meaning to vacate this space, which includes both the physical and mental dimensions. While there exist different versions of etymology and original usage of these terms, the point here is that tourism can be used to broadly subsume many different types of travellers, travel situations, and travel activities. The book therefore adopts the term *tourism*, in the interests of parsimony, to represent a diversity of *travel situations*, such as: holidays/vacations, staycations, foodtripping, visiting friends and relatives (VFR), medical travel, dark tourism, cruising, pilgrimage, day trips, road trips, trekking, stopovers, events, entertainment, short break, business, special interest, international and domestic travel, education, sex and romance, volunteering and sports. However, rather than use the term *tourist*, which can have a derogatory meaning, as in the cases of 'tourist class' and 'bloody tourists', or be used in reference to large groups from overseas on organised tours, the terms *visitors, guests,* and *travellers* are more welcoming descriptors. In this regard, *visitor industry* is also an apt term.

Characteristics of tourism services

The majority of commercial activities in the tourism industry are in the form of *services*. It is important to recognise how the distinguishing characteristics of tourism services, relative to consumer *products*, have implications for the marketing planning process and the marketing mix. These key characteristics are:

■ intangibility, risk, and the critical role of consumer perceptions
■ the role of people
■ variability of service quality
■ perishability and seasonality
■ the social stage setting.

Intangibility, risk, and the critical role of consumer perceptions

Whereas consumer products can usually be inspected or trialled prior to purchase, this isn't possible for tourism services because they are *intangible*. The only physical evidence of a service we haven't previously experienced will be in the form of the information source, such as an advertisement, brochure, or friend's social media post. Therefore the customer's expectations can only be realised after purchasing and travelling to the service. There are two major implications of this. First, the lack of physical evidence means the consumer can only base their purchase decisions on the perceptions they hold in their mind about the alternative options. These perceptions might or might not be correct, but they will influence their decision making. The need to understand consumers' perceptions and how to influence them, is a major thread weaved throughout the book. For example, there is a range of tactical options for small tourism businesses to try and counter intangibility, including: promotion of any tourism or business awards won by the organisation or staff, promotion of any quality standards accreditation, promotion of a high consumer rating achieved from online communities, customer endorsement quotes, money back guarantee, virtual reality, celebrity endorsement, development of a photo/video opportunity, or offering a tangible memento of the experience such as a souvenir or small gift or certificate of achievement.

Industry insight: Tangiblising a bungy jump

Memorabilia, such as souvenirs, and photos/videos, are the most popular way to tangiblise an experience. The world's first commercial bungy jump operator, www.ajhackett.com, used this approach from the outset. One tactic was using black humour by asking customers to write their name on a morgue-type toe tag, which was used to build on the fear factor in the lead up to the jump. Customers got to keep the toe tag as a tangible memento of the experience. Another initiative the business used to good effect was the add-on sale of video footage of the customer's jump; which begins with footage of AJ Hackett's early publicity-building escapades, such as being arrested by police after illegally jumping off Paris' Eiffel Tower. The customers then become ambassadors for the brand when they show their friends their bravery via social media. Perceptions developed though this type of word of mouth have higher credibility than advertising by marketers.

The second consequence for the consumer when purchasing an intangible service is *perceived risk*, and so an important part of tourism marketing is managing perceptions of risk. There is a range of different types of perceived risks than can impact on tourism service purchase decisions:

- **Financial risk**. Will the experience represent good value for money? The bigger the investment, the greater the risk, and therefore a higher level of involvement in the information search.
- **Performance risk**. Will the service meet my expectations?
- **Physical risk**. Is there a risk of personal harm, if something goes wrong?
- **Psychological risk**. Is there a risk of social embarrassment? For example, when joining a group situation, such as a Contiki Tour of Europe for 18-35 year olds, there can be a risk of not being accepted by the cool kids.

Critical point: Tourism activities often represent discretionary spending

For many people, tourism purchases represent discretionary spending. That is, non-essential spending relative to indispensable budget items such as mortgage repayments, medical expenses, and children's education fees. A holiday might be a psychological necessity, but will often be a lower priority after budgeting for essential items. In this regard the tourism industry is competing with major consumer goods (e.g. cars, televisions, smart phones, etc) for this discretionary spending, and the marketing budgets of these brands (e.g. BMW, Sony, Apple, etc) are far bigger than that of 99% of travel and tourism brands. Also, discretionary spending is susceptible to external financial shocks that can occur periodically, such as a stock market crash, an interest rate rise or a currency devaluation.

The role of people

The tourism provider and the customer have traditionally been *inseparable* in the delivery of the tourism service, with production and consumption occurring more or less simultaneously. Service is viewed as an interactive process of doing something for someone, which is valued (Vargo & Lusch, 2004). One of the reasons tourism development is usually encouraged by government is that it is a labour intensive industry. People have been required to make tourism services happen, and this means jobs for the community. Also, in recent years, travellers have been seeking increasing involvement in tourism services, as participants rather than passive observers (Crouch, 2000; Pike & Page, 2014). Research reporting the concept of service dominant logic and applications in tourism marketing highlight a shift in thinking towards co-creation and co-production between service providers and visitors (Shaw et al., 2011).

While technological advances are leading to disruptions in the delivery of many tourism services, there will likely be limits to the extent that technology will replace human interaction, such as hotel robot concierges and driverless buses. In the short term *people* will continue to play a critical role in making most tourism services happen. This has implications, of course, for ensuring that the promises made to consumers in marketing communications are delivered consistently to customers, at realistic prices. For example a dining experience might represent a special occasion for the customer, but an ordinary day for the waiter. In many tourism service situations, the stars of the show are the serving staff, who are also the lowest paid and often working in stressful situations. So there is a trade-off between stimulating a great service culture and being able to afford to reward outstanding service. This is where the labour-intensive nature of tourism services can be a double-edged sword. For example, in Australia the issue of *penalty rates* for staff working on weekends and public holidays, sometimes up to double the standard hourly rate, means that hospitality businesses are forced to add a surcharge on some occasions. On public holidays, up to half of all restaurants in some areas stay closed because of the expense of higher wage rates, which can't always be realistically passed on to customers. The tourism industry in Australia has long argued penalty rates impact on Australia's competitiveness as a destination by contributing to making the country an expensive place to visit, by international standards.

Activity 1.1: A restaurant with no humans?

It is possible to design a restaurant experience that doesn't involve the customer interacting with any other humans. Imagine a restaurant where you make a reservation online and are given a pin code that you use to open the door when you arrive. The pin code activates beaded lights on the floor directing you to your private booth. The menu is displayed on an electronic device, with which you use to place your order. The meals are then delivered by some form of sushi train mechanism, via a hole in the wall. You end the experience by tapping your credit card or smart phone. Alternatively, insert a robot to any of these service delivery stages.

There are occasions when everyone likes a bit of solitude and privacy, but would there be sufficient demand for a restaurant to provide this? How interested would you be with such an experience? What are the potential advantages and disadvantages for customers?

Variability of service quality

The *inseparability* of tourism services also leads to the potential for *variability* in delivery. Travellers aren't a homogenous group all sharing the same needs, budgets, previous experiences and expectations. Therefore, perceptions of the quality of the service delivery can vary between customers. The same service person can vary their performance over the course of a shift or a week, depending on their own mood and energy, as well as the type of customer they are dealing with. Service delivery quality can also vary greatly between different staff. Even if we have previously enjoyed a particular tourism service, there is no guarantee the experience will be exactly the same next time, because of the role of people. Also, the service experience can vary for different customers who are all involved in the same service situation at the same time. For example, imagine a newlywed couple wanting a romantic honeymoon but finding themselves sharing a resort area with 20,000 high school graduates partying hard to celebrate their coming of age, an actual experience reported by the Gold Coast Bulletin (2012). Thus service quality is as interpreted by the individual guest during consumption.

Perishability and seasonality

A tourism service experience can't be stored for future use. Each day represents a new opportunity to sell the service capacity for that day only. Any unused capacity at the end of the day is considered perished because the potential cash flow has been lost. A major influence on perishability is *seasonality*. Seasonality represents fluctuations in demand over time, which can occur over the course of a day, a week, and between seasons during the year. Seasonality affects most tourism businesses, often in different ways. For example, hospitality businesses in capital cities are usually busy Monday to Friday when the government's politicians are attending parliamentary sessions, but then face a quiet weekend when the politicians and lobbyists have returned to their electorates. This is the opposite to winery destinations, which have busy weekends but quieter periods during the week. Some destinations are affected by seasonality more than others, particularly where climate plays a key role in attracting visitors such as ski or beach resorts. As is discussed in *Chapter 8 Pricing Tourism Services*, an implication of perishability and seasonality is the need for yield management, where pricing is flexible to match fluctuating demand levels.

The social stage setting

Many tourism services are performances acted out by suppliers and customers on a social stage (Crang, 1997). Whereas intangible services in many other sectors, such as financial services for example, take place in a private setting, travellers frequently share the experience with other guests. Issues that impact on appeal and satisfaction in this regard include: segregation of customer classes; congestion; experiences of the senses; making new friends; learning from others; and the behaviour of other guests.

The challenge of differentiating tourism services

Tourism is fiercely competitive, for two key reasons. First, in most markets there are low barriers to entry for small business start-ups. In free markets, there are no rules dictating how many competing businesses are permitted to operate, which is wonderful for entrepreneurs wanting to have a go with small family businesses. The financial reality is that in free markets the average return on investment for small tourism ventures is no more than the risk free bank interest rate. However, in some cases a tourism business might be a lifestyle choice, while in other cases it might be to create self-employment. Second, there is little if any legal protection from imitation of a good service idea. Really innovative tourism services emerge infrequently, and when they do they are quickly copied by competitors.

Industry insight: The demise of an innovative start-up low cost airline

In 1996 a small upstart airline, Kiwi Air, collapsed with debts of $8 million. The failure occurred even though the operation was cleverly addressing a much-needed gap in the New Zealand market for a low cost carrier, similar to those that had emerged in Europe and America, and targeting a new market of travellers. Having a great idea and a differentiated position in the market was not enough to save Kiwi Air from retaliation by the major carriers. Former Air New Zealand CEO Jim Scott had this to say on Kiwi Air's poor strategic planning, which lacked any tactics to deal with the retaliation:

"The message for new entrants is very clear – spend as much time on understanding the position and likely responses from your main competitors as you spend preparing your own strategy before you launch. Your ultimate success will depend at least as much on your own preparedness and ability to cover your competitors' responses as on the extent of your operating knowledge of the industry you are about to enter".

Substitutability

It is very difficult then, for small tourism businesses in particular, to gain a competitive edge in markets crowded with *me too* services, including larger corporate brands, offering similar features and benefits. This environment means that in so many purchase situations one tourism service brand is *substitutable* for another in the mind of the consumer. When brands are easily substitutable they are commodities that can only compete on price and volume.

Small business

Despite the dominance of big travel related corporations in the media and stock market, such as airlines, hotel chains and theme parks, the overwhelming majority of players in the travel industry are small businesses. Small and medium sized enterprises (SME) represent 99% of all businesses in the European Union (European Commission, 2017) and in the USA (Ward, 2017). Marketing of the big corporations is well covered in other tourism and hospitality text books. Small businesses can't follow the strategies of the big brands, when they don't have the same resources at their disposal. Reading cases about the successes of a major airline or hotel chain is not always going to be useful to the owner of a small business. That's why this book focuses on theory and practices of practical value to small ventures and not-for-profit organisations. While references are made to big brands in terms of their leadership on certain marketing concepts (e.g. Walt Disney as the leader in the tourism *experience* economy in *Chapter 6 Designing Tourism Services and Experiences*, no marketing tactics that are beyond the realm of implementation by small businesses are proposed.

Surprisingly, given the scale and economic importance of small businesses in tourism, there has been relatively limited research published by academic researchers. A major review of this literature in this under-researched field identified a lack of international agreement on the definition of small businesses in tourism, which makes comparative work across different parts of the world difficult (Thomas et al., 2011).

Resource scarcity and lean marketing

A key characteristic of small tourism firms, relative to the major brands, is resource scarcity. A *resource* is a tangible or intangible asset owned or controlled by the firm (Amit & Schoemaker, 1993). The resource-based view of the firm (Barney, 1991, 1996; Hamel & Prahalad, 1993) holds that it is the ability of the firm to maximise the effectiveness of the application of these resources that is the basis for competitive advantage. This underpins much of the discussion in *4: Tourism Marketing Planning* to enhance your understanding of how to identify which resources represent a potential source of competitive edge. Small tourism businesses are forced to compete in crowded markets with limited resources. *Lean marketing* is therefore a thread that is woven throughout the book.

Cooperating to compete

A key lean marketing theme in *Chapter 2 Destination Marketing Organisations* is developing a cooperative community approach to promoting the destination. Small tourism businesses have much to gain from working cooperatively, not only with the destination marketing organisation (DMO), but also with other local businesses by sharing promotional resources and creating a bigger impact in the marketplace than they could individually.

Case 1.1: Austin's Arts et Metier Hotel, Paris

Austin's Arts et Metier Hotel is a small 3-star bed and breakfast establishment with 31 rooms. The hotel is located in a quiet street in the heart of the Marais district in Paris, France. The hotel has an underground Metro rail station across the road, and is surrounded by licensed cafes. The historic Republique Square is only 500 metres walking distance, while Notre Dame Cathedral and the Latin Quarter are a comfortable two kilometre stroll away.

Most of the hotel's business is generated through listings with online travel agents, such as Hotels.com. During 2016 business at the hotel was down on the previous year. As with many other tourism organisations in Paris, the business was feeling the effects of a drop in international visitor arrivals that year. Although Paris is the second most visited city in the world, after London, visitors to the city in 2016 were down by over one million, due to the negative publicity surrounding a number of terrorist acts. This is an example of how the success of a tourism business is reliant to some extent on the competitiveness of the destination; and where a decline in business has been caused by events beyond the control of the hotel management.

Adjacent to the hotel is a unique higher education facility, the Conservatoire National des Arts et Metiers (Cnam) and the Musee des Arts et Metiers. The Musee des Arts et Metiers houses the oldest industrial and technological collection in the world. A product of the French revolution, the original Conservatoire des Arts et Metiers was founded in 1794 in what was a monastery that dated back to the 5th century. While the more famous Louvre was established to showcase the arts, the Musee des Arts et Metiers was dedicated to industrial technology. The museum's collection now includes over 8,000 machines, tools and scientific instruments dating back to the Renaissance. Among these are: Foucault's 1851 pendulum which was the first to be used to demonstrate the Earth's rotation on its axis; a 1:16 scale model of the Statue of Liberty, made by the French sculptor Auguste Bartholdi, who designed the monument that was inaugurated in New York in 1886; the world's first steam driven vehicle, built in 1770; and the Avion number 3, an 1890 flying machine. What makes the museum even more special is that it is part of a tertiary education institute, because the purpose of the original 1794 legislation establishing the conservatory was to educate workers in emerging technology to "improve the nation's industry, cultivate engineering methods, teach widely and illuminate ignorance". Cnam attracts both local and international students. The Director of the Museum, Professor Yves Winkin, regularly invites visiting academics and engineers to give seminars on the premises, and classes are taught within the museum building.

Discussion question

How could the hotel collaborate with nearby businesses, in a mutually beneficial way, to stimulate new customers?

Marketing orientation

The key challenge facing tourism businesses in the current competitive environment is to effectively cut through the clutter of competition and differentiate in the minds of consumers at the time a purchase choice is being considered. *A marketing orientation is an outward and forward thinking philosophy of making decisions with the needs of the target consumer in mind.* In general the tourism industry has been slow to evolve to this level of thinking (see for example Medlik & Middleton, 1973; Pike, 2008). Typically, industries evolve through four stages:

1   A *production orientation* is common when a new product category is developed and the level of demand exceeds available goods or services. This shortage creates a seller's market. The organisation's focus is on *current* and *internal* issues such as increasing output to meet demand, rather than on future market needs. Most of the tourism industry was at this stage until the 1950s.

2   A *sales orientation* takes over when there is increased imitation and competition, which leads to lower prices and the supply of goods or services exceeds the level of consumer demand. This is now a buyer's market, where the focus of the organisation is still internal, in the form of running sales promotions to sell the increased output. The development of passenger jet aircraft in the 1960s (e.g. Boeing 707) and 1970s (e.g. Boeing 747), and the resultant development of large hotel chains, stimulated the start of this stage in the tourism industry.

3   A *marketing orientation* is needed to cater for increasingly sophisticated consumers. Today's consumers are the most sophisticated in history, having been exposed to more marketing communications than any generation before them. We therefore don't believe everything we see in advertising, even if we noticed it in the first place. Therefore the organisation has to adopt an outward thinking approach about understanding the current and future needs of target consumers, and work on ways of communicating and delivering better value than rivals. Any sustained competitive edge necessitates having a marketing orientation; a philosophy of making all marketing decisions with target consumers in mind. A marketing orientation is easy to espouse, but it has been suggested that marketers in general have only applied the concept half-heartedly; and that rather than being customer-centric have actually been supplier ego-centric (Gummeson, 2008).

4   A further level of marketing evolution is manifesting as a *societal marketing orientation*. This is outward thinking and forward thinking, representative of a marketing orientation thinking about target consumers, but in a way that holistically takes into account the well-being of society and the environment. In this regard, Gummesson (2008) argued that a firm's stakeholders also contribute to perceived service value, and that there is a need to reorient marketing thinking from being customer-centric to balanced-centric, where the needs of stakeholders also need to be considered and satisfied.

Key points

1: The distinguishing characteristics of tourism services

The majority of commercial activities in the tourism industry are in the form of *services*. It is important to recognise how the distinguishing characteristics of tourism services, relative to consumer *products*, have implications for the marketing planning process and the marketing mix. These key characteristics are: intangibility, risk, and the critical role of consumer perceptions; the role of people; variability of service quality; perishability, seasonality, and the social stage setting.

2: The challenge of differentiating tourism services

The tourism industry is fiercely competitive. Most markets have low barriers to entry for small business start-ups, and there is little legal protection from imitation of a good service idea. It is very difficult then, for small tourism businesses to gain a competitive edge in markets crowded with services offering similar features benefits, among consumers who are spoilt by choice. In so many purchase situations one tourism service offering is easily *substitutable* for another.

3: The importance of a marketing orientation

Today's consumers are the most sophisticated in history, having been exposed to more marketing communications than any other generation in history. Tourism enterprises have to adopt an outward and forward thinking approach about understanding the current and future needs of target consumers, and work on ways of communicating and delivering value more effectively than rivals. Any sustained competitive edge necessitates having a marketing orientation, a philosophy of making all marketing decisions with target consumers in mind.

Discussion questions

1. Why does tourism represent discretionary spending for many consumers?

2. Why do consumers' perceptions play such an important role in tourism marketing?

3. Why is the role of people such an important factor in tourism?

References

Amit, R. & Schoemaker, P.J.H. (1993). Strategic assets and organisational rent. *Strategic Management Journal*, **14**: 33-46.

Barney, J. (1991). Firm resources and sustained competitive advantage. *Journal of Management,* **17** (1): 99-120.

Barney, J. (1996). *Gaining and Sustaining Competitive Advantage*. Reading, Massachusetts: Addison-Wesley.

Crang, P. (1997). Performing the tourist product. In Rojek, C., & Urry, J. (Eds). *Touring Cultures*. London: Routledge, pp. 137-154.

Crouch, G.I. (2000). Services research in destination marketing: a retrospective appraisal. *International Journal of Hospitality & Tourism Administration*, **1**(2) : 65-85.

European Commission. (2017). *What is an SME?* Accessed online at http://ec.europa.eu/ growth/smes/business-friendly-environment/sme-definition_en, 1/3/17.

Gold Coast Bulletin. (2012). Schoolies holiday shocker. *Gold Coast Bulletin*. pp. 1, 5.

Gummesson, E. (2008). Extending the service-dominant logic: from customer centricity to balanced centricity. *Journal of the Academy of Marketing Sciences*, **36**: 15-17.

Hamel, G. & Prahalad, C. K. (1989). Strategic intent. *Harvard Business Review*. May-June: 63-76.

Medlik, S. & Middleton, V. T. C. (1973). The tourist product and its marketing implications. *International Tourism Quarterly*, **3**: 28-35.

Pike, S. (2004). *Destination Marketing Organisations*. Oxford: Elsevier Science.

Pike, S. (2008). *Destination Marketing*. Burlington, MA: Butterworth-Heinemann.

Pike, S. (2009). Destination brand positions of a competitive set of near-home destinations. *Tourism Management*, **30**(6): 857-866.

Pike, S. (2010). *Marketing Turistickog Odredista*. Turizmoteka: Zagreb.

Pike, S. (2016). *Destination Marketing Essentials*. (2nd Ed). Abingdon, Oxon: Routledge.

Pike, S. & Page, S. (2014). Destination Marketing Organizations and destination marketing: A narrative analysis of the literature. *Tourism Management*, **1**:202-227.

Shaffer, M.S. (2001). *See America First: Tourism and National Identity, 1880-1940*. Washington: Smithsonian Institution Press.

Shaw, G., Williams, A. & Bailey, A. (2011). Aspects of service-dominant logic and its implications for tourism management: Examples from the hotel industry. *Tourism Management*, **32**(2): 207-214.

Thomas, R., Shaw, G. & Page, S. J. (2011). Understanding small firms in tourism: A perspective on research trends and challenges. *Tourism Management*, **32**(5): 963-976.

Vargo, S.L. & Lusch, R.F. (2004). Evolving to a new dominant logic for marketing. *Journal of Marketing*, **68**(January): 1-17.

Ward, S. (2017). SME definition. *The Balance*. 17 January. Accessed online at https:// www.thebalance.com/sme-small-to-medium-enterprise-definition-2947962, 1/3/17.

1

Appendix: Literature reviews

There are an estimated 150+ academic journals related to tourism research (see Goeldner, C.R. (2011). Reflecting on 50 years of the Journal of Travel Research. *Journal of Travel Research*, **50**(6): 583-586). Reviews of the academic literature related to key topics in the book are listed in Table 1.1.

Table 1.1: Literature reviews of key topics

Topic	References	Ch.
Small businesses in tourism	Thomas, R., Shaw, G. & Page, S. J. (2011). Understanding small firms in tourism: A perspective on research trends and challenges. *Tourism Management*, **32**(5): 963-976.	1
Destination marketing and the DMO	Pike, S. & Page, S. (2014). Destination Marketing Organizations and destination marketing: A narrative analysis of the literature. *Tourism Management*, **1**:202-227.	2
Destination image	Pike, S. (2002). Destination Image Analysis: A Review of 142 Papers from 1973-2000. *Tourism Management*, **23**(5): 541-549.	
	Pike, S. (2007). Destination image literature: 2001 – 2007. *Acta Turistica*. 19(2): 107-125.	
Consumer behaviour in tourism	Cohen, S.A., Prayag, G. & Moital, M. (2014). Consumer behaviour in tourism: Concepts, influences and opportunities. *Current Issues in Tourism*, **17**(10): 872-909.	3
Innovation in tourism	Hjalager, A.M. (2010). A review of innovation research in tourism. *Tourism Management*, **31**: 1-12.	6
HRM in tourism	Baum, T. (2007). Human resources in tourism: Still waiting for change. *Tourism Management*, **28**(6): 1383-1399.	
Destination branding	Pike, S. (2009). Destination brand positions of a competitive set of near-home destinations. *Tourism Management*, **30**(6): 857-866.	7
Social media in tourism	Leung, D., Law, R., van Hoof, H. & Buhalis, D. (2013). Social media in tourism and hospitality: A literature review. *Journal of Travel & Tourism Marketing*, **30**(1/2): 3-22.	10
Tourism eWOM (word of mouth)	Luo, Q. & Zhong, D. (2015). Using social network analysis to explain communication characteristics of travel-related electronic word-of-mouth on social media networking sites. *Tourism Management*, **46**: 274-282.	
Public relations (PR) in tourism	L'Etang, J., Falkheimer, J. & Lugo, J. (2007). Public relations and tourism : Critical reflections and a research agenda. *Public Relations Review*, **33**(1): 68-76.	11
Customer relationship management (CRM) in tourism	Maggon, M. & Chaudry, H. (2015). Revisiting relationship marketing and customer relationship management in leading tourism and hospitality journals: Research trends from 2001 to 2013. *Journal of Relationship Marketing*, **14**: 53-77.	12
	Rahimi, R., Koseoglu, M.A., Ersoy, A.B., & Okumus, F. (2017). Customer relationship management research in tourism and hospitality: A state-of-the-art. *Tourism Review*, **72**(2): 209-220.	

Books

Table 1.2 lists specialist books on the tourism marketing themes addressed in the book.

Table 1.2: Relevant books on specialist tourism marketing topics

Topic	References	Ch.
Destination marketing	Pike, S. (2004). *Destination Marketing Organisations.* Oxford: Elsevier Science. Pike, S. (2008). *Destination Marketing.* Burlington, MA: Butterworth-Heinemann. Pike, S. (2010). *Marketing Turistickog Odredista.* Turizmoteka: Zagreb. Pike, S. (2016). *Destination Marketing Essentials.* (2nd Ed). Abingdon, Oxon: Routledge.	2
Consumer behaviour in tourism	Horner, S. & Swarbrooke, J. (2016). *Consumer Behaviour in Tourism.* (3rd ed). London: Routledge Pearce, P.L. (2013). *The Social Psychology of Tourist Behaviour: International Series in Experimental Social Psychology (Volume 3).* Oxford: Pergamon Press.	3
Strategic planning in tourism	Tribe, J. (2016). *Strategy for Tourism.* (2nd Edition). Oxford: Goodfellow.	4
Tourism research	Nunkoo, R. (2017). *Handbook of Research Methods for Tourism and Hospitality Management.* Abingdon, Oxon: Edward Elgar Publishing. Brotherton, B. (2015). *Researching Hospitality and Tourism.* (2nd Edition). London: Sage.	5
Tourism service Talent management	Hudson, S. & Hudson, L. (2017). *Customer Service for Hospitality and Tourism.* (2nd Edition). Oxford: Goodfellow. Horner, S. (2017). *Talent Management in Hospitality and Tourism.* Oxford: Goodfellow Publishers Ltd.	6
Tourism pricing and revenue management	Burgess, C. (2014). *Essential Financial Techniques for Hospitality Managers.* Oxford: Goodfellow. Dopson, L.R., & Hayes, D.K. (2009). *Managerial Accounting for the Hospitality Industry.* Hoboken, NJ: John Wiley & Sons. Yeoman, I. & McMahon-Beattie, U. (2004). *Revenue Management and Pricing: Case Studies and Applications.* London: Thomson.	8
Social media in tourism	Sigala, M., Christou, E. & Gretzel, U. (2012). *Social Media in Travel, Tourism and Hospitality: Theory, Practice and Cases.* Farnham, Surrey: Ashgate Publishing.	10
Customer relationship management in tourism	Kumar, C. (2016). *Relationship Management in Hospitality & Tourism : A Professional Approach of RM for Hospitality and Tourism Professionals.* (Self published).	12
Tourism distribution	Buhalis, D. & Laws, E. (eds.). (2001). *Tourism Distribution Channels – Practices, Issues and Transformations.* London: Cengage Learning EMEA.	13

2 Destination Marketing Organisations

Chapter outline

The success of individual tourism businesses is reliant to some extent on the competitiveness of their destination. For any given travel situation, consumers are spoilt for choice of available destinations that offer similar features and benefits. Therefore the majority of destinations are substitutable in consumers' minds, and so becoming competitive, and staying competitive, is challenging. A key success factor is having an effective destination marketing organisation (DMO), the consequence of a community recognising the need to become organised to create a bigger impact in the marketplace than could be achieved by the efforts of individual businesses. The role of the DMO is to impartially coordinate the promotion of the destination, in a holistic manner that enhances economic and social benefits for the wider community. Individual tourism businesses need to understand how to take advantage of promotional opportunities presented by the DMO, and in doing so aid destination competitiveness through a cooperative community approach. Developing a mutually beneficial working relationship with the DMO necessitates stakeholders understanding the unique challenges and constraints facing destination marketers. Underpinning all of this is the need for government financial support, without which the DMO would struggle to survive. Long term funding is never a certainty, and so stakeholders should be able to debate the merits of government funding of their DMO with others in the community who might take the view that this is *subsidizing* the tourism industry.

Learning aims

To enhance your understanding of:

- the role of the DMO in enhancing destination competitiveness

- opportunities for small tourism businesses to work with the DMO

- key challenges faced by DMOs.

Key terms

Destination competitiveness

A competitive destination features an effective market position, an attractive environment, satisfactory visitor experiences, profitable tourism businesses, and supportive local residents.

Destination image

Images held by travellers of a destination are as important as the tangible attractions and services. Whether the travellers' perceptions are correct or not, they do influence travel planning decision making and therefore impact on the destination's competitiveness.

Destination marketing organisation (DMO)

A destination *marketing* organisation (DMO) coordinates the impartial and collaborative promotion of a geo-political boundary, in a holistic manner that enhances economic and social benefits for the wider community.

Destination competitiveness

The success of individual tourism businesses is reliant to some extent on the competitiveness of their destination (Pike, 2016). Travellers are spoilt by the choice of an almost unlimited number of destinations. However, the top 10 most visited countries in the world accounted for around 50% of all international air arrivals in 2017. This means the vast majority of the world's 193 countries (member states of the United Nations) are left to compete for the remaining 50% of travellers. At a domestic level, the situation is often even more competitive. In the USA for example, it has been estimated there are 20,000 cities, 3400 counties, 126 America's Byways and 12,800 National Historical Districts competing for visitors (Baker, 2007:16).

For any travel situation the competitive set of available destinations will offer similar features and benefits, and so the majority of places are substitutable in consumers' minds. That is, individuals can switch their preference for one destination to another, depending on which is perceived to offer the best value at decision time. Therefore, even the most successful destinations cannot take future potential visitation for granted. For example, Brisbane, with a population of around 2 million is the sub-tropical capital of the state of Queensland in Australia, where short break beach holidays by car are popular all year round. Brisbane residents take an average of three such holidays per year, and have a choice of over 100 beach destinations (e.g. Surfers Paradise, Byron Bay and Noosa) on offer within a comfortable drive (Pike, 2006).

There can be many contributing factors to the (un)competitiveness of a destination that are beyond the control of individual tourism businesses:

- Destination life-cycle
- Disasters and crises
- Government travel advisories
- Emergence of new types of competition
- Power of travel trade intermediaries
- Destination image.

Destination life-cycle

Just like commercial products and living things, destinations usually evolve through a life-cycle, from creation to growth to stagnation and eventually potential decline (Butler, 1980). The life-cycle stage of the destination attracts different types and numbers of travellers (Plog, 1974), and therefore presents differing opportunities and challenges for individual tourism businesses. During the development of a destination, competitiveness can seem illusory, as has been reported for Cambodia (Pich et al., 2016), sub-Saharan Africa (Kadel et al., 2011) and Jordan (Hazbun, 2000). Also, many cases of destinations at the stagnation or decline stages have been documented in the literature, including: Hamm, Germany (Buckly & Witt, 1985), Majorca, Spain (Morgan, 1991), Gold Coast, Australia (Faulkner, 2002), Atlantic City, USA (Cross & Walton, 2005), Rotorua, New Zealand (Pike, 2007a), and Blackpool, England (Clarke, 2008). For a more comprehensive list of destinations suffering a decline in competitiveness see Pike (2016:37). There have been far fewer studies published about destinations that have reversed the fortunes from an uncompetitive position (see for example Pritchard & Morgan, 1998; Gilmore, 2002), which is indicative of the challenge.

Disasters and crises

There have been many cases of disasters rendering destinations uncompetitive. How well the community is able to respond to a disaster will influence the degree of severity of the resultant crisis. For a review of 64 publications concerning post-disaster recovery at destinations see Mair et al. (2016). Such events can be a phenomenon of nature or man-made, and the diversity of disasters that have negatively affected a destination's success for years afterwards has included:

- 2012 earthquake in Christchurch, New Zealand (Lane, 2016)
- 2011 Fukushima nuclear disaster (Chew & Jahari, 2014)
- 2010 BP Gulf oil spill in the USA (Ritchie et al., 2014)
- Ongoing conflicts in Israel (Beirman, 2003, 2008)
- Civil war in Sri Lanka (Beirman (2003)
- 2001 September 11 attack on America (Goodrich, 2002)
- 1997/1998 Asian economic crisis (Henderson, 2002)
- Violent crime levels in in Florida (Pizam, 1999)
- decades of terrorism in Northern Ireland, referred to as 'the troubles' (Leslie, 1999)

A recent survey of tourism stakeholders in Australia found that tourism businesses perceived destinations did not adequately engage in disaster preparedness activities, which had implications for disaster response and recovery (Granville et al., 2016). This suggests businesses should be proactive in their local community by stimulating discussion about possible disaster situations and responses.

Industry insight : Tear gas, tanks and water cannons in Taksim Square, Istanbul

Delegates at the 8th Consumer Psychology in Tourism, Hospitality & Leisure Symposium held in Istanbul, Turkey during June 2013, experienced a destination disaster unfold first-hand. The conference hotel was located off Taksim Square, where one million protestors had assembled for a peaceful demonstration. The demonstration began a week earlier in response to the use of teargas by police to remove 50 environmentalists staging a sit-in to halt the demolition of Gezi Park. The Turkish government took a dim view of the protest and brought in the military to disperse the massive crowd with tear gas, rubber bullets and water cannons. The night I arrived I got to within 100 metres of the conference hotel, before being forced back by teargas. When I eventually made it to the hotel the next morning, I had no idea we would be forced to remain indoors for nearly three days due to the tanks and teargas immediately outside. The scale of the protest and the brutality of the military actions made media headlines around the world, although there was a media blackout imposed in Turkey. Considered to be the heart of the European side of Istanbul, Taksim Square is a popular tourism district and houses the city's central Metro station. The conference hotel manager advised us his property was facing an uncertain future given they were receiving cancellations for months ahead. Ironically, visitors to old part of Istanbul (Sultanahmet), just across the Bosphorous River from the Taksim Square district were unaffected. So those tourism businesses located in Sultanahmet, near famous sites such as the Blue Mosque, Grand Bazaar and Topkapi Palace were still trading during the unrest. The case is a useful example of how random unexpected events beyond the control of tourism businesses can have immediate negative impact, with lasting repercussions.

Government travel advisories

Governments have a moral obligation to update their citizens about international travel risks, commonly communicated via a travel advisory website (for example https://www.gov.uk/foreign-travel-advice). Negative travel advisories can have a damaging effect on a destination's popularity, such as reported in the cases of:

- Australian government advisories against travel to Bali (Sobocinska, 2011)
- World Health Organization travel advisories against travel to a number of destinations during the 2003 SARS outbreak (Hollingsworth et al., 2006)
- UK and USA government advisories against travel to Kenya (Opanga, 2003)

- UK and USA government advisories against travel to Caribbean destinations (de Albuquerque & McElroy, 1999)

Industry insight: Paris loses one million visitors in a year

"In the wake of the November 13, 2015 terrorist attacks in Paris and continued threats against France and Europe detailed in the Department's Worldwide Caution, we strongly urge U.S. citizens to maintain a high level of vigilance, be aware of local events, and take appropriate steps to bolster their personal security. Authorities believe the likelihood of terror attacks in Europe will continue as European members of ISIL return from Syria and Iraq".

This was the travel advisory posted by the U.S. Embassy in Paris on November 15, 2015. With many countries posting similar warnings to their citizens, following this and other terrorist attacks in the region, it was not surprising to see international visitor arrivals decrease in 2015 and 2016. Though Paris remained the second most visited city in the world, a decrease of one million visitors in a year had a major impact on local businesses, and a negative flow-on effect in the regions (Office du Tourisme et des Congrés, 2015).

Emergence of new types of competitors

The 1970s' emergence of Mediterranean sun and sea destinations, made more accessible by the arrival of low cost air carriers, eventually led to the demise of traditional British seaside resorts such as Blackpool (Clarke, 2008). More recently in Australia, many of the once popular island resorts along Queensland's Great Barrier Reef have closed, due to the emergence of much cheaper alternatives in Asia, such as Bali and Vietnam, which have become more accessible through the advent of low cost air carriers. Cruise ships have emerged as serious competition for destinations, with an estimated 25.3 million annual cruise passengers worldwide by 2019 (http://www.statista.com/statistics/270605/cruise-passengers-worldwide/).

Power of travel trade intermediaries

Sun and sea resort destinations, which are highly substitutable, are at the mercy of a relatively small number of international tour wholesalers and low cost airlines that control the flow of multitudes of package tourists. In the case of Alanya in the Turkish Mediterranean, the effect of the destination's lack of control over visitor traffic was such that the area's major hotels have been forced to close for the three months of the winter off-season (Okumus & Karamustafa, 2005; Pike 2016:294-295). The flow-on effects of this were felt throughout the local community, from shopkeepers in the bazaar to local produce growers. Similarly, the Algarve region in Portugal has become increasingly reliant on European low cost air carriers in recent years, to the extent that the winter off season is exacerbated when these carriers cut the number of services during winter.

Destination image

The topic of destination image is one of the most popular in the tourism literature. For a list of 262 destination image studies published between 1973 and 2007,
see Pike (2002, 2007a). The reason for the ongoing interest in this topic is the
proposition that the images held by travellers are as important as the tangible
attractions and services. Whether the travellers' perceptions are correct or not,
they do influence travel planning decision making and can therefore impact on
the competitiveness of the destination. Since positive destination image change
occurs only slowly over time (Pike et al., 2016; Pike, 2017), it is in the interests of
all stakeholders to ensure market perceptions are monitored regularly because a
decline in destination image can occur quickly, but take years to reverse.

Case 2.1: The rise, fall and resurgence of Rotorua's destination image

In a rather unique situation, Rotorua was developed as New Zealand's first international
tourism destination by that country's government. New Zealand established the world's
first national tourism office in 1901, and the focus was the development and management
of the new Rotorua township as a geothermal spa to rival the likes of Bath in England. The
New Zealand Department of Tourist & Health Resorts governed almost all aspects of the
town for 50 years, providing a level of support rarely afforded to any destination. Rotorua
was the flagship destination in all international promotion of New Zealand. The key
problem that would later slowly emerge was that Rotorua tourism stakeholders appear
to have taken this privileged position for granted. Rotorua suffered a spectacular fall from
grace, from the 1960s to the 1990s, through the gradual withdrawal of the government's
support and resources; and the fortunes of the destination were almost left to chance.
As a result, new and more competitive destinations such as Queenstown and Taupo
emerged, at a time when Rotorua's tourism infrastructure and tourism offerings declined
in quality, with little reinvestment. National media headlines during this era included:

- "Death of a tourist town"

- "The most squalid place in the country"

- "Rotorua losing its oomph"

- "Lake Rotorua is an unflushed toilet"

The combination of a decline in the quality of the Rotorua experience, and the resultant bad publicity, led to an increasingly negative image of the destination in the most
important domestic market and in the minds of influential travel trade intermediaries
serving international markets. In 1988 a crisis point was reached when the tourism industry forced the local government to finally recognise the significance of the decline in
Rotorua's reputation and the impact this was having on the wider community through
business closures, the highest unemployment rate in New Zealand, and increasing crime

levels. Tourism has always been Rotorua's most important industry and the leading source of revenue and jobs. The 1988 crisis was also in recognition of the low level of civic pride held by local residents.

Since 1988, major investments have been made by the local government in infrastructure and destination marketing, in the attempt to reverse the destination's image. These efforts have been successful in stimulating private sector investments and a gradual return to competitiveness. However, history does have a way of repeating, and so it will be interesting to monitor whether Rotorua's stakeholders allow the mistakes of the past to happen again.

Further reading

Pike (2007b), Pike, May and Bolton (2011)

Discussion question

How can a decline in destination image impact on local tourism businesses?

Destination marketing organisations

A competitive destination is one featuring an effective market position, an attractive environment, satisfactory visitor experiences, profitable tourism businesses, and supportive local residents (Pike, 2008:41). It is unlikely these will occur either by chance, or if left to local tourism businesses. A cooperative destination approach necessitates a champion with an impartial and holistic perspective, because if destination marketing was left to the local tourism industry, individual businesses would do what was best for their operation.

The establishment of a destination marketing organisation (DMO) is the result of a community becoming organised to be more competitive (Pike, 2016), and is defined as the entity officially recognised by stakeholders as being responsible for coordinating the tourism marketing communications for a geographic boundary. For practical reasons this is commonly a political boundary, rather than based on the traveller's perspective, as it is related to government funding of the DMO. Without government funding, DMOs would struggle to survive, and such funding comes with the caveat that it is used to benefit the community that provided the tax revenue.

Critical point: DMOs are NOT destination *management* organisations

A term sometimes used in reference to DMOs is destination *management* organisation. However, this a misnomer as few DMOs have the mandate or resources to manage their destination. The term therefore sets up false expectations of the nature of destination leadership able to be provided by the DMO, particularly during periods of crisis or economic downturn (Pike & Page, 2014). Usually the only element of the marketing mix the DMO has direct control over is promotion. Destination marketers rarely have control over other marketing functions such as new product development, pricing, distribution or quality of service delivery.

Cooperating to compete

The central role of the DMO is to coordinate the promotion of the destination, in a holistic manner that stimulates economic and social benefits for the wider community. The mantra *promote the destination first and your business second* can be difficult concept to grasp for new entrants in the tourism industry. Tourism is fiercely competitive between businesses within a destination. The main priority for any tourism business is to generate tomorrow's cash flow, in competition with rivals chasing the same visitor spending. However, working with local rivals to promote the destination in a cooperative manner can increase the competitiveness of the destination.

Lean marketing: Cooperative media advertising

The sales manager for a national newspaper came up with the simple idea for a destination to have a feature spread of three pages in the weekend edition. If the DMO would contribute 25% of the cost of a two-page advertisement, the newspaper sales manager would sell the remaining 75% of space to individual tourism businesses. The DMO would use the half a page of space to provide a generic destination message with a call to action. Businesses would all be offered the same coupon size space at a discounted price (e.g. $200), and were encouraged to promote an offer of some sort, the effectiveness of which could be tracked. If all space was sold, the newspaper would include an additional full page of travel editorial on the destination. Even the smallest tourism businesses were able to afford an advertisement, and the collective presence created a far greater impact than would the sum of the parts of individual businesses advertising separately.

DMO funding

The purpose of the DMO is to enhance destination competitiveness for the benefit of all stakeholders, including the host community. The main source of funding for DMOs is from government, either by way of an annual grant or through a bed tax or other levy. Other business sectors often regard this as a *subsidy* for the tourism industry. This negative public perception has at times resulted in the reduction or withdrawal of government funding for a DMO. Therefore it is important for anyone with a vested interest in the tourism industry to understand the arguments for and against government support for tourism. While detailed discussion about this argument can be found elsewhere (e.g. Piko 2016:59-67), the key benefit of a flourishing tourism industry is as an economic enabler. Tourism is labour-intensive, and visitor spending leads to job creation, with the resultant wider socio-cultural benefits for the community beyond tourism businesses. At every destination there is a multiplier effect of direct, indirect and induced spending that leads to direct, indirect and induced employment (e.g. Page & Connell, 2009: 385-402).

Categories of DMOs

There is no widely accepted definition of a *destination* (Pike & Page, 2014). From the consumer perspective a destination can be as diverse as a precinct, an island, a village, a city, a state, a country or a continent. However, as mentioned, from the tourism industry perspective the destination is usually representative of a geo-political boundary. There are five main categories of DMOs, which present differing types of collaborative opportunities for tourism businesses:

National tourism office (NTO)

The agency officially recognised as responsible for coordinating the tourism marketing for a country. Many nations also have a Ministry of Tourism (government department), which has a broader role in providing policy advice to the government on all issues relating to productive and sustainable tourism development that have implications for legislation relating to issues such as border controls, environmental impacts, employment conditions, land use zoning, and so on. The NTO and Ministry of Tourism work together closely on the development of the long term tourism strategy. The first NTO was set up in New Zealand in 1901 (NZTPD, 1976).

State tourism office (STO)

The agency officially recognised as responsible for coordinating the tourism marketing for a state (e.g. Hawaii Tourism Authority, USA), province (e.g. Ontario Tourism Marketing Partnership, Canada), or territory (e.g. Tourism Northern Territory, Australia) in a country with a federal political system. The first STO was established by Hawaii in 1903 (Choy, 1993).

Regional tourism office (RTO)

The agency officially recognised as responsible for coordinating the tourism marketing for a concentrated tourism area such as a city or town. There are variations in different parts the world such Convention and Visitors Bureau (CVB) and

Regional Tourism Board (RTB). The first official RTO is thought to be have been launched in Switzerland at St. Moritz in 1864 (Laesser, 2000), while the first CVBs opened in 1888 in the USA (Ford & Peeper, 2008).

Local tourism association (LTA)

Commonly a cooperative partnership of tourism stakeholders in a sub-destination within an RTO or STO boundary, such as a village or a precinct with a cluster of tourism-related businesses. Such entities might receive little if any government funding and rely on membership fees.

Macro-region tourism organisation (MTO)

Competing NTOs sometimes form a cooperative alliance with neighbouring countries to promote a macro region, such as the Scandinavian Tourism Board, Confederación de Organizaciones Turísticas de la America Latina, Caribbean Tourism Organization and the South Pacific Tourism Association. The first to be established was the European Travel Commission in 1948 (Pike, 2016).

DMO activities

As discussed, DMOs generally lack direct control over most aspects of the marketing mix other than promotion. The key activities of DMOs include the following, where the approach is to create a platform for individual businesses to take advantage of:

- Championing destination branding.
- Coordinating joint venture promotions with local stakeholders and travel trade intermediaries.
- Consumer and travel trade promotions.
- Coordinating the digital and social media presence for the destination.
- Public relations and publicity, such as a visiting media programme.
- Bidding for conferences, exhibitions and special events to be staged at the destination.
- Lobbying government agencies for funding and legislation supporting tourism growth and sustainability.
- Lobbying major airlines and other major transport operators (eg cruise lines) for increased capacity.
- Championing service quality programmes for local businesses.
- Promoting opportunities for new product development.
- At the RTO level, operating a visitor information centre.
- Providing networking opportunities for stakeholders, such as information sharing seminars.
- Undertaking marketing research, and monitoring destination performance metrics such as visitor arrivals, length of stay, spending, and satisfaction.

Unique challenges faced by the DMO

Many tourism businesses benefit from engaging with their DMO. A mutually beneficial working relationship requires both parties to understand the goals of the other. For example, DMO staff should understand that tourism businesses operate in a competitive markets where some information is commercially sensitive, and that they are focused on generating profit. On the other hand tourism operators need to understand that DMO staff are concerned with generating wider community benefits and/or business opportunities for financial members, and should not expect preferential treatment.

Destination marketers face a unique set of challenges not faced by other organisations. To develop an effective working relationship with the DMO means stakeholders need an understanding of:

- Over-reliance on government funding
- Destination branding complexity
- Politics of DMO decision making
- Measuring DMO performance.

Over-reliance on government funding

DMOs have an over-reliance on government funding, without which they would struggle to survive. DMOs do not take government backing for granted, and also understand they might not be guaranteed such funding over the longer term. At a national level for example, in 2014 Brand USA received federal government support only until 2020, at which time the Travel Promotion Act might or might not be re-enacted. At a state level, the government of Queensland in 2016 confirmed funding for the STO for four more years, which does not provide long term certainty. The negative impacts of such funding cuts have been reported in the cases of Maine, Colorado and Illinois, USA (Bonham & Mak, 1996; Bolson, 2005), Waikato in New Zealand (Coventry, 2006), the UK (Hays et al., 2013), Greece (Trihas et al., 2013), Portugal (Oliveira & Panyak, 2015), and Italy (Reinhold et al., 2015).

Industry insight: Colorado visitor numbers drop following withdrawal of government funding for the STO

The Colorado state government de-established the state's DMO in 1993, making it the only American state without an STO. Tourism was Colorado's second largest industry at this time, worth over US$6 billion per annum. There was a dramatic impact of the withdrawal of funding for Colorado's destination marketing, with pleasure travellers dropping 10% the following year. Colorado's share of domestic pleasure travel declined 30% between 1993 and 1997.

Destination branding complexity

Destination branding is complex, and for a detailed discussion on ten key issues in this regard see Pike (2005, 2016:193-195). The DMO must somehow develop a *succinct* and *propositional* slogan that encapsulates the *sense of place* in a way that is *meaningful* to the target market, effectively *differentiates* against rival places offering similar benefits, and *represents* the interests of stakeholders. The brand proposition must be *truthful*, since the DMO has no control over the actual delivery of the brand promise by local businesses and the host community. What is also critical is that the brand is seen as a long term investment that serves as an umbrella brand for individual tourism businesses to incorporate in their own marketing collateral. Destination marketers and stakeholders must resist the urge to regularly change the theme, due to the length of time it takes to gain traction in the market.

Activity 2.1: What's the destination slogan?

Without using Google, draw an arrow between each of these destinations and the corresponding brand slogan you think has recently been used by that destination.

Las Vegas	100% pure
New Zealand	There's nowhere like…..
New York	I ♥ …
Scotland	What happens here, stays here
Australia	Dream big
California	A spirit of its own

After checking your responses, discuss why you recognised the brand slogan(s) and not the others.

Politics of DMO decision making

Governments provide DMOs with funding to stimulate economic and social benefits for the wider community, and thus governance of DMOs requires impartiality. However, the structure of most DMOs as public-private partnerships or qangos, means that governance also features a majority of private sector tourism business representatives on the board of directors. Anyone who has worked for a DMO understands that politics in DMO decision making is unavoidable, given that the vested interests of such diverse stakeholders as government bureaucrats, tourism businesses, travel intermediaries, developers, host community, and conservationists will not always converge. After all, politics is about "the striving for power, and power is about who gets what, when and how in the political and administrative system and in the tourism sector" (Elliott, 1997:10). Politics has potential to undermine both the effectiveness of the DMO, along with perceptions of fairness by stakeholders.

Activity 2.2: Funding decision

Place yourself in the shoes of a marketing manager for a small RTO that has limited resources funded by the local government. The owner of one of the largest visitor attractions has met with you and offered a substantial amount of funding for the RTO on a monthly basis, with the proviso that their business has first rights to feature in all future promotional activity. For example, when the RTO hosts a visiting travel writer, the attraction must be included in their itinerary. The business owner argues this is a win/win situation because the destination will benefit from having more RTO funding, and since the largest tourism businesses employ more staff and spend more in the community, they should feature a lot more than small businesses in RTO promotions. What is your response?

Measuring DMO performance

Since the destination marketing literature commenced in 1973 there has been a lack of research that addresses the question "to what extent are DMOs responsible for increases in visitor arrivals, length of stay, spending and other performance metrics" (Pike & Page, 2014:211). The central problem is the difficulty in isolating cause and effect relationships for key destination performance metrics such as visitor arrivals, length of stay, and spending; and isolating the effect of extraneous variables such as: user-generated content on social media; economic factors in source markets, including exchange rates and interest rates; travel intermediaries' activities; other stakeholders' promotional activities; special events, the media; the weather, and so forth. Given increasing pressure on governments to defend public spending on non-essential services, the lack of ability to precisely demonstrate the market impact specifically caused by the DMO will inhibit future government funding consideration.

Opportunities for small businesses to work with the DMO

There are many ways for individual business operators to get involved with their DMO, for mutual benefit. Working with the DMO presents increased opportunities for networking, information gathering and market exposure. A summary of examples is listed in Table 2.1.

Table 2.1: Opportunities to work with the DMO

DMO activity	Description	Example
Industry briefings	Seminars to update stakeholders on key markets and campaign strategies.	Visit Britain (www.visitbritain.org) organises annualseminars. Enter 'seminar' in the NTO website search box for the latest.
Newsletter	Subscription to free monthly email newsletter about topical issues related to the destination	Quebec City and Area provides an archive of previous newsletters (www.quebecregion. com/en/travel-trade/services/travel-news-archives/)
Product database	A digital database of local tourism information, enabling businesses to list their services	The Australian Tourism Data Warehouse (www.atdw.au) has over 40,000 product listings, which are freely accessible for travel wholesalers, retailers and other distributors.
Digital library	A collection of story angles and high quality images and videos for free use by the travel trade and media to promote the destination.	Tourism New Zealand's Visual Library (http://visuals.newzealand.com/#/)
Visiting media program	Targeting media with story ideas and hosting visiting media on familiarisation visits, requires input of story ideas and hosting of media crews.	NYC & Company (http://www. nycandcompany.org/press)
Social media program	Contributing images and news to the DMO's conversations on platforms such Facebook, Twitter and Instagram, WeChat and Sina Weibo.	Visit Sweden's digital media strategy (http:// corporate.visitsweden.com/vart-uppdrag/vara-prioriteringar/417-2/)
Educating travel agents	Training programme for travel agents and wholesalers specialising in the destination.	Tourism Ireland's Ireland Specialists programme (www.irelandspecialists.com/)
Travel trade events and exhibitions	Participation in consumer travel expos, trade expos, and travel industry exchanges.	America's IPW travel trade exchange (https://www.ipw.com/)
Contra prizes	DMO partnering with a television or radio network to offer a competition for consumers with travel prize to the destination.	
Cooperative advertising	Umbrella consumer advertising campaign offering individual businesses the chance to participate in a collective campaign.	RTOs have commonly used this approach in newspaper features for example (see Lean marketing 2.1).
Destination branding collateral	Using the DMO's destination brand style guide to incorporate the destination brand into individual business' marketing	Cumbria Tourism's destination brand guidelines (www.cumbriatourism.org/wp-content/uploads/2015/07/brand-guidelines.pdf)
URL link	Opportunity to support the destination by providing a URL link to the official destination website.	Visit Florida provides instructions on how to provide a link to the STO website on stakeholders' websites. (www.visitflorida. com/en-us/link-to-us.html)

Key points

1: The role of the DMO in enhancing destination competitiveness
The success of individual tourism businesses is reliant to some extent on the competitiveness of their destination. For any given travel situation, consumers are spoilt by the choice of available destinations that offer similar features, and so most places are substitutable in consumers' minds. A critical success factor is having an effective DMO.

2: Opportunities for small businesses to work with the DMO
A DMO is the consequence of a community becoming organised to create a bigger impact in the marketplace than could be achieved by the efforts of individual businesses. The central role of the DMO is to coordinate the promotion of the destination, in a holistic manner that provides economic and social benefits for the wider community. It is important for individual tourism businesses to understand how take advantage of promotional opportunities presented by their DMO, and in doing so help to enhance destination competitiveness through a cooperative community.

3: Key challenges faced by DMOs
To enhance the prospects of developing a mutually beneficial working relationship with their DMO necessitates stakeholders understanding the unique challenges facing DMOs. Underpinning all of this is the need for government financial support, without which the DMO would struggle to survive; which in turn can impact on destination competitiveness and therefore the success of individual businesses. Since long term funding is not certain, stakeholders should to be able to debate the merits of government funding of their DMO with those who take the view that this is *subsidizing* the tourism industry.

Discussion questions

1. What is meant by the mantra: *promote the destination first, and your business second?*

2. Why is it important for local tourism businesses to understand key challenges faced by their DMO?

3. Why are DMOs so reliant on government funding?

Further reading

Pike, S. (2004). *Destination Marketing Organisations*. Oxford: Elsevier Science.

References

Baker, B. (2007). *Destination Branding for Small Cities: The Essentials for Successful Place Branding*. Portland, Oregon: Creative Leap Books.

Beirman, D. (2003). *Restoring Destinations in Crisis*. Crows Nest, NSW: Allen & Unwin.

Beirman, D. (2008). Israel tourism's marketing recovery 2001-July 2006. In S. Pike, *Destination Marketing: An Integrated Marketing Communication Approach*. Oxford: Butterworth-Heinemann. pp. 321-325.

Bolson, F. (2005). Alliances. In Harrill, R. (Ed). *Fundamentals of Destination Management and Marketing*. Washington: IACVB. pp. 219-228.

Bonham, C. & Mak, J. (1996). Private versus public financing of state destination promotion. *Journal of Travel Research*. Fall: 3-10.

Buckley, P. J. & Witt, S. F. (1985). Tourism in difficult areas: case studies of Bradford, Bristol, Glasgow and Hamm. *Tourism Management*. **6**(3): 205-213.

Butler, R.W. (1980). The concept of a tourist area cycle of evolution: implications for management of resources. *Canadian Geographer*. **24**(1): 5-12.

Chew, E.Y.T. & Jahari, S.A. (2014). Destination image as a mediator between perceived risks and revisit intention: A case of post-disaster Japan. *Tourism Management*. 40 (February): 382-393.

Choy, D.J.L. (1993) Alternative roles of national tourism organizations. *Tourism Management*. 14(5): 357-365.

Clarke, J. (2008). Blackpool's next 'resort cycle' stage: Rejuvenation or decline? In S. Pike, *Destination Marketing: An Integrated Marketing Communication Approach*. Oxford: Butterworth-Heinemann, pp. 321-325.

Coventry, N. (2006). *Inside Tourism*. 621. December 1.

Cross, G.S. & Walton, J.K. (2005). *The Playful Crowd – Pleasure Places in the Twentieth Century*. New York: Columbia University Press.

de Albuquerque, K. & McElroy, J. (1999). Tourism and crime in the Caribbean. *Annals of Tourism Research*. **26**(4): 968-984.

Elliott, J. (1997). *Tourism - Politics and Public Sector Management*. London: Routledge

Faulkner, B. (2002). *Rejuvenating a Maturing Destination – The Case of the Gold Coast*. Altona, Vic: Common Ground Publishing.

Ford, R.C. & Peeper, W.C. (2008). *Managing Destination Marketing Organizations*. Orlando: ForPer Publications.

Gilmore, F. (2002). Branding for success. In Morgan, N., Pritchard, A. & Pride, R. (Eds). *Destination Branding: Creating the unique Destination Proposition*. 57-65.

Goodrich, J. (2002). September 11, 2001 attack on America: A record of immediate impacts and reactions in the USA travel and tourism industry. *Tourism Management*. 23: 573-580.

Granville, F., Mehta, A. & Pike, S. (2016). Destinations, disasters and public relations: Stakeholder engagement in multi-phase disaster management. *Journal of Hospitality and Tourism Management*. 28: 73-79.

Henderson, J. (2002). Managing a tourism crisis in Southeast Asia: The role of national tourism organisations. *International Journal of Hospitality & Tourism Administration*, **3**(1): 85-105.

Hazbun, W. (2000). Enclave orientalism: the state, tourism, and the politics of post-national development in the Arab world. In In Robinson, M., Evans, N., Long, P. Sharpley, R.,& Swarbrooke, J. (Eds). *Management, Marketing and the Political Economy of Travel and Tourism*. Sunderland: The Centre for Travel & Tourism, pp.191-205.

Hays, S., Page, S.J. & Buhalis, D. (2013) Social media as a destination marketing tool: its use by national tourism organisations. *Current Issues in Tourism.* **16**(3): 211-239.

Hollingsworth, T.D., Ferguson, N.M. & Anderson, R.M. (2006). Will travel restrictions control the international spread of pandemic influenza? *Nature Medicine*, **12**:497- 499.

Kadel, R., Rodl, M. & Wollenzien, T. (2011). Tourism tackles poverty – A case study of Africa. In Conrady, R. & Muck, M. (Eds). *Trends and Issues in Global Tourism 2011.* Heidelberg: Springer-Verlag.

Laesser, C. (2000). Implementing destination-structures: experiences with Swiss cases. In Manete, M. & Cerato, M. (Eds) *From Destination to Destination Marketing and Management*. Venice: CISET. 111-126.

Lane, A. (2016). Tours to Christchurch's earthquake Red Zone. In Pike, S. *Destination Marketing Essentials*. (2nd Ed). Abingdon, Oxon: Routledge. pp. 155-156.

Leslie, D. (1999). Terrorism and tourism: the Northern Ireland situation - a look behind the veil of certainty. *Journal of Travel Research.* **38**: 37-40.

Mair, J., Ritchie, B.W. & Walters, G. (2016). Towards a research agenda for post-disaster and post-crisis recovery strategies for tourist destinations: a narrative review. *Current Issues in Tourism.* **19**(1): 1-26.

Morgan, M. (1991). Dressing up to survive - marketing Majorca anew. *Tourism Management.* March: 15-20.

NZTPD. (1976). *75 Years of Tourism*. Wellington: New Zealand Tourist & Publicity Department.

Office du Tourisme et des Congrés. (2015). *Le Tourisme* à Paris *Chiffres clé*s. Accessed online at www.parisinfo.com, 16/1/17.

Okumus, F. & Karamustafa, K. (2005). Impact of an economic crisis – evidence from Turkey. *Annals of Tourism Research.* **32**(4): 942-961.

Oliveira, E. & Panyik, E. (2015). Content, context and co-creation: Digital challenges in destination branding with references to Portugal as a tourist destination. *Journal of Vacation Marketing.* **21**(1): 53-74.

Opanga, K. (2003). *Kenya suffers for the US and because of America*. 24 June. Available at: www.eTurboNews.com.

Page, S. & Connell, J. (2009). *Tourism: A Modern Synthesis*. (3rd Edition). Andover, Hampshire: Cengage.

Pich, P., Cheab, P., Phoem, M. & Sok, P. (2016). Cambodia, an add-on destination. In Pike, S. *Destination Marketing Essentials*. (2nd Ed). Abingdon: Routledge. pp. 38-39.

Pike, S. (2002). Destination image analysis: A review of 142 Papers from 1973-2000. *Tourism Management,* **23**(5): 541-549.

Pike, S. (2005). Tourism destination branding complexity. *Journal of Product & Brand Management,* **14**(4): 258-9.

Pike, S. (2006). Destination decision sets: A longitudinal comparison of stated destination preferences and actual travel. *Journal of Vacation Marketing,* **12**(4): 319-328.

Pike, S. (2007a). Destination image literature: 2001 – 2007. *Acta Turistica,* **19**(2): 107-125.

Pike, S. (2007b). A cautionary tale of a resort destination's self-inflicted crisis. *Journal of Travel & Tourism Marketing,* **23**(2/3/4): 73-82.

Pike, S. (2008). *Destination Marketing.* Burlington, MA: Butterworth-Heinemann.

Pike, S. (2016). *Destination Marketing Essentials.* (2nd Ed). Abingdon, Oxon: Routledge.

Pike, S. (2017). Destination image temporality – Tracking perceived strengths and weaknesses over time. *Journal of Hospitality & Tourism Management,* **31**: 126-133.

Pike, S., Gentle, J., Kelly, L. & Beatson, A. (2016). Tracking brand positioning for an emerging destination during the advent of the social media era: 2003 to 2015. *Tourism and Hospitality Research.* (In press).

Pike, S., May, T. & Bolton, R. (2011). RTO governance: Reflections from a former marketing team. *Journal of Travel & Tourism Research.* Fall: 117-133.

Pike, S. & Page, S. (2014). Destination Marketing Organizations and destination marketing: A narrative analysis of the literature. *Tourism Management.* **41**:202- 227.

Pizam, A. (1999). A comprehensive approach to classifying acts of crime and violence at tourism destinations. *Journal of Travel Research.* **38**: 5-12.

Plog, S.T. (1974). Why destination areas rise and fall in popularity. *The Cornell HRA Quarterly.* **14**(4): 55-58.

Pritchard, A. & Morgan, N. (1998). Mood marketing - the new destination branding strategy: a case of Wales the brand. *Journal of Vacation Marketing.* **4**(3): 215- 29.

Reinhold, S., Laesser, C. & Beritelli, P. (2015). 2014 St. Gallen consensus on destination management. *Journal of Destination Marketing & Management.* **4**(2): 137-142.

Ritchie, B,W., Crotts, J.C., Zehrer, A. & Volsky, G.T. (2014). Understanding the effects of a tourism crisis: The impact of the BP oil spill on regional lodging demand. *Journal of Travel Research.* **53**(1): 12-25.

Sobocinska, A. (2011). Innocence lost and regained: Tourism to Bali and Australian perceptions of Asia. *History Australia.* **8**(2): 199-222.

Trihas, N., Perakakis, E., Venitourakis, M., Mastorakis, G. & Kopanakis, I. (2013). Social media as a marketing tool for tourism destinations: The case of Greek municipalities. *Journal of Marketing Vistas.* **3**(2): 38-48.

3 Tourism Consumer Behaviour

Chapter outline

A marketing orientation dictates all decisions are made with the interests of target consumers in mind. Consumer behaviour is the most important and complex issue faced
by marketers. Attempting to understand the needs, motivations and decision making
processes (*the why of buy*) of unique individuals in mass markets, is central to the development, implementation and evaluation of marketing activities. The chapter presents
concepts about consumer behaviour that have practical implications for small tourism
businesses. A five-stage model of tourism consumer behaviour is presented, commencing with the recognition of a need or want by an individual, leading to purchase decision
making, anticipation and expectations, travel and on-site experiences and satisfaction,
and culminating in post-trip reflections. This process is influenced by a range of internal
and external forces. The main external influences discussed are destination attractiveness, culture and societal norms, and social networks. Key internal influences presented
are individual consumers' demographics, perceptions, travel experience, personality, personal values, travel context and motivation. These personal characteristics are not static
over time, since we re-arrange our thinking and attitudes over a lifetime as we learn from
our travel experiences.

Learning aims

To enhance your understanding of:

■ Consumer behaviour as central to the development, implementation and evaluation
of tourism marketing activities.

■ A model of consumer behaviour in tourism.

■ The key internal and external influences on an individual's tourism buying behaviour.

Key terms

Consumer

The term is used to encapsulate existing customers, potential customers, and non-customers (those who have chosen to not purchase our service).

Needs, wants and demand

A *need* is something an individual has to have to satisfy a felt state of deprivation (e.g. a drink to quench a thirst), and a *want* is how an individual communicates a need (e.g. a green tea). A want plus buying power represents *demand*.

Motivation

Motivation for a tourism experience represents a *want* arising that can't be met at home. This should not be confused with the reason for the travel experience, such as 'to visit friends and relatives'. Tourism motivations can be physiological (e.g. relaxation), psychological (e.g. break from routine) or intellectual (e.g. to learn); and they generally relate to pleasure seeking, self-improvement or spirituality.

Introduction

A core theme throughout the book is that a marketing orientation, which is essential in the pursuit of a competitive edge in overcrowded markets, dictates all decisions are made with the interests of *target consumers* in mind. The term *consumer* is used to encapsulate existing customers, potential customers, and non-customers (those who have chosen to not to purchase our service). Theories on human behaviour are well established, and based on over a century of research in the psychology literature. However, while entire books disseminate the implications of such theories in the marketing context (e.g. Solomon, 2017) the study of consumer behaviour is not an exact science. We attempt to understand the minds and behaviour of unique individuals in mass markets. It is worth remembering the words of British philosopher Emerson Pugh who suggested that if the human mind was simple enough to understand, we would be too simple to understand it!

For an extensive review of the tourism consumer behaviour literature see Cohen et al. (2014). This chapter focuses on those aspects of buyer behaviour likely to be of practical relevance to marketers of small tourism businesses. The concepts introduced in the chapter underpin much of the discussion in other chapters.

While every human is a unique individual, in many aspects of tourism there will be a shared commonality of needs, motivations and behaviour. A model of consumer behaviour in tourism is presented in Figure 3.1, where there are five key stages in a tourism experience.

1 Needs and wants recognition

2 Purchase decision making

3 Anticipation and expectations

4 Travel to the service location/On-site experiences/Return travel

5 Post-trip satisfaction, memories and reflections.

The tourism experience commences with recognition of needs and wants, which are stimulated by a combination of external and internal influences. This model differs from that for many consumer goods products, where there might not be as much anticipation and/or return experience. Also, as can be seen, the consumer-traveller is not acting in isolation. Tourism is a communal activity, often acted out on a social stage. On one level the consumer becomes an influencer through sharing their experiences with other consumers and/or significant others in their personal life. On another level, the traveller creates impacts on society and the environment, through the travel consumption process and through encounters with service staff and interactions with fellow guests. For a comprehensive analysis of the wider implications of tourist consumption behaviour beyond the buying process see the work of Pearce (2013).

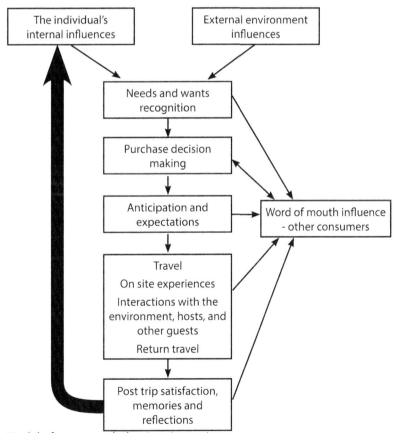

Figure 3.1: Model of consumer behaviour in tourism

External influences on consumer behaviour

There are a range of external forces influencing consumers' tourism behaviour. In *4: Tourism Marketing Planning Framework*, key macro environment forces, over which marketers have no control, but which impact either positively or negatively on overall tourism demand, are analysed by using the STEEPL framework: Socio-cultural, Technological, Economic, Environmental, Political, and Legislative. In this chapter, the key influences on an individual's tourism consumer behaviour of most interest to small businesses include:

- Destination attractiveness
- Culture and societal norms
- Social networks.

Destination attractiveness

There are three important issues in this regard.

1 As was discussed in *2: Destination Marketing Organisations*, the success of individual tourism businesses is reliant to some extent on the competitiveness of their destination. Destination attractiveness plays a major role in influencing travel decisions, due to the strong influence of consumers' perceptions (Pike 2016).

2 The destination lifecycle stage will attract different types of travellers and for different lengths of stay (Plog, 1974). For example, mature destinations will tend to attract short break holiday visitors rather than longer stays (Pike, 2002).

3 Many holiday decisions are made on the basis of the activity first (the *want*) and the destination second (Gilmore, 2002). For example, travellers on a sun and sea package often have low awareness of the destination to which they are travelling, since the package product deal was more important in the purchase decision than the actual destination.

Culture and societal norms

Other people in our community impact on our decision making, with the main social forces being: the values, ideas and attitudes within our *culture* and *sub-cultures* which provide reference points for societal norms of behaviour; the hierarchy of *social classes* in which we are positioned will dictate certain standards of expected behaviour; and *reference groups* to which we aspire to belong (or not!).

A recent phenomenon influencing tourism behaviour, particularly in affluent economies, is concern about ethical consumption (Cohen et al., 2014: 891): "For marketers, understanding the motivations and attitudes for ethical consumption offers opportunities to differentiate and position brands successfully". Consumers' purchase decisions are influenced by their own ethical concerns about consumption, and there is no doubt that in developed economies there is increasing pressure to conform to societal norms relating to issues such as the environment, consumption constraint, and fair working conditions for service staff. However, there has been a lack of tourism research about the main barrier to ethical consumption, which is the attitude-behaviour gap; while individuals might espouse positive consumption practices as being important to them, this is not reflected in their actual purchase decisions and consumption behaviour.

Social networks

The consumer-traveller is influenced by, and influences, other individuals. Humans are social animals and most have a supportive network of significant others, where there is a sharing of experiences. The influence of the social network on tourism behaviour has arguably never been so prominent as in the Web 2.0 era, where user-generated content on social media has exploded to the point where the mass and credibility of this organic information source now swamps that of the marketing communications of the tourism industry.

Internal influences on consumer-traveller behaviour

There is a complex array of internal factors influencing individuals in different ways. Issues relating to tourism buying behaviour discussed here are consumers' demographics, perceptions, personality, motivation, and the travel context.

Demographics

Demographics are the most observable population characteristics shaping consumer behaviour, and therefore form the starting point for most market segmentation approaches. Key demographic variables influencing consumer behaviour in tourism are:

- *Age*, where there will be differences in travel preferences between different age groups. As if understanding consumer behaviour is not complex enough, Pearce (2005) warns that what it means to be of any particular generation today (e.g. a teenager) is different to what it meant to the previous generation and will mean to future generations.

- *Family life-cycle stage*, where for example the role of children in influencing tourism decisions is an important consideration. There will clearly be differences in travel patterns and the decision making process between seniors with no dependent children and plenty of free time, and families with young children who are constrained by school and work schedules.

Industry insight: Grey nomads' outback touring app

Increasing life expectancy and length of retirement in affluent societies has led to a demand for longer duration travel services catering to seniors. In North America there is the *Snowbirds* market of over 55 year olds from colder regions who leave their homes for a three to five month period to spend subtropical winters at destinations such as Florida, Texas and California (Crompton et al., 1992). Similarly there are the phenomena of German seniors buying second homes in the Canary Islands (Breuer, 2005), and UK and Swiss elderly residents retiring to Spanish beach areas (Huber & O'Reilly, 2004). In Australia there is a large *grey nomad* market of retirees who purchase a motor home and spend around two years roaming around the continent (Hillman, 2013). Travel apps for smartphones and tablets, such as 'Outback Touring' (www.greynomadsapp.com.au), are now regarded as a necessity by grey nomads. Specifically tailored to suit the unique needs of these older travellers, the app is essentially a navigation tool, but goes beyond just touring maps, to including features such as social network forums with user-generated content as well as friendship requests, route sharing with family, options to avoid toll roads, and pet friendly camping grounds.

- *Place of residence*, where there will be difference in the type and level demand by variables such as nationality, country of residence, domestic versus foreign origin and market catchment areas. The environment in which we live will also shape our travel aspirations. There will often be differences in destination attractiveness between residents of large cities versus small rural towns, and between residents of polar/tundra climates versus tropical climates.

- *Gender*, including decision making roles within a relationship. Also, the sizeable markets of gay and lesbian travellers, and solo travellers has led to the emergence of specialist travel intermediaries and tourism businesses catering to their needs.

Other demographic variables that can influence consumer-traveller behaviour, but which are less directly observable, include occupation, income and education levels.

Perceptions

Our tourism buying behaviour is influenced by our perceptions. *Perceptions*, *beliefs*, *attitudes*, and *brand images* are used interchangeably to describe the internal views held by individuals about the world around them, including other people, brands and destinations. It is important to recognise the different meanings for the terms perceptions/images, beliefs and attitudes.

Types of perceptions/images – beliefs and attitudes

When considering the issue of brand image, it is important to consider the difference between an individual's beliefs and attitudes. *Beliefs* represent information held about a brand, otherwise referred to as knowledge, whereas an *attitude* is an evaluation of the object, or level of liking. Beliefs and attitudes form a hierarchy of three levels of perceptions: cognition, affect and conation.

■ *Cognition* is what is known about the brand, from organic and/or induced sources. This knowledge is about the brand's features, which are also known as functional attributes. For a cafe this might include features such as: an outdoor dining area, gluten free food options, opening hours, air conditioning, views, location, prices etc. Clearly an individual must be aware of the brand to have any cognitive image (beliefs/knowledge).

■ *Affect* represents feelings towards the brand, in the form of an attitudinal evaluation that will be positive, negative or neutral. For the café, examples of affect might include terms such as: 'fun atmosphere', 'friendly', 'trendy', 'old fashioned' etc. An individual should have some cognition of the business' tangible attributes to be able to develop any affective *attitude*.

■ *Conation* represents actions such as behavioural intent, based on the affective attitude toward the brand. For the café, this might result in (non)intent to (re) visit, and/or (non)intent to recommend the business to others.

Perceptions/image formation

Given the influence a consumer's perceptions have in decision making, of interest to marketers is understanding how such images are formed, to enable consideration of ways to influence them. There are two main sources of image formation, and the level of influence of the marketer varies greatly between the two.

Organic (natural) image formation occurs through an individual's everyday assimilation of sensory information. We are born with no perceptions. Apart from an innate need to explore our surroundings, every other motivation related to travel is learned from our own unique experiences. For instance, none of us was born with the need for status, which can manifest in *wants* for travel experiences that have brag value. Organic images are developed from exposure to a wide range of stimuli as we go through life, regardless of whether we are consciously thinking about a future purchase decision. As well as our own travel experiences, the diverse mediums from which we develop images of tourism destinations, for example, includes: media editorial, movies and television, word of mouth, school geography and history classes, fiction and non-fiction books, magazines, museums, art galleries, festivals and sporting events.

Induced (forced) image formation is stimulated through the efforts of marketers, where marketing communications are used in the attempt to *persuade* us to form desired images of brands. This is more likely to be effective when we are actively sourcing travel information. Organic images are more influential in overcoming intangibility and risk, because they are more credible than induced image sources. Today's consumers are the most sophisticated in history, having been exposed to more marketing communications than previous generations, and do not necessarily believe everything seen in advertising. Also, it is difficult to force people to change their minds through advertising.

Critical point: It is difficult to change people's perceptions

When it comes to beliefs and attitudes, most people are generally dogmatic. It is difficult to change an individual's perceptions, and so marketers should be aware of the challenge of this approach. The easiest route to the mind is to identify and reinforce already existing positive perceptions, rather than to try and correct a negative perception.

One of the major challenges (and opportunities) for marketers in the Web 2.0 era has been the rise of user-generated content (UGC) on social media, the mass of which now swamps the level of tourism advertising. For marketers it is worthwhile considering how there is a continuum of image information agents between overt induced and completely organic, as shown in Table 3.1.

Table 3.1: Image formation agents. Source: Adapted from Gartner (1993)

Agent category	Examples
Overt induced 1	Traditional advertising
Overt induced 2	Information sourced from a travel agent
Covert induced 1	Blatant celebrity endorsement on traditional advertising
Covert induced 2	Disguised celebrity endorsement through seemingly unbiased reports, such as mass media editorial articles or product placement
Autonomous	News editorial and popular culture such as movies and television shows
Unsolicited organic	Unsolicited information received from friends, such as social media posts
Solicited organic	Information solicited from friends
Completely organic	Actual experience, such as when travelling

Travel experience

British philosopher John Locke (1632-1704) noted that when we are born our mind is like a blank canvas; we have no innate ideas (Levene, 2013). At first, we start developing simple ideas from our senses, and then gain knowledge over time from reflecting on our sensory experiences. Therefore our own knowledge, perceptions and attitudes influencing our tourism buying behaviour, are based on our unique travel experiences over our lifetime.

Personality

Typically, when personality is discussed in an inter-personal context, it is about an individual's outward persona, such as extrovert, flirty, adventurous, confident etc. However, the personality construct is much more complex in relation to consumer behaviour in tourism. One of the most commonly discussed theories in marketing is the *self-concept* (Grubb & Stern, 1971), which posits an individual will gravitate towards brands with images that are congruent with their own self-image. However, while there have been investigations about the relationship between self-concept and destination attractiveness (Beerli et al., 2007), there has been a lack research in relation to practical implcations for small tourism businesses. There are two other key aspects of this most complex of topics that will be of practical interest to marketers of small tourism businesses: personal values and learning styles.

Personal values

A personal value is "an enduring belief that a particular mode of conduct or a particular end-state of existence is personally and socially preferable to alternative modes of conduct or end-states of existence" (Rokeach, 1968-69: 550); a preference for a mode of behavior for an experience or travel situation (instrumental value), or a desired state of being (terminal value). Rokeach proposed that a similarity in value systems will occur in a population. To identify the small set of personal values guiding consumer behavior, marketers often refer to the process of *laddering* in a Means-End Chain, following the work of Gutman (1982). Laddering Analysis was developed by Hinkle (1965) as an extension of the Repertory Test in Personal Construct Theory (Kelly, 1955). Laddering enables understanding of how cognitive attributes are perceived to provide benefits or consequences, which in turn satisfy personal values.

In the example shown in Figure 3.2, an individual might differentiate destinations on the basis of good beaches (salient attribute), which offers the potential benefit of relaxation/recharging (consequence/benefit), to enhance happiness (personal value). In this way consumers are thought to consider certain brands (pull) that will achieve a desired outcome (push). An understanding of consumer values therefore aids understanding of buyer behavior, through an understanding of linkages between the product and the relevant role it plays in the consumer's life (Reynolds & Gutman, 1988).

Good beaches → To relax/recharge → Happiness
(Attribute)   (Benefit/consequence)   (Personal value)

Figure 3.2: Example of a means-end ladder

For examples of how the laddering technique has been used in tourism research to identify personal values in travel decision making see Watkins and Gnoth (2011), and my own study (Pike, 2012) that identified the following personal values from a sample of consumers considering a short break holiday: happiness, healthy life, get close to family, self-fulfilment, broaden the mind, rewarding self, status and safety.

Learning styles

Individuals vary in their cognitive learning styles; the way in which they will notice, absorb and retain information. We are therefore selective about the stimuli we notice, the data we absorb, and about information we retain in memory. While we employ a mix of learning styles there is usually one that dominates.

The travel context

Travel context is the *situation* for which tourism services are being considered, such as the reason for travel, time of year, type of trip, or geographic travel range. The set of determinant attributes the influence destination selection will vary depending on situational context. For example, destination attractiveness will likely differ between the context of a honeymoon and an end of season football team trip. Restaurant attractiveness will differ between the context of a business lunch and a romantic dinner.

Motivation

Motivation for an individual's travel experiences is one of the most difficult aspects to analyse. Even though motivation begins the tourism decision process, it is easier to investigate the *who* and *how* and *what* and *where* and *when* of tourism activities, than to gain an understanding into the *why* of buy. Motivation is an over-used term in the tourism industry and it is important to note here that the reason for travel should not be confused with the motivation for travel. For example, the following reasons for travel do not represent motivation for travel: 'for a short break', 'for a family summer vacation', 'to visit friends or relatives'. Researchers have consistently reported the lack of agreed understanding of tourism motivations (e.g. Dann, 1977; Pearce, 2013). Part of the problem in understanding this issue is that it can be very difficult for a consumer to recall and articulate what motivated their recognition of the need for travel.

Extensive modelling by Pearce (2005: 85) pointed to 14 possible tourism motivation categories, with the strongest being *novelty*, *escape/relax* and *relationship* (to strengthen). The other categories were: autonomy, self-actualisation, nature, kinship, self enhancement, romance, nostalgia, self-development, stimulation, isolation and social status. Given the complexity of understanding human motivations, in terms of practical implications for marketers of small tourism businesses, a worthwhile starting point is the succinct categorisation of tourism motivations proposed by Gilmore (2002), where the three underlying motivations are the need for:

- hedonism (pleasure seeking)
- self-improvement
- spiritual growth

Another simplified approach uses three key categories of tourism motivations. As shown in Table 3.2, Mill and Morrison (1992) proposed three categories of tourism needs and wants being *physical*, *psychological* or *intellectual*, with the wants being representative of motives.

Table 3.2: Tourism needs and wants. Source: Adapted from Mill & Morrison (1992, p. 20)

Need	Want (Motive)
Physical Physiological Safety	Relaxation Security
Psychological Belonging Esteem Self-actualisation	Love Achievement, status Be true to one's own nature
Intellectual To know and understand Aesthetics	Knowledge Appreciation of beauty

For a deeper analysis of models that have been developed to explain motivation in tourism see Plog's (1974) allocentric-psychocentric continuum, Dann's (1977) push-pull model, and Pearce's (2005) travel career ladder.

Needs and wants recognition

This is the eureka moment (aha!), like a lightbulb switching on, when there is felt recognition of some form of deprivation. Motivation for a tourism experience represents a *want* arising that can't be met at home (Gartner, 1993). In Chapter 1 it was suggested the term *vacation* originated from the Latin meaning *to vacate this space*. This has mental implications as well as the physical aspect, since for many busy individuals pleasure travel is now a *psychological necessity* (Pike, 2016: 208). A *need* is something an individual has to have to satisfy a felt state of deprivation (eg a drink to quench a thirst), and a *want* is how an individual communicates a need (eg a green tea). Motivation is representative of an individual wanting to satisfy a need. When wants are backed by buying power, this is representative of *demand*, and a *product* is anything offered to meet that demand. Tourism services can therefore be viewed as *bundles of benefits* to meet needs, as well as a set of tangible product features.

Purchase decision making

When tourism consumers are motivated to act they become decision makers. Decisions must be made about where to go, when to go, how to travel there, and what to do there. Such decisions take place in the consumer's *black box* in the mind. We know information goes into the black box and what decisions come out; but understanding how the decision is made represents one of the greatest challenges in consumer psychology. Most of the consumer behaviour research in tourism has been underpinned by the view that we are rational decision makers, based on concepts such as the Theory of Planned Behaviour (Cohen et al., 2014). For example, decisions about which tourism services providers to select will involve an assessment of alternative brands on the consumer's choice criteria in memory. There has been criticism that this approach doesn't take into account the complexity of the multiplicity of decisions made in the travel planning context, which are not made in isolation from other consumption decisions. Cohen et al. further argued that most consumer behaviour research in tourism assumes thoroughly planned decisions, and that this is not necessarily the case for frequent travellers and repeat visitors, for example. Also, there will be many spontaneous buying decisions made during a holiday.

Memory, and decision sets

Associative Network Theory suggests memory as consisting as nodes (neurons) that have links to other nodes (Anderson, 1983). A node represents stored information about a concept, and forms part of a network of links to other node concepts. Activation of a link between nodes is sparked by processing external information or when retrieving information from memory. When a node concept is recalled (e.g. restaurants), links to a range of other nodes (e.g. desired features and benefits) will be activated from memory. There are two key implications of this for tourism marketers. The first is *brand salience* (top of mind awareness). When a purchase situation is being considered only a small number (an average of 4 +/- 2) of brands will come to mind that form the consumer's decision set (Pike & Ryan, 2004). While an individual will likely be aware of many more available brands, evaluating the positives and negatives of all of these is not practical, and so the decision set represents a form of self-defence for the mind. Therefore a major goal in marketing is to position the brand in consumers' decision sets, since these brands have a higher probability of being selected for purchase (Wilson, 1981; Pike, 2006). Decision set membership represents a competitive advantage over those brands not being considered. It is important then to remember that brand salience is far more powerful than awareness per se, since this represents being remembered for the right reasons.

3

Activity 3.3: Your next short break holiday destination?

A short break holiday is a trip away from home of between one and four nights, and has been one of the fastest growing segments around the world in recent years. *For your next short break, of all the destinations that are available to you, what is the first destination that comes to mind? What other destinations would you probably consider?* The destinations you have listed in response to these two questions represent your decision set at this point in time. Decision Set Theory (Howard & Sheth, 1969) suggests there will be a mean of between 2 and 6 destinations. For the rationale behind the design of these two questions to operationalise Decision Set Theory see Pike (2006).

Anticipation and expectations

A useful lens for understanding this process in the context of how travel experience shapes anticipation and expectations is Personal Construct Theory (PCT) developed by Kelly (1955). Kelly viewed humans as scientists, whose ultimate aim was to predict and control their own world. Underpinning PCT is constructive alternativism, which proposed that an individual has the creative capacity to interpret his environment, rather than simply respond to it in a stimulus-response manner. We all construe the universe in different ways, and are open to reconstruction. Our world is viewed through patterns that we individually create and attempt to fit over the environment. Kelly referred to these patterns, which allow us to chart a course, as personal constructs. Our individual construct system guides our behaviour. Kelly's fundamental assumption was that "a person's processes are psychologically channelized by the ways in which he anticipates events" (1955:46). Therefore, *anticipation* is the reason for construing. "If we were not anticipating regularities in behavior, why should we become upset about sudden change?" (Landfield & Leitner, 1980: 5).

Activity 3.4: When and why were you last disappointed with a service?

Think back to the last time you were disappointed with a service experience. Why were you disappointed? To what extent was your disappointment the result of your expectations? Now think back to the last time you were disappointed by a friend or colleague or relative. Why were you disappointed? To what extent was your disappointment the result of your expectations?

Experience comes from the act of construing (interpreting) a series of events, not merely by being a participant in, or exposure to them. Experience is a cycle of five phases: anticipation, investment, encounter, confirmation or disconfirmation, and revision. I have used PCT as a basis for research investigating consumers' personal values in travel decision making (Pike, 2012), as well as perceptions of international stopover destinations (Pike & Kotsi, 2016) and short break holiday destinations (Pike 2003, 2007). As well as student satisfaction (Pike & Larkin) and students' university decision criteria (Pike, 2004).

Travel/on-site experiences

A concept that can be helpful in trying to understand the feelings and behaviours of people when they are travelling is *liminality*. With roots in anthropology, this refers to the transitioning of an individual's state of being (Pearce, 2005). An individual will have a normal state of everyday living at home, then a liminoid phase during travel when life is not normal, and in some cases possibilities in life are expanded, and then a post-liminoid state when the individual returns to the routine of normal life. The liminoid state of visitors might be of particular interest in situations that are challenging, novel, sacred or spiritual. There are a number of practical implications of this state, which can impact on the level of comfort and satisfaction, including: culture shock, acclimatisation (e.g. to altitude, temperature), sense of fitting in with the locals (e.g. language, fashion), epiphany or spiritual awakening, and post-travel restlessness.

Another perspective on liminality relates to our transitioning through various life stages, such as during an individual's lifetime, for example when we reach adolescence or the coming of age. The travel behaviour of school leavers and college students on hedonic experiences such as spring break in North America, gap year in Europe and schoolies week in Australasia is a uniquely distinctive transitioning into adulthood. The phenomenon of grey nomads, mentioned earlier in the chapter, represents transitioning into retirement.

Involvement

A strong wish to derive enjoyment from the travel experience becomes a determinant of their behaviour. In other words, a desire to have a great time. This desire influences anticipation, expectations and ultimately satisfaction. The level of involvement in tourism experiences is higher than for most other service. The practical implications of this for small tourism businesses are twofold. First, so much of tourism is hedonic, where we are dealing with happy pleasure seekers who are in the mood to have fun. Second, this sets up a high risk of potential dissatisfaction from guests with high expectations, particularly in high involvement situations such as an annual holiday.

Industry insight: Catering to luminoid men at the cellar door

In a wine tourism region, the *cellar door* (shop/visitor centre) is often the first personal contact travellers have with a winery. The cellar door is the front of house reception and retail outlet for the winery. Wine regions comprise many small wineries, and the cellar door is an important outlet for generating sales of wine, and central to building ongoing customer loyalty. For most of these small businesses, cellar door sales are critical to profitability because of the high margins and low distribution costs. The design and operation of the cellar door is critically important, because it is here that visitors develop their first impressions of the winery. When visitors enter the shop they will be influenced by the layout and appearance, and the friendliness of the staff. For some travellers, particularly those new to the wine tourism experience, approaching the cellar door can be a confronting experience. There is a phenomenon in some men for example when they are in new surroundings, to not want to ask for directions or help as much as a woman might. In this *luminoid* state, such men are likely to leave the cellar door if it appears confronting and unwelcoming. In particular, if a visitor's own wine knowledge is limited or developing, some cellar doors can appear intimidating.

For a study investigating this aspect of consumer behaviour in the Margaret River wine region in Western Australia, and recommendations for cellar door service quality, see O'Neill and Charters (2000).

Post trip reflections

Satisfaction is a post-experience attitude (Pearce, 2005). What is relevant in the context of this chapter is that post-experience reflections influence future decision making, not only for the traveller, but also potentially for others in their social network. As discussed, Personal Construct Theory (Kelly, 1955) holds that an individual's experiences guide their future decision making. We make predictions about the outcomes of different scenarios being considered in a purchase decision, and this anticipation is based on our life experiences. Travel is one of life's great educational experiences, and contributes to a broadening of our thinking, and personal growth, through new experiences involving all the senses, interacting and bonding with fellow guests, service providers, and people from different cultures. There are few industries outside tourism where learning more about the world and re-arranging our attitudes has an influence on future purchase decisions (Pearce, 2005). New knowledge will be gained from every experience, and we often share that knowledge, good and bad, with others in our social network.

Key points

1: Consumer behaviour is central to the development, implementation and evaluation of tourism marketing activities

A marketing orientation dictates all marketing decisions are made with target consumers in mind. Consumer behaviour is the most important and most complex issue faced by marketers. Attempting to understand the needs, motivations and decision making processes (*the why of buy*) of unique individuals in mass markets, is central to the development, implementation and evaluation of marketing activities.

2: A model of consumer behaviour in tourism

A five-stage model of tourism consumer behaviour was presented, commencing with the recognition of a need or want, leading to purchase decision making, anticipation and expectations, travel and on-site experiences, and then culminating in post-trip reflections.

3: The key internal and external influences on an individual's tourism buying behaviour

The model of consumer behaviour is influenced by a complex range of internal and external forces. The main external influences discussed were: destination attractiveness; culture and societal norms; and social networks. Key internal influences presented were individual consumers' demographics, perceptions, travel experience, personality, personal values, motivation, and the travel context.

Discussion questions

1. Why does brand salience, in the form of membership of a consumer's decision set, represent a source of competitive advantage?

2. Explain the difference between a belief and an attitude about a brand, and the key implications of this for marketers.

3. Why is it suggested that marketers should reinforce positively held perceptions of the brand, rather than try to correct a negative brand image?

References

Anderson, J.R. (1983), *The Architecture of Cognition,* Harvard University Press, Cambridge, MA.

Beerli, A., Meneses, G.D. & Gil, S.M. (2007). Self-congruity and destination choice. *Annals of Tourism Research,* **34**(3): 571-587.

Breuer, T. (2005). Retirement migration or rather second-home tourism? German senior citizens in the Canary Islands. *Contributions to Human Geography,* **3**: 313-333.

Cohen, S.A., Prayag, G. & Moital, M. (2014). Consumer behaviour in tourism: Concepts, influences and opportunities. *Current Issues in Tourism,* **17**(10): 872-909.

Crompton, J.L., Fakeye, P. C. & Lue, C. (1992). Positioning: The example of the Lower Rio Grande Valley in the winter long stay destination market. *Journal of Travel Research,* Fall: 20-26.

Dann, G.M.S. (1977). Anomie, ego-enhancement and tourism. *Annals of Tourism Research,* **4**: 184-194.

Gartner, W.C. (1993). Image information process. *Journal of Travel & Tourism Marketing,* **2** (2/3): 191-215.

Gilmore, F. (2002). Branding for success. In Morgan, N., Pritchard, A. & Pride, R. (Eds). *Destination Branding: Creating the unique Destination Proposition,* pp. 57-65.

Grubb, E.L. & Stern, B.L. (1971). Self-concept and significant others. *Journal of Marketing Research,* **8**(3): 382-385.

Gutman, J. (1982). A means end chain model based on consumer categorization processes. *Journal of Marketing,* **46**(2): 60-72.

Hillman, W. (2013). Grey Nomads travelling in Queensland, Australia: social and health needs. *Aging & Society,* **33**(4): 579-597.

Hinkle, D.N., (1965). *The Change of Personal Constructs from the Viewpoint of a Theory of Construct Implications.* Unpublished PhD thesis. Ohio State Univeristy.

Howard, J.A. & Sheth, J.N. (1969). *The Theory of Buyer Behavior.* New York: John Wiley & Sons.

Huber, A. & O'Reilly, K. (2004). The construction of *Heimat* under conditions of individualised modernity: Swiss and British elderly migrants in Spain. *Aging & Society,* **24**: 327-351.

Kelly, G. A. (1955). *The Psychology of Personal Constructs.* New York: Norton.

Landfield, A.W. & Leitner, L.M. (1980), (eds). *Personal Construct Psychology: Psychotherapy and Personality.* New York: John Wiley & Sons

Levene, L. (2013). *I Think, Therefore I Am.* London: Michael Omara Books Ltd.

Mill, R.C. & Morrison, A.M. (1992). *The Tourism System: An Introductory Text.* (2nd Ed). Englewood Cliffs, NJ: Prentice Hall

O'Neill, M. & Charters, S. (2000). Service quality at the cellar door: implications for Western Australia's developing wine tourism industry. *Managing Service Quality,* **10**(2): 112-122.

Pearce, P.L. (2005). *Tourist Behaviour: Themes and Conceptual Schemes.* Clevedon, Channel View Publications.

Pearce, P.L. (2013). *The Social Psychology of Tourist Behaviour: International Series in Experimental Social Psychology (Volume 3).* Oxford: Pergamon Press.

Pike, S. (2002). *Positioning as a Source of Competitive Advantage – Benchmarking Rotorua's Position as a Domestic Short Break Holiday Destination.* PhD Thesis. University of Waikato. November.

Pike, S. (2003). The use of Repertory Grid Analysis to elicit salient short break holiday attributes. *Journal of Travel Research,* **41**(3): 326-330.

Pike, S. (2004), The use of repertory grid analysis and importance-performance analysis to identify potential determinant university attributes, *Journal of Marketing for Higher Education,* **14**(2): 1-18.

Pike, S. (2006). Destination decision sets: A longitudinal comparison of stated destination preferences and actual travel. *Journal of Vacation Marketing,* **12**(4): 319-328.

Pike, S. (2007). Repertory Grid Analysis in group settings to elicit salient destination brand attributes. *Current Issues in Tourism,* **10**(4): 378-392.

Pike, S. (2012). Destination positioning opportunities using personal values elicited through the Repertory Test and Laddering Analysis. *Tourism Management,* **33**(1): 100-107.

Pike, S. (2016). *Destination Marketing Essentials.* (2nd Ed). Abingdon, Oxon: Routledge.

Pike, S. & Kotsi, F. (2016). Stopover destination image – Using the Repertory Test to identify salient attributes. *Tourism Management Perspectives,* **18**: 68-73.

Pike, S. & Ryan, C. (2004). Destination positioning analysis through a comparison of cognitive, affective and conative perceptions. *Journal of Travel Research,* **42**(4): 333-342.

Plog, S.T. (1974). Why destination areas rise and fall in popularity. *The Cornell HRA Quarterly,* **14**(4): 55-58.

Reynolds, T.J. & Gutman, J. (1988). Laddering theory, method, analysis, and interpretation. *Journal of Advertising Research,* **28**(1): 11-31.

Rokeach, M. (1968-69). The role of values in public opinion research. *The Public Opinion Quarterly,* **32**(4): 547-559.

Solomon, M.R., (2017). *Consumer Behaviour: Buying, Having, and Being.* (12th Ed.). Upper Saddle River, NJ: Pearson.

Watkins, L. & Gnoth, J. (2011). The value orientation approach to understanding culture. *Annals of Tourism Research,* **38**(4): 1274-1299.

Wilson, C.E. (1981). A procedure for the analysis of consumer decision making. *Journal of Advertising Research,* **21**(2): 31-36.

4 Tourism Marketing Planning

Chapter outline

Marketers need to be forward thinking. Tourism businesses operate in an increasingly dynamic (changing) environment, over which they have no control. Every business needs some form of marketing plan to charter a course through an uncertain future. For any travel purchase situation, consumers are spoilt for choice of products offering similar features and benefits. Business success is dependent on the ability to develop *strengths* to take advantage of *opportunities* ahead of rivals. First mover advantage doesn't last forever however, with imitators quick to follow the lead, and so the quest for a competitive edge is ongoing. Marketing planning is not an exact science, and requires skills in both critical analysis and creative thinking. The chapter outlines a structured process for developing a marketing plan to differentiate from competitors and strive for a competitive edge. The structure of this planning approach enables stakeholders, such as staff and investors, to follow the rationale for the proposed marketing objectives and ensuing tactics. At the core of the marketing planning framework are three tools: the STEEPL Analysis is used to scan the macro-environment for forces beyond the control of the firm that represent sources of opportunities and threats; the VRIO Model is used to identify resources controlled by the firm that can be regarded as strengths; and the SWOT Matrix is a visual tool for developing objectives by matching strengths with opportunities, and then demonstrating the rationale for the marketing objectives to stakeholders.

Learning aims

To enhance your understanding of:

■ Marketing planning as a forward thinking process

■ The importance of marketing planning in striving to gain a competitive edge

■ The key stages in marketing planning.

Key terms

Competitive edge

While competitive advantage is a common term, a competitive edge is a more realistic ambition for small tourism businesses. A competitive edge is gained when the business uses a *strength* to take advantage of an *opportunity* before rivals do.

Strength

A resource controlled by the firm, which is valuable in terms of either increasing revenue or decreasing costs, and is relatively rare among competitors in a target market.

Opportunity

A positive force in the external macro-environment, over which the firm has no control.

Introduction

Richard Branson once wrote how he started his Virgin business empire without any formal marketing plan. While a business absolutely can have a successful start without a formal marketing plan, there will have been an informal planning process where an *opportunity* was identified and an idea formulated on how to exploit it. An informal approach might be fine in the start-up stage, but it is unusual for any business that has been successful over the long term to not have a formal marketing plan. Most successful people write down their goals, in manageable chunks, and re-evaluate them regularly (Pease & Pease, 2016). These days any business venture needing finance (e.g. bank loan) or equity investors (e.g. shareholders) will need to be able to articulate the success potential of the strategy. Both informal and formal marketing plans follow the structure of four key questions shown in Table 4.1.

Table 4.1: Marketing planning stages

Stage	Informal question	Formal term
1	Where are we now?	Situation analysis
2	Where do we want to go?	Development of objectives
3	How do we get there?	Tactics implementation
4	How will we know we got there?	Performance monitoring

Two points are worth remembering here.

1 First, the marketing plan is not set in stone, because of the dynamic (constantly changing) nature of the operating environment. We live in a world of continuous *discontinuous* change; where change is constant but is disruptive rather than evolving incrementally. For example, wristwatches have declined in sales worldwide every month since 2015, due to the ubiquitous smartphone…what will replace the smartphone?

2   Second, the marketing plan does not need to be a lengthy document, but should succinctly guide the reader seamlessly through each of the four stages, as indicated in the marketing planning, implementation and evaluation cycle in Figure 4.1. It should be clear to the reader how each stage logically builds on the previous section, so that:

■ The *objectives* clearly emerge from the situation analysis

■ The *tactics* clearly address the objectives

■ The *performance* measures clearly address the effectiveness of the tactics.

Figure 4.1: Marketing planning, implementation and evaluation cycle

Situation analysis (*Where are we now?*)

This is an exercise in critical thinking. What is required is an analysis of the current situation facing the business, from both internal and external perspectives. The traditional way of structuring thinking is to undertake a SWOT Analysis, which identifies i) strengths and weaknesses, and ii) opportunities and threats. The tool is more effective when it is extended to a *SWOT Matrix,* which facilitates the development of marketing objectives and the ensuing tactics. The SWOT Matrix is also valuable for justifying the proposed objectives and tactics to stakeholders.

Critical point: The difference between the internal/external components of the SWOT

Strengths and **W**eaknesses are resources that are directly controlled by the firm, in the internal operating environment. **O**pportunities and **T**hreats on the other are forces in the external environment, over which the business has no control. Understanding this is fundamental to undertaking an effective situation analysis.

Strengths and weaknesses

The quest for differentiation in the tourism industry is challenging, particularly since it is usually difficult to patent a service idea. When a new service concept is launched, it can be quickly imitated, and so tourism markets are crowded with *me too* products that offer similar features and benefits. This leads to competitive parity between rivals, and commodity-based substitutability in consumers' minds, where one product offering can be easily and quickly substituted for another, based on price.

Activity 1.1: How to differentiate?

Consider the options for how the following businesses in your nearest city could differentiate the offering from rivals:

■ Local sightseeing bus operator

■ Hotel in the central business district

What could be done to make the service different to local competing businesses? How difficult would it be for competitors to copy your suggestions?

Competitive advantage/competitive edge

While the term *competitive advantage* is commonly used in business and the academic literature, *competitive edge* is probably a more realistic aim for small tourism businesses. It is important to recognise that achieving differentiation is difficult even for big businesses, and so no SWOT analysis will realistically contain a long list of *strengths*. One way to focus thinking about potential options for gaining a competitive edge is to ask yourself this question:

What do you value most as a customer?

At a basic level, there will likely be three key sources of value that are salient when we are making a purchase decision involving a competitive set of brands. What gets our attention is an offer featuring one of the following benefits:

■ Cheaper than rivals

■ Faster than rivals

■ Better than rivals.

Rarely would a small business be able to offer more than one of these. Possessing a resource that delivers one of these benefits is merely the ticket to enter the game. Three further conditions are required to achieve a competitive edge in the market. First, the consumer must be aware that there is a difference between competing firms. Second, this difference must represent a competency gap that competitors are not able to match. Third, the competency gap must endure over time.

VRIO resource model for classifying *strengths*

Barney's (1991, 1996) VRIO resource model is a practical tool for assessing whether a resource controlled by the firm represents a source of competitive advantage, and therefore worthy of being labelled a *strength* in the SWOT analysis. To develop the VRIO model, Jay Barney interviewed hundreds of successful businesses and asked management what it was they did that gave them a competitive advantage. The most common reply was: "We worked hard, took risks, and surrounded ourselves with the best people". However, this is not a source of advantage because if all businesses did this, they would all have the same strengths.

Barney's proposition underpinning the development of the VRIO resource model is that strengths are heterogeneous, and immobile between firms. That is, a strength is a resource that is relatively unique, and can't be easily transferred to another firm. For a resource to be considered capable of achieving a sustainable competitive advantage, Barney argued the following characteristics must exist:

1 Valuable to the firm

The resource is valuable to the firm if it has the potential to either increase revenue or reduce costs.

2 Rare

The resource represents a unique selling point (USP), because is relatively rare. It doesn't have to be the rarest on the planet, but is not offered by close competitors in a given market. For example, a competing set of beach destinations within a short drive of a major city will need to identify something that is unique about their beach to standout. *Nice beach*, for example, would not be a strength in such a situation, but rather a source of parity with competing places, since a beach is a beach is a beach.

3 Imitation is difficult

Competitors should not be able to replicate the resource in the short term.

4 Organisation

The firm must be organised in a way that capitalises on the resource's competitive potential.

Critical point: True *strengths* are few in number

Strengths are difficult to obtain and will be small in number; one or a few at best. The business might have a resource that is attractive to consumers, but if competing businesses have the same resource it is not a strength. A strength is a resource that is attractive to consumers and differentiates the business from competitors. So a long bullet point list of *strengths* is not appropriate in a SWOT analysis.

Case 4.1: The world's most exciting jet boat ride

Table 4.2 demonstrates how the VRIO can be applied to a tourism business, using the example of Shotover Jet in Queenstown, New Zealand (www.shotoverjet.com). Positioned as *the world's most exciting jet boat ride*, Shotover Jet has achieved a sustainable competitive advantage over rivals since 1965. While the business was not the first jet boat operation in Queenstown, and has a dozen competitors, Shotover Jet is the best known brand. The jet boat concept was invented in New Zealand to enable boats to travel up shallow rivers, where outboard motors cannot be used. In 1960 two entrepreneurs saw the opportunity to use the technology to provide a thrill ride for visitors. Today, experienced drivers carry groups of passengers in fiberglass boats at speeds up to 85 kilometres per hour through the narrow Shotover Canyon, missing rocks and cliffs by centimetres. The company has held a long term lease of the most spectacular stretch of river in the canyon that no other operator has access to. No other stretch of river in the region offers the same dramatic scenery and thrills.

Of the many resources controlled by Shotover Jet, there are five listed in Table 4.2 to demonstrate how the VRIO model can be applied. Each resource must first be assessed in terms of its value to the firm for increasing income or reducing costs. If a resource is not valuable it should be removed from consideration in the VRIO. You will see all five resources in the table are considered valuable. Next, it must be decided if the resource is rare in the competitive situation. While the firm's drivers are exceptionally skilled, competitors have also been able develop the same resource. So driver skills represents a source of *competitive parity*, and would not be considered a *strength* in the SWOT analysis. To be a strength would require something different about the skills that competitors' drivers don't possess and might provide a short term first mover advantage until competitors catch up (e.g. Arabic language skills). At times in Shotover Jet's history there have been advances in boat design and engine technology such as the introduction of multiple LPG fuelled motors, which provided a short term advantage in attracting visitors and reducing operating costs. At the time of writing, the boat technology was not rare and so is also an example of competitive parity and not representative of a *strength*. However a temporary competitive advantage did exist in terms of having more jet boats than any competitor.

The Shotover Jet brand has become one of the best known in New Zealand tourism. This resource is both valuable and rare, and so is categorised a representing a source of *sustainable competitive advantage*. This is where the subjectivity of assessment is highlighted. On one hand, as shown, developing a rival brand would require a major effort over a long period of time and so it could be argued the brand can't be imitated and would therefore be categorised as representing a source of sustainable competitive advantage over the long term. On the other hand, it could be argued that if a billionaire with a recognised tourism brand such as Trump or Virgin entered the game, they could develop brand awareness in a relatively short time frame.

The other key resource for Shotover Jet, which has led to the strong brand awareness, is the renewable 20 year lease over the important stretch of river in Shotover Canyon. This is valuable, rare, and not able to be imitated by competitors. The firm has decades of experience in the industry, has the management skills and financial resources to be organised to exploit the resource. So in this example three *strengths* for inclusion in the SW/OT analysis are the river lease, brand awareness, and number of boats.

Table 4.2: VRIO for Shotover Jet

Resource	Valuable	Rare?	Unimitable?	Organised?	Competitive status
River lease	✓	✓	✓	✓	SCA
Brand awareness	✓	✓	✓		SCA
Number of boats	✓	✓			CA
Boat technology	✓				CP
Driver skills	✓				CP

Notes: SCA = sustainable competitive advantage
CA = competitive advantage
CP = competitive parity

Discussion question

Using the VRIO format, analyse a nearby tourism business near you. Are there any strengths?

Categories of resources controlled by the firm

There are at least nine key categories of resources that are potential sources of strengths for tourism service providers, because they are difficult to obtain:

- Recognised brand
- Access to a unique resource
- Innovative use of technology
- Unique or patented offering
- Unique access to customers and/or travel trade suppliers
- Location, location, location
- Unique history
- Operant resources
- Access to capital
- Famous host.

Recognised brand

As discussed in the case of Shotover Jet, the firm's brand represents a source of competitive advantage. Branding principles are discussed in *7: Tourism Branding*, while brand equity is discussed in *14: Tourism Marketing Performance Measurement*.

Access to a unique resource

Obtaining sole rights to use a unique resource, such as in the case of Shotover Jet's lease of the Shotover Canyon stretch of waterway, can create a competitive edge when there is consumer demand. Examples include:

- Sole access rights to an area that is environmentally sensitive for eco tourism, such as the Falealupo Canopy Walk in Samoa's Falealupo Rainforest Reserve.

- Sole access rights to a historical site, such as the Avebury ancient stone monuments in the county of Wiltshire England.

- Obtaining the lease of a city's major bridge for bridge climbs. At the time of writing there were only three cities in the world where visitors can participate in a climb to the top of a major bridge. These are the Sydney Harbour Bridge and Brisbane Story Bridge in Australia, and the Auckland Harbour Bridge in New Zealand.

- Securing the lease to use the site of a disaster for dark tourism, such as The Buried Village, near Rotorua in New Zealand, where archaeological digs have unearthed remnants of the village of Te Wairoa. Te Wairoa was one of three villages buried in ash from the 1886 volcanic eruption of Mount Tarawera.

- Obtaining the lease to use a disused government facility, such as a prison, for hostel accommodation. Creative examples in different parts of the world include: PRISON at Anjuna in Goa, India; Hotel Celica in Ljubljana, Slovenia; The Art Prison in Prague, Czech Republic; and the HI-Ottawa Jail Hostel in Canada.

Innovative use of technology

There can be first mover advantages in applying innovative use of technology. Being the first to commercialise bungy jumping technology created a global edge for AJ Hackett Ltd (www.ajahackett.com). For a small tourism business, opportunities are as diverse as developing a customer relationship management (CRM) database system enabling the stimulation of more repeat visitation than competitors, or a clean energy application resulting in lower costs, such as Shotover Jet's early adoption of LPG technology for their jet boats.

Unique or patented offering

For the owners of a new invention, a patent can provide protection from imitation in one country for a given period of time, such as in the case of Zorb globe riding (www.zorb.com). A separate patent must be applied for in different countries, which means it is rare for a small business owner to be able to afford global patents, and so imitation can't be stopped. Also, in many countries a service cannot be patented. Indeed not all tangible products can be patented. Clothing for example can't be patented, which is why new releases by famous designer brands are copied and on sale within hours.

In practice: There is only one Sally Lunn's bun

Sally Lunn's Historic Eating House in Bath, England is a famous eating place, based on Sally's secret 300 year old recipe for the first Bath bun. This type of bun is fondly referred to as a *Sally Lunn* in the UK. While *Sally Lunn* has become a generic term (along the lines of *Xerox a copy*, *Google it* etc) for this style of bun made in many other parts of the world, Sally Lunn's Historic Eating House remains one of the must-see attractions in Bath. When in Bath, the original and famous Sally Lunn's bun can only be enjoyed at this small historic eatery. Still in the original house, built in 1482, the eatery also features a museum where visitors can view Sally's original kitchen.

Unique access to customers and/or travel trade suppliers

As is discussed in *12: Customer Relationship Management in Tourism*, loyal customers are valuable to a business because they reduce promotional costs and increase yield. However, many small businesses don't invest time in developing even a rudimentary loyalty programme. An effective CRM programme that fosters customer loyalty not only represents a source of competitive advantage, but also has a financial value as an intangible asset on the balance sheet. Also, it is common for travel agency chains to have *preferred* suppliers, who pay extra commission for the privilege of being recommended first by their travel consultants. The opportunity/challenge for small tourism businesses is to gain inclusion in the wholesalers' packages represented in the travel agencies' preferred supplier brochures.

Location, location, location

The real estate adage *location, location, location* is just as applicable for tourism businesses. Access to visitors at high density areas is a potential source of competitive edge. A location in a high traffic visitor spot creates advantages (at a cost). Examples include: public squares, central train, ferry and bus depots, major theme parks, popular walking/biking routes, airport and cruise ship terminals and so forth. Sometimes this can manifest as a result of good luck or timing, rather than good management. For example the augmented reality game Pokemon Go craze that started in 2016 provided a bonanza for food and beverage businesses that by chance were located adjacent Pokestops and Pokemons.

Industry insight: Selling shoes in Puerto del Sol, Madrid

Puerto del Sol is the most famous public square in Madrid, Spain. This is one of the busiest places in the city, connecting several recreation and business precincts. The square, which is actually the shape of a semi-circle, is crowded day and night with visitors and locals. Puerto del Sol is the focal point for major public demonstrations, and also the televised New Year's Eve celebrations. There are many streets and alleys leading off the square, filled with hostels, shops and eateries. One of the most common types of shops in this area are those selling shoes and handbags. Spain is famous for the good quality and value of leather products, and it is almost as if every second shop in this area is in the shoe business. While there are many high quality (and not so high quality) shoe stores on the Sol area, the ones that attract the most visitors are those closest to the square near the entrances of two streets in particular, Calle de la Monterra and Calle de Carritas. While these small stores pay high rents, they are able to compete with the nearby big name department stores on the basis of price due to the high level of foot traffic day and night, particularly from travellers. A high volume, low yield strategy based on foot traffic at a prime location.

Unique history

That many of the world's most popular attractions are historical sites bears testimony to our innate curiosity about life in the past. There are many creative ways in which tourism businesses can tap into historical events of interest to visitors. Travellers taking selfies on the front steps of the hotel in Ocean Drive in South Beach, Florida where Italian fashion designer Gianni Versace was shot dead. The Jane Austin suite at the Dolphin Hotel in Southampton, England where the author celebrated her 18th birthday. In Venice, a simple plaque on the wall outside a restaurant denoting the spot where famous Italian lothario Casanova had one of his many romantic trysts. Conference gala dinners in the ballroom at the Hollywood Roosevelt Hotel, California where the first academy awards were staged in 1927. Duke's Bar in London, where author Ian Fleming took inspiration for agent 007 James Bond's preference for a martini that is *shaken not stirred*.

Operant resources

These resources represent intangible skills and knowledge possessed by staff members. Examples include foreign language skills, advanced technology skills, and close relationships with important travel trade intermediaries.

Access to capital

Small tourism businesses operate with scarce resources, and the focus is always on tomorrow's cash flow. Securing access to a large capital funding source, such as private equity investors, represents an advantage over competitors.

Famous host

Businesses owned or partly owned by famous personalities can be a drawcard. Probably the most common are restaurants with links to celebrity chefs, and nightclubs linked to celebrities. There are also opportunities for tourism businesses to develop unique characters who become an attraction in themselves. One example is Australia Zoo, now one of the best known and most visited theme parks in south east Queensland. The attraction had humble beginnings as Beerwah Reptile Park in 1970. The park had the advantage of being located on the main highway linking Brisbane with the Sunshine Coast. Even though the attraction suffered a major setback when the new national highway bypassed the area, the transformation into Australia Zoo owes much to the late son of the founder of the original park. Steve Irwin, nicknamed *the Crocodile Hunter*, became a famous television personality on the back of his unique personality, and in between his outback television adventures was a popular host at the park until his death from a stingray attack in 2006. Irwin's image and memory is still celebrated at Australia Zoo, and the highway on which it is located was renamed Steve Irwin Way by the government.

Weaknesses

A weakness is a resource controlled by the firm, which could lead to a competitive disadvantage. Awareness of potential weaknesses can emerge from a variety of sources, such as customer feedback, competitor analysis, and marketing research. Given tourism services are labour intensive, a temporary weakness can emerge suddenly through human error. For example, in the case of New Zealand's Shotover Jet, the death of a Japanese passenger in 1999 was a temporary weakness, particularly in the Japan market. The best way to monitor perceived weaknesses is by using surveys that compare perceptions of the business with local competitors.

Opportunities and threats

All organisations operate in an external macro-environment, over which they have no control. Critical to the success of marketing planning are trends and events that represent potential sources of opportunities and threats for the firm. Most external forces might not be directly related to travel and tourism, but have the potential to influence levels of consumer demand. Those forces with the potential to impact positively on the firm are representative of *opportunities*, while negative external forces are considered *threats*.

Critical point: An *opportunity* is not a tactic

An *opportunity* is an external force over which the business has no control (e.g. a decrease in bank interest rates). It is important to understand an *opportunity* is not to do something (e.g. to advertise in bus shelters), since that is a tactic.

Disruption/paradigm shifts

As will be discussed in Chapter 6, disruption to industries and economies is not a new phenomenon. There have been many historic paradigm shifts that have created new opportunities and threats. What is new is the sheer speed of disruptions since the emergence of the internet and Web 2.0 technologies. The purpose of mentioning this here, is that it is easy for each generation to scoff at the antiquated practices of previous generations. For example, my children and students are amused to hear about the following milestones in my life:

- When I was at primary school in New Zealand there was only one television channel, broadcast in black and white, which didn't start until 5pm each day. Also during this period all pubs had to close at 6pm by law, and couldn't open on a Sunday.
- Cell phones weren't available until I was 28.
- The internet was not commercially available until I was 36, and at this time we were using 3.5 inch floppy discs for storing data (1.44 megabytes!).
- Social media wasn't available until I was 44.

Why do I share this with you? Well, you might want to sit back and reflect on how new technologies, which are unknown to you at the moment, but are going to change your life in the future. Are you a forward thinking marketer? Will you be able to spot emerging technological trends that represent *opportunities* for you?

Activity 4.2: Your world in 30 years' time?

People tend to think about incremental improvements that might be made to existing practices, rather than imagine a revolutionary concept that might replace current technologies. Ask yourself how technology might differ in your world in 10, 20 or 30 years, in ways that make your current practices seem amusing to the generation growing up behind you.

Industry insight: What will New York be like in 1960?

In 1860 a community meeting was held in New York to discuss ideas about what the city might be like 100 years in the future. In the end the consensus was New York would cease to be inhabited in 1960. In 1860 the main form of transportation was horse and carriage. To cope with predicted population growth, it was estimated that 6 million horses would be needed to cater to transport needs in 1960. The droppings from 6 million horses would clog up all the roads (this was already a problem in 1860), rendering the city impossible to live in. Interestingly, by 1900 there were 1001 car manufacturers in the USA and in 1903 the world's best subway system opened in New York. With the benefit of hindsight we can understand how difficult it can be to forecast future disruptors, such as cars and underground trains in the case of New York.

Scenario thinking

Scenario planning was introduced by Wack (1985) and championed by Schwartz (1992) as a structured way for firms to think about the future, by attempting to construct plots about what could happen. Different strategic choices can be made based on how the different scenarios might unfold. There is a relatively small but growing literature about scenario planning in the tourism industry. For a detailed range of scenarios for global tourism in the year 2050 see Yeoman (2012).

Lean marketing: Follow the futurists

Even though we can't predict the future, marketing is still as much a forward thinking exercise about unmet consumer needs as it is about catering to current customers' wants. There is a rich resource of ideas about the future offered by professional futurists. Their ideas can be accessed inexpensively through their websites and books. Well-known futurists and organisations include: World Future Society (www.wfs.org), Alvin Toffler (www.tofflerassociates.com), Faith Popcorn (www.faithpopcorn.com), John and Doris Naisbitt (www.naisbitt.com), and Ray Kurzweil (www.kurzweilai.net).

4

STEEPL Analysis

An effective tool for structuring thinking about the future is the STEEPL Analysis. Forces in the external macro-environment can be analysed using the following categories: Socio-cultural, Technology, Economic, Ecological, Political and Legal (STEEPL); also known as PLEETS, PESTE, PEST or STEP. This systematic approach to scanning the macro-environment helps to identify those forces, over which the organisation has no control, that have the potential to impact on the local tourism operating environment, either positively or negatively. It is from the STEEPL Analysis that the *opportunities* and *threats* are selected. The STEEPL Analysis will differ between tourism businesses, depending on where they are located and which markets are targeted.

Socio-cultural

Many socio-cultural changes can influence levels of demand and consumer behaviour. These need to be analysed in relation to the key markets of interest to the firm, since circumstances might differ between geographic regions. Important factors to consider in each market include changes in: demographics; cultural values and preferences; perceptions of the destination; lifestyles; leisure trends; consumer sophistication levels.

Technological

In analysing the time lag from technological invention to wide market use, strategy guru Peter Drucker (1995) proposed the future is already here. Drucker suggested we should look to the fringes of society to identify future technologies that in the exploratory design stages; since everything that will be in common use in 30 years' time already exists in some form today, being developed somewhere on the *fringes of society*. Current examples of the range of forces for consideration here include: consumer influence on social media; disruption; intermediation; self-driving vehicles, drones and aircraft; virtual and augmented reality; robotics; smart clothing; nanotechnology; technology interoperability; bio fuels and clean energy; sub-orbital travel.

Lean marketing – Look back to the future

Look to the past for failed ideas that were ahead of their time. For example, virtual reality technology experiences were around in the 1980s, but not successfully commercialised for 30 years.

Economic

Travel is often discretionary spending, and so economic conditions plays a significant role in determining demand. Also, on the supply side the economic situation impacts on the business' ability to compete efficiently. Key economic indicators influencing the demand and supply sides include: bank interest rates, at the destination and in target markets; currency exchange rates; consumer confidence surveys; competition levels; employment levels; the share market; taxation policies; innovations in the sharing economy; business alliances, mergers and acquisitions; the value of consumer information; increasing competition; retirement incomes.

Ecological/Environmental

The attractiveness of many destinations is based on environmental resources, which need to be managed sustainably. Also, the global travel industry is one of the biggest producers of carbon emissions, particularly by aircraft. With over 100,000 flights every day, any changes to the taxing of carbon emissions would have significant impact on global tourism. The range of factors to be monitored include: effects of climate change; renewable energy options; the green movement; overcrowding and pollution levels; biosecurity; organics; threats of natural disasters.

Political

All business markets are more likely to flourish in times of political stability, and suffer in times of uncertainty, such as prior to elections and during terrorist events and military action. For example, travel movements declined worldwide by 10% in the year following the events of September 11, 2001, even though the attacks occurred in one country. So it is important to be aware of the political environment and the effects of various levels of government. Forces to monitor include: threats of terrorism at the destination and along transit routes; effects of upcoming local and national elections on consumer confidence; change of government;

government stability; relationships between the destination country and target market countries; international government trading alliances and protectionism; government travel advisories.

Legislative

Changes in legislation can impact on tourism, such as in relation to: visas and border controls; land use zoning; environmental protection legislation; deregulation; industry (de)regulations; health and safety; funding of the DMO, relative to competing destinations; personal information privacy; international government foreign exchange movement regulations; visa policies; employment legislation such as minimum wages; taxation.

4

Critical point: How to write up the STEEPL Analysis

The best way to tabulate ideas is to create a bullet point list of possible trends/forces for each section. File this away in the appendix of the marketing plan, so that it can be reviewed again and updated later. From the bullet point list only select the few that will be most relevant for the business at this time in terms of representing potential opportunities and threats in the foreseeable future. Provide a brief description of each in the body of the plan, so that stakeholders such as staff and financiers understand the rationale.

Developing objectives (Where do we want to go?)

An effective tool for developing objectives, and ensuing tactics, is to extend the SW/OT analysis into a matrix. The SW/OT Matrix focuses thinking in a structured way, which enables readers to follow the logic of the resultant objectives and tactics. The structure is also ideal for brainstorming tactical ideas to achieve the objectives, by asking:

- How do we leverage this strength to take advantage of that opportunity?
- What can we do about this weaknesses to minimise that threat?

BHAGS, goals and objectives

A BHAG (big hairy audacious goal) is useful way to capture the attention of stakeholders, and to motivate and inspire them (Collins & Poras, 1997, p. 94). A BHAG might seem impossible, but it can be a catalyst for stimulating increased creativity:

- The 1915 Coca-Cola bottle design brief: "A bottle so distinct that it could be recognised by touch in the dark or when lying broken on the ground".
- Henry Ford's BHAG was to democratise the automobile.
- Bill Gates had a vision for a computer in every household.

■ The Ford Motor Company once developed a state-of-the-art automobile suspension system, based on the BHAG of designing a car that could run on square wheels

Goals are broad strategic statements about how to achieve the organisation's mission statement. Goals have a longer term focus than just this year's marketing plan. For example, a goal might be to explore opportunities for franchising the business. Another might be to develop an entry into a new market. Objectives are quantifiable targets of the goals, where the outcome is SMART: **S**pecific, **M**easurable, **A**greed by those who must achieve them, **R**ealistic, and **T**ime-bound. As discussed in *Chapter 14 – Tourism Marketing Performance Measurement*, it is also important to identify the performance indicators (see Table 14.1 for a list of key performance indicators). Performance indicators are measurable markers that indicate the level of effectiveness in achieving marketing objectives. This section is concerned with the use of the SW/OT Matrix to develop marketing objectives.

Figure 4.2 shows a hypothetical application of a SWOT Matrix for Shotover Jet, the business discussed in Case 4.1. The opportunities and threats are selected from a STEEPL Analysis, strengths are selected from a VRIO analysis, and weaknesses from analysing the operating environment. Offensive objectives are developed by matching opportunities with strengths, while defensive objectives are to mitigate the effect of threats on weaknesses. For the purpose of demonstrating how the SW/OT Matrix works, in this example only one example is provided in each box.

Figure 4.2: SWOT matrix

Tactics (How do we get there?)

Once the objectives have been set, the creative process of brainstorming and developing tactics to achieve them begins. It is beneficial to involve staff in this process, rather than be left to one person who is responsible for marketing. A diversity of age, gender, culture and experience can also be valuable. There are structured techniques available that can help focus creative thinking. These include mind mapping (e.g. Buzan & Buzan, 1995), decision trees (e.g. Magee, 1964) and associative memory brainstorming (e.g. Brown & Paulus, 2002). Marketing tactics are explored in later chapters.

Critical point: The golden rule of brainstorming

4

To really tap the creative potential of the group, the atmosphere must feel inclusive, with everyone encouraged to participate equally. Any power imbalances between a senior owner and a new young team member must be left at the door. The golden rule for effective brainstorming is that when an idea has been floated, it may be built on but not criticised. In particular, avoid the temptation to say "that's been tried before and it didn't work". Remember the session is to feed off each other to discover new ideas. Feasibility of these ideas can be considered at another time.

Performance monitoring (How will we know we got there?)

A marketing plan is never set in stone. Due to the dynamic nature of the marketing environment, any plan should have the scope for flexibility to adapt. In this regard small businesses have an advantage over big corporations by being more agile in responding quickly to shifting circumstances. The issues around measuring performance are addressed in *14:Tourism Marketing Performance Measurement*.

Key points

1: Marketing planning as a forward thinking process

Marketers need to be forward thinking. Tourism businesses operate in an increasingly dynamic environment, over which they have no control. Every business needs some form of marketing plan to chart a course through an uncertain future.

2: The importance of marketing planning is striving to gain a competitive edge

For any travel purchase situation, consumers are usually spoilt by choice of products offering similar features and benefits. So business success is dependent on the ability to develop *strengths* to take advantage of *opportunities* before rivals. First mover advantage doesn't last forever however, with imitators quick to follow the lead, and so the quest for a competitive edge is ongoing.

3: The key stages in marketing planning

Marketing planning is not an exact science, and requires skills in both critical analysis and creative thinking. The chapter outlines a structured process for developing a marketing plan to differentiate from competitors and strive for a competitive edge. The structure of this planning approach enables stakeholders such as staff and investors to follow the rationale for the proposed marketing objectives and ensuing tactics.

Discussion questions

1. Why will a small tourism business only realistically have one or a few *strengths*?

2. Why are the following not representative of an *opportunity* in the SWOT Matrix?

    ■ To create a virtual reality experience.

    ■ To advertise on nearby bus shelters.

    ■ To develop a Facebook page.

3. Why is a situation analysis so important in the marketing planning process?

References

Barney, J. (1991). Firm resources and sustained competitive advantage. *Journal of Management,* **17**(1): 99-120.

Barney, J. (1996). *Gaining and Sustaining Competitive Advantage.* Reading, Massachusetts: Addison-Wesley.

Brown, V.R. & Paulus, P.B. (2002). Making group brainstorming more effective: Recommendations from an associative memory perspective. *Current Directions in Psychological Science.* **11**(6): 208-212.

Buzan, T. & Buzan, B. (1995). *The Mindmap Book.* London: BBC Books.

Collins, J.C. & Porras, J.I (1997). *Built to Last.* New York: HarperCollins.

Drucker, P. (1995). *Managing in a Time of Great Change.* Oxford: Butterworth-Heinemann.

Magee, J.F. (1964). Decision trees for decision making. *Harvard Business Review.* **42**: 126-138.

Pease, A. & Pease, B. (2016). *The Answer: How to Take Charge of your Life and become the Person you want to be.* Orion Publishing Group.

Schwartz, P. (1992). *The Art of the Long View.* London: Century Business.

Wack, P. (1985). Scenarios: uncharted waters ahead. *Harvard Business Review.* September-October: 73-89.

Yeoman, I. (2012). *2050 – Tomorrow's Tourism.* Bristol, UK: Channelview Publications.

5 Tourism Marketing Research

Chapter outline

A marketing orientation dictates decisions be made with target consumers in mind. This requires gathering *information* that will provide insights into the experience of current customers, and the needs of target consumers. Marketing research is an essential activity, even for small tourism businesses with limited resources, because information reduces uncertainty in decision making. However, marketing research is often under-utilised by small tourism businesses, due to lack of training, negative perceptions of the practical value, or lack of resources. This chapter presents a six-stage process for gathering information to enhance marketing decision making. The process starts with the identification of the marketing decision problem (MDP) and then articulating the marketing research question (MRQ) that will guide the research design. For any MRQ there will be a range of data collection options, and so understanding the strengths and weaknesses of different research techniques is important. The argument is made for the use of a mixed methods research design, which combines qualitative and quantitative data collection techniques, to provide a richer depth and breadth of information than could be obtained from using a single method.

Learning aims

To enhance your understanding of:

- The role of marketing research in management decision making

- A six-step marketing research process

- The value of using a mixed methods research design.

Key terms

Primary data
New data being collected for the first time for a specific purpose, through interacting with, and/or observing participants, using qualitative and/or or quantitative methods.

Secondary data
Existing data that has been collected for a purpose other than the current research.

Mixed methods
A research design employing both qualitative and quantitative data collection methods.

Introduction

Information reduces uncertainty and enhances management decision making. Therefore, marketing research is an essential ongoing activity for all small businesses. Either informally or formally, information needs to be collated about environment *opportunities* (see 4:*Tourism Marketing Planning*), competitors' activities, the experience of current customers, and the needs of target consumers (including those who choose competitors' offerings). Remember that *perception is reality*; what people believe to be true will be real in its consequences (Thomas & Thomas, 1928 in Patton, 2002). This theory underpins the need for information about people's perceptions given the influence in purchase decisions.

Critical point: Develop an interest in numbers

Anyone involved in operating or marketing a small business needs to have an understanding of the principles of marketing research, as well as basic accounting. Otherwise, how will you be able to trust your marketing researcher or accountant if you don't understand the strengths and weaknesses of different options being recommended to you? Putting aside a fear of numbers and being prepared to engage with data, to find useful information, can lead to a competitive edge in the marketplace over those who shy away.

Marketing research has been defined as (Burns et al., 2017):

> The process of designing, gathering, analysing, and reporting information that may be used to solve a specific marketing problem.

This means any collection of information can be regarded as research, including informal approaches such as talking to customers or suppliers. The more complex the problem, the more detailed the information and the more systematic the research design. What is important is that the information generated for marketing decision making is: relevant, accurate, reliable, valid, timely, and efficient (Malhotra et al., 2006).

Formal marketing research is a six stage process, beginning with identifying the marketing decision problem (MDP), as shown in Figure 5.1. The stages are shown here in a cyclical format, to indicate that marketing research can be an ongoing process rather than a linear one that stops at stage 6. The findings often lead to a revised MDP that requires more research. An understanding of each of the stages in this process is important for a small business, whether undertaking research in house or outsourcing.

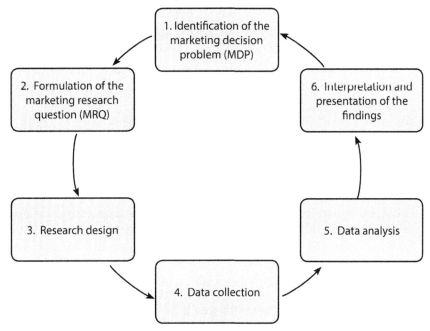

Figure 5.1: Stages in the marketing research process

Marketing decision problem

The first and most important stage in the marketing research process is identifying and succinctly articulating the marketing decision problem (MDP). The MDP is a one sentence description of the *decision facing management* in relation to a problem or opportunity. In this chapter, the decision problem relates to both problems and opportunities, which exist in each part of the marketing mix. These can be in relation to either the need to identify whether there is a problem/opportunity, or identifying how to solve the problem or take advantage of an opportunity. Typically the MDP is related to one of the following:

■ Improving profitability through increasing sales and/or reducing costs

■ Improving promotion effectiveness

■ Developing new markets/segments

■ Developing and pricing new service offerings

- Improving service standards
- Identifying market characteristics
- Understanding consumer behaviour
- Analysing competitors

The MDP is action oriented, and written from the perspective of management, rather than the researcher, such as:

- Should we enter the China market? (Problem solving)
- Are our existing customers happy with our service during the rush hour? (Problem identification)
- What price should we charge for this new product? (Problem solving)
- How do we know if our billboard advertising is working? (Problem identification)

Formulating the marketing research question

The marketing research question (MRQ) is a broad description of the information required to address the MDP, which can be broken down into manageable objectives. The MRQ is *information-oriented* and therefore written from the perspective of the researcher. Examples of differences between the wording of an MDP with a MRQ are listed in Table 5.1. It's helpful to start the MRQ with one of the six Ws: what, where, why, who, what, when.

Table 5.1: Examples of the relationship between MDP and MRQ

Marketing decision problem (MDP)	Marketing research question (MRQ)
Is there a problem with our service quality?	What are the perceptions of our service quality by customers and non-customers?
Develop packaging for new souvenir product	How are alternative package designs perceived by consumers?
Should we change the brand logo and slogan?	What are the perceptions of the brand, relative to competitors, in the minds of target consumers?

Consider a marketing decision needing to be made about whether to introduce a new product. A general example of the MDP, MRQ and research objectives is summarised in Table 5.2.

Table 5.2: Example of relationship between the MDP, MRQ and research objectives

MDP	Should the new product be launched in the market?
MRQ	What are consumer perceptions of the product?
Research objectives	To identify consumer preferences for this type of product. To identify consumers' potential purchase intent for this type of product. To identify the range of similar offerings by competitors.

Critical point: The importance of asking the right question

Getting the MDP and MRQ is critical to the success of the project, because they lay the foundation for the remaining stages. The best data collection and analysis will be meaningless if based on the wrong question. As Dr Karl Kruszelnichi reminds us: "It's not the answer that gets you the prize, it's the question".

Research design and data collection

The research design sets out the collection of primary and secondary data that will generate information to address the marketing decision problem.

Secondary data

The starting point in research design is undertaking a search of secondary data. This is existing data that has previously been collected for a purpose other than the current research project. The range of secondary data sources is vast and includes such diversity as government census data, industry reports, news media, blogs and other social media, DMO websites, geographic information systems, internal customer database, and the academic literature.

Lean marketing: Are we making the most of the firm's existing data?

A basic customer database can easily be set up and maintained. For example, accommodation businesses have guest registration cards, restaurants have reservations details, cafes and retailers have a record of what is selling and when; and all should have a complaints file. It also doesn't take much to add a question at the register/checkout (e.g. What is your post code? What was the main reason for your visit?), or having a suggestion box for example, when there is a captive customer audience. Depending on the marketing research problem, there may already exist some useful information already held by the firm. As is discussed in *12: Customer Relationship Management in Tourism*, loyalty programmes that record transactions of frequent customers can be a valuable source of data on purchase behaviour and effectiveness of rewards offers such as short term coupons.

Secondary data analysis is often referred to as *desk research*, given the ease at which electronic sources can be accessed from the desktop computer or laptop. This is an important step prior to undertaking primary data collection, which can save a lot of time and resources. We might find some of the information we need already exists.

Industry insight: It's all about the bed!

A content analysis of over 60,000 hotel review comments on Expedia.com found lower customer ratings for a hotel were most frequently attributed to negative comments about the bed. Interestingly however, the bed was not attributed to positive reviews (Stringham & Gerdes, 2010). This secondary data has important implications for all accommodation providers.

Lean marketing: Subscribe to free travel industry newsletters

There is a range of freely available tourism newsletters, providing updates on industry developments around the world. These include: www.skift.com, www.travelwirenews. com, www.eturbonews.com, www.thebyte.com.au, and www.travelindustrywire.com. It is also worthwhile subscribing to email newsletters from the local DMO and tourism industry association.

Primary data collection

Primary data is that being collected for the first time for a specific purpose through interacting with and/or observing participants using qualitative and/or quantitative methods.

Ethics

Every marketing research project should be undertaken in an ethical manner, particularly during primary data collection when we are dealing with human beings. While some ethical research issues are not black and white, two important considerations are that the research should not break any laws, particularly in relation to participants' privacy and any research involving children, and that no one will suffer hurt or loss. Researchers must adopt the view that it is a privilege to have people participate, and that we should treat them with respect in a spirit of reciprocity. Codes of research ethics usually include the following principles (Jennings, 2001):

- Voluntary participation
- Informed consent
- The right to refuse to answer any question
- The right to withdraw at any time
- Confidentiality
- Participants' access to the findings.

Mixed methods

Mixed methods is a research design employing both qualitative and quantitative data collection methods. Using mixed methods provides a greater depth and breadth of data than could be generated by using either qualitative or quantitative, as highlighted in Figure 5.2.

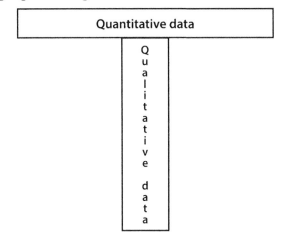

Figure 5.2: Mixed methods give breadth and depth

Quantitative methods have the potential to generate a great breadth of data through a large sample of participants responding to a large number of multiple choice questions. However, a disadvantage of this type of data is that the multiple choice format generates responses that are just descriptive numbers. We don't have the ability to analyse the 'why' behind participants' responses. Quantitative data does not have as great a depth as qualitative.

Qualitative methods generate a greater depth of information through conversations with participants, where meanings are elicited in their own language rather than the researcher's language being imposed on them as in a questionnaire. However, because of the labour intense nature of data collection and interpretation, qualitative samples are relatively small, and therefore lack the breadth of quantitative data. In a mixed methods research design, the qualitative stage is commonly undertaken prior to the quantitative stage. For example, personal interviews with customers could be used to help design a questionnaire about service satisfaction. However, a qualitative stage could also follow the quantitative stage. For example, focus groups could be convened to gain insights on specific findings that emerged from the questionnaire. The key characteristics of qualitative and quantitative research are compared and contrasted in Table 5.3.

Table 5.3: Key characteristics of qualitative and quantitative methods

	Qualitative research	Quantitative research
Purpose	To find meaning in a phenomenon or situation from an inside perspective.	To measure the phenomenon or situation and generalise results to the wider population of interest.
Sample	Relatively small in number. Non-probability methods. Not representative of the wider population of interest.	Relatively large in number. Probability methods. Representative of the wider population of interest.
Methods	Unstructured or semi-structured data collection, through personal interviews, focus groups, or observation.	Structured data collection, through observation, surveys, or experiments.
Data	Non-numerical.	Numerical.
Data analysis	Subjective interpretation.	Objective statistical analysis.
Outcome	An initial understanding of a situation, which may be tested through quantitative research.	Marketing implementation recommendations.
Practical tourism applications	Identifying items to include in a questionnaire. Testing creative concepts such as new branding, advertising and packaging. Exploring views and price impressions for a new product. Generating new ideas for an old product. Exploring motivations for an activity. Observing a phenomenon, such as queueing for service. Exploring barriers to purchase by non-customers. Exploring issues that emerged from a questionnaire.	Measuring: - brand awareness - brand positioning - brand loyalty - service quality - customer satisfaction - differences between groups Identifying different segments in the population. Identifying associations between variables.

Qualitative research methods

The role of science and philosophy has always been to attempt to explain the world we live in. Such explanations are referred to as theories, which help to simplify our complex existence. Theories are developed through the scientific method, which involves observation of a phenomenon, hypothesis development and then rigorous testing. The starting point is qualitative research, which is exploratory in nature. Qualitative methods enable us to *explore* a phenomenon to a depth not possible with a quantitative approach, by either observing actual behaviour or conversing with people and asking them to express their views in their terms, and then interpreting their beliefs and/or behaviour. The strengths of qualitative research methods are that the research can take place in natural settings, the emphasis is on the participants' meanings, and there is a high degree of flexibility.

Critical point: There is nothing so practical as good theory!

Marketing research is underpinned by theory. The value of reviewing the academic literature is that it can guide us about theories relevant to our marketing research question (MRQ). If our MRQ contains a construct, such as *brand awareness* or *market position*, for example, we can look for a theory that will guide our research design. A theory is practical when it helps determine how the construct can be measured.

Purpose

The purpose of qualitative research is to find meaning in a phenomenon or situation from an insider's perspective.

Sample

A relatively small number of people, who are representative of the wider population of interest. Non-probability sampling methods are used, such as convenience sampling, quota sampling and snowball sampling. It is important that the small number of participants are selected purposively, which means they should be knowledgeable about the research topic matter. The general rule is to continue sampling until a point of data saturation is reached, which is when the addition of any new participants does not generate any new data. While there is no set number of what constitutes a small sample, in general it might be expected there would be between 10 and 30 participants, depending on the interview method.

Methods

The three most common qualitative research methods are personal interviews, focus groups and observation. Each enables an unstructured approach to data collection. The unstructured approach enables greater flexibility, and so the researcher starts with one or a few questions, but can then shape the discussion depending on the responses. This is more conducive for understanding the situation from the insider's perspective, in their words.

Personal interviews involve a one-on-one in-depth conversation, using detailed probing, commonly for between 30 minutes and an hour. This is particularly valuable for discussion around sensitive topics, and where indirect forms of questioning can be used to tap the subconscious. These include: hidden issue questioning; word association; and sentence, picture or story completion. A disadvantage is that it is very time consuming to conduct the interviews, and then transcribe and interpret the data.

A *focus group* involves 8-12 participants being led in a discussion by a trained moderator. The value of this approach lies in the interaction between participants in a free-flowing discussion, similar to a brain storming exercise. Challenges include the over reliance on a skilled moderator, the danger of group-think, and the transcription and interpretation the mass of audio and visual data.

Observation research can be qualitative or quantitative, depending on the level of structure. A highly structured quantitative approach is where the researcher knows what to look for in advance, such as counting foot traffic or vehicles at a specific location. An unstructured qualitative approach seeks to understand behaviour taking place in a situation. Examples include examining shop camera footage of customers' browsing patterns and focus group videos. Variations of these approaches used in tourism research include:

- Social media web crawlers such as Salesforce to explore what consumers are posting about a situation (Stringham & Gerdes, 2010).
- Mystery shopper technique to explore the customer experience in hospitality and retail (Miller et al., 2005)

Data

Qualitative data is non-numerical, and may take a range of forms that are textual, oral or visual, including: interview transcripts, focus group video footage, participants' drawings, video diaries, photos, and the researcher's field notes.

Data analysis and interpretation

Qualitative research does not attempt to measure anything. Due to the non-numerical nature of the data, analysis is by subjective interpretation and can be more challenging and messy than quantitative data analysis. As we are all unique individuals with different life-experiences, when we are interpreting qualitative data we acknowledge our biases. Therefore the interpretation is subjective and depends upon who is undertaking the analysis; different researchers might reach different conclusions. For this reason it is helpful if triangulation is utilised, so that a comparative consensus can be reached. Triangulation involves analysing different data sources to arrive more confidently at a finding than from one source alone. This can also involve data analysis being undertaken by two or three co-researchers, or by analysing a combination of data sources such as personal interviews and secondary data.

There are computer software programmes now available to assist analysis of qualitative data, such as NVivo, CATPAC, Atlas.ti, and Leximancer. These programs don't automate the analysis as the output generated relies on the researcher to instruct the software on what to search for and code into themes. A useful analogy in this regard is to consider the validity of a machine marking your next major written assignment or essay. Marking an essay is subject to the interpretation of the marker, and it is difficult to program software to do this accurately.

The first step is assembling the data, which commonly requires a transcription of audio recordings from personal interviews and focus groups. The second step is to reduce the data, and this is generally undertaken by thematic analysis. Key themes gradually emerge through the researcher deciding what is most relevant through the coding of patterns. The third step is to display the data. This is usually in the form of graphics such as word clouds and flowcharts where the relationships between key themes can be structured. The fourth step is to verify the findings, because of the subjective nature of the analysis, by questioning whether there are alternative explanations. This is where triangulation of sources of data or interpretation by co-researchers is invaluable. For detailed discussion on qualitative data evaluation see Patton (2015).

Outcome

The final outcome of qualitative research is the development of an initial under-standing of what might be happening in a particular situation, since the sample size and characteristics do not enable the findings to be generalised to other situations or the wider population of interest. The findings only apply to that unique situation and group of participants, although they can be used to generate hypotheses or research questions to be tested in a quantitative research stage.

5

Activity 5.1: Would you rely on one focus group to make a marketing decision?

Imagine you were developing a new brand logo and slogan, and had been supplied with three options from a graphic designer. A colleague has suggested you run a focus group meeting of customers or target consumers to pick the most popular theme. What are the advantages and disadvantages of using a focus group to help you make a decision regarding the new brand? Overall would you rely on one focus group to make such a strategic decision?

Practical tourism applications

As shown in Table 5.3 there is a wide range of practical uses for qualitative research methods. In general, because the data analysis is subjectively interpreted and the sample size is small, the findings cannot be generalised to the wider target population, and so these methods are most applicable for tactical decisions where the decision outcome does not represent a long term and major investment by the firm; or the qualitative research is part of a wider project, combined with quantitative research, aimed at enabling a major strategic marketing decision.

Quantitative research methods

Quantitative research is commonly undertaken in the form of a *descriptive* approach, which involves surveys and observation. This approach is used to describe the characteristics of a population (e.g. a target market) or a phenomenon (e.g. short break holidays). Descriptive research can be used to describe *who, what, where, when and how* of consumer behaviour, but can't be used to address the *why* questions (e.g. the *why* of *buy*). Experimental research designs, also referred to as causal research, are used to measure relationships between variables, and therefore can be used to address the *why* questions. Experimental designs are rare for small tourism businesses due to the level of complexity involved.

Purpose

The purpose of quantitative research methods is to *measure* the phenomenon or situation and *generalise* the results to the wider population of interest; that is, to infer that the findings from the sample can be applied to the wider population with a good level of confidence. This helps marketers make predictions about future events.

Sample

To generalise results to the wider population of interest, and maximise the level of confidence, necessitate obtaining a large and representative sample. A *census*, which surveys the entire population, is rarely practical nor feasible in marketing research. Probability sampling techniques, where every member of the population has a known and equal chance of being chosen, include simple random sampling, stratified sampling and cluster sampling. There is no single rule for what constitutes a large sample. While most samples in quantitative marketing research are in the range of 350+, small businesses with limited resources should aim for sample of at least 100 for small tactical marketing decision problems. Sample size can vary according to a range of issues, such as: the available budget; the importance of the marketing decision problem; the number of variables (scale items) in the questionnaire; the type of data analysis to be used; and the level of confidence required in the statistics. The demographic characteristics of the sample should also be representative of the wider population of interest.

Traditionally the starting point for obtaining a sample is to use a *sample frame*. A sample frame is the source from which a participants can be randomly selected. Ideally this is in the form of a list, such as a customer database, membership list, map or telephone directory. However, rarely will the sample frame contain an up to date and complete listing of all members of the target population, and so there will be a margin of error between the findings from the sample and that which might be expected from the wider population. An increasingly practical option, budget permitting, is to use a research panel. Many marketing research firms have developed large panels of participants who have agreed to participate in regular online surveys. These participants are rewarded by the marketing research firm for their loyalty based on how many surveys they complete. The costs for accessing a panel will depend on the number of participants sought and the length of time the survey will take to complete. Data turnaround is very quick when using panels, with results usually available in a few days.

Methods

The three main quantitative methods are observation, surveys, and experiments. Observation is commonly used for counting foot traffic, such as in a retail precinct, and vehicle movements past a specific location, such as a billboard advertising sign. Surveys are the most common form of quantitative research, with questionnaires in an online or paper-based self-complete format or undertaken by researchers in interviews by phone or in intercept surveys. The majority of questionnaire items are in the form of closed-ended questions, where the participants selects one response from fixed alternatives. Examples of the most popular closed-ended questions are shown in Table 5.4.

Table 5.4: Popular types of questionnaire scale items

Dichotomous Two choice options	What is your gender? Male Female
Likert-type Indicating level of agreement with a statement about a functional attribute, along a continuum	This restaurant provides great service Strongly disagree Strongly agree 1 2 3 4 5
Semantic differential A continuum of bi-polar (opposite) attitudes (feelings)	This attraction is: Boring Exciting ☐ ☐ ☐ ☐ ☐
Multiple choice	How often did you use the hotel pool during your stay? Never Once Twice Three or more times

Open-ended questions can also be used. These allow the participant to respond in their own words, which is more time-consuming to analyse in a large sample, but can provide a richer understanding. Indirect forms of open-ended questioning can also be used, such as story, picture or sentence completion.

Most surveys are a snapshot of participants' perceptions at one point of time, and so it must be recognised that results might be different if investigated at another time. Longitudinal studies, which involve multiple surveys of the same participants over time, are rare due to time and resource constraints (Pike, 2006; Pike & Larkin, 2010). However, this approach is extremely valuable in studies investigating the relationship between what people say (stated intent) and what they actually do (behaviour).

Lean marketing: Free online surveys

Free online surveys can be undertaken using online tools such as www.surveymonkey.com. The site enables you to quickly set up a basic online questionnaire, the URL link for which can then be emailed to potential participants. Participants' responses are automatically pooled to provide descriptive data such as frequencies and means. While there are limitations to what can be undertaken with the free membership option, SurveyMonkey is a very user friendly, efficient and effective option for basic marketing research.

Data

Quantitative data is numerical. Even the responses to open ended questions can be coded numerically.

Data analysis

Data is loaded onto a spreadsheet or statistical software package for analysis. While statistical software licenses can be expensive, Microsoft Excel is an effective option for small businesses. For more detailed discussion on the use of spreadsheets for data analysis see Burns and Bush (2012). The two main types of data analysis are descriptive and inferential, and the type used will depend on the characteristics of the data collected and the sample size. Basic descriptive data analysis includes frequencies and means, from which differences between groups in the sample can be explored through common techniques such as t-tests and Analysis of Variance (ANOVA). More advanced techniques include cluster analysis for segmenting a population, Exploratory Factor Analysis for reducing a long list of attributes into a reduced set of common themes, and Regression Analysis, and Structural Equation Modelling for testing the relationships between independent variables and a dependent variable.

Outcome

The outcome of the quantitative research stage should be to make practical recommendations in relation to the marketing decision problem.

Practical tourism applications

As shown in Table 5.3 (p. 80) there is a range of important marketing issues that can be addressed using a quantitative research design.

Case 5.1: Surf's up 咱们进去冲浪吧！

Sarah Gardiner and Noel Scott, Griffith University, Gold Coast, Australia

To remain competitive in changing tourism markets, Destination Marketing Organisations need to support and encourage small businesses to evolve their services to meet the needs of a changing visitor mix. The Gold Coast is one of Australia's major leisure tourism destinations, providing a fun holiday environment built around the core resources of surf beaches, waterways, theme parks and hinterland environments. Gold Coast tourism experiences have historically catered for predominantly Western markets, chiefly domestic visitors from Brisbane, Sydney and Melbourne, and international visitors from New Zealand (the number one international source of visitors), North America and Europe. However, the recent dramatic growth in Japanese (1980s onwards) and later in Chinese visitors (2000s onwards) has presented challenges for tourism businesses, in terms of evolving their service offerings to accommodate the important cultural differences of these new markets.

China is the fastest growing international travel market in the world and many Australian destinations, like the Gold Coast, have benefited from this boom in Chinese travellers. China will soon become Australia's largest source of international visitor arrivals. However, some of the needs of Chinese visitors are quite different to those from more traditional markets, and so product development is a strategic issue.

Gold Coast tourism businesses are aware of the opportunity to grow their business by attracting more Chinese visitors, but require insightful and actionable research on the preferences of Chinese visitors to make the experiences offered by local businesses *China-ready*. Accordingly, research is needed to investigate ways Gold Coast tourism businesses could make changes to their guest experience to better accommodate Chinese visitors, in particular youth and student travellers. This case is particularly interested in practical and actionable research for a surfing school business that is interested in getting into the China market. Chinese university students living in Brisbane (an hour drive) and the Gold Coast are the sample of interest, for an investigation into perceptions and attitude towards participating in a surf lesson as part of a Gold Coast visit.

Preliminary research suggests Chinese international students really like the beach and it is one of their main reasons for visiting and studying in the Brisbane/Gold Coast region. However, most of the time, they just tended to look and visit the beach, and didn't enter the water, because they were unfamiliar with the surf and had a fear of the waves. The surf school wonders if it needs to modify its product offering to something different to better appeal to Chinese visitors, since they are currently not attracting many at all. Currently the product offers a brief instruction on the beach and then straight into the surf.

Discussion questions

- Describe the management decision problem (MDP)?
- Articulate a marketing research question (MRQ) to address the MDP.
- Briefly describe how a mixed methods approach could be applied.

Source: Adapted from Gardiner and Scott (2016).

Interpreting and presenting the findings

The research process does not end with the data analysis and the presentation of statistics. What is required is careful thinking about what the results mean in relation to the marketing decision problem. Interpreting the results therefore requires both critical analysis and creative thinking. Unlike qualitative data interpretation, quantitative data analysis is objective, which is to say that if different researchers generally follow the same data analysis procedures on the same data set, the output should be the same or similar. However, creative thinking is required, first to determine the most appropriate data analysis techniques, and second to generate effective real world recommendations from the mass of data.

Critical point: *So what?*

The critical question to ask when the data analysis is being undertaken is: *So what?* What do the findings all mean, in relation to the marketing decision problem?

Limitations of marketing research

In most competitive tourism markets there is no such thing as perfect information, in terms of providing the ability to eliminate all uncertainty about a decision. Managers are often making decisions at pace, and never have the luxury of having access to all the information needed at the time a decision must be made. Rarely is a research design perfect, and so all research projects have limitations. The value of the academic literature in this regard is that every good journal article will discuss the limitations of the project and offer some suggestions for future research. Common examples of limitations of marketing research projects that have otherwise been carefully planned and executed include:

- The characteristics of the sample may not be completely representative of the wider population of interest.
- The results are what participants have stated, such as purchase intent for example, but do not measure actual behaviour. Studies that measure both stated intent and actual behaviour are rare.

■ Most studies are in the form a snapshot at one point in time, and results might be different if investigated at another time. Longitudinal studies, which involve multiple surveys of the same participants over time, are rare.

Activity 5.2: Fake news? It must be true because I read it in a newspaper!

In traditional newspapers a large proportion of editorial content presents the findings of research. Often there is a sensational headline to grab attention. Many people read the headline and maybe the first paragraph, and then might spread the news through word of mouth. In the post Web 2.0 era, where investigative journalists have declined in number, many newspaper articles are simply a published press release. Can you trust the sensational headline, just because it's in a newspaper, and might be just a corporate press release? A way to test your understanding of research methods is to read these types of articles and determine whether you believe the findings are valid, based on the details (or lack of) reported on how the research was conducted. What questions might you ask to validate the reported results?

5

Key points

1: The role of marketing research in management decision making

A marketing orientation requires that all decision making be made with the consumer in mind. This requires gathering information that will provide insights into the experience of current customers and the needs of target consumers. Marketing research is an essential activity, even for small tourism businesses with limited resources, because information reduces uncertainty in decision making.

2: A six-step marketing research process

This chapter presented a six-stage process for gathering information to enhance marketing decision making. The process starts with the identification of the marketing decision problem (MDP) and then articulating the marketing research question (MRQ) that will guide the research design. For any MRQ there will be a range of data collection options, and so an understanding of the strengths and weaknesses of different research techniques is important.

3: The value of using a mixed methods research design

The argument is made for the use of mixed methods, which is a combination of qualitative and quantitative data collection techniques, to provide a richer depth and breadth of information than could be obtained from using a single method.

Discussion questions

1. Why is it essential that all tourism business owners and marketing managers have an understanding of the principles of marketing research?

2. How would you decide whether to use a qualitative or quantitative stage in the research design?

3. Explain why it is acceptable to acknowledge the limitations of the findings in a marketing research project to stakeholders, such as management, staff, investors or financiers?

References

Burns, A.C. & Bush, R.F. (2012). *Basic Marketing Research – Using Microsoft Excel Data Analysis*. (3rd Edition). Upper Saddle River, NJ: Pearson.

Burns, A.C., Veeck, A. & Bush, R. (2017). *Marketing Research*. (8th Edition). Harlow, Essex: Pearson Education Ltd.

Gardiner, S. & Scott, N. (2016). Collaborative marketing research for product development. In Pike, S. *Destination Marketing Essentials*. Abingdon, Oxon: Routledge, pp. 168- 170.

Jennings, G. (2001). *Tourism Research*. Milton, Qld: Wiley.

Malhotra, N., Hall, J., Shaw, M. & Oppenheim, P. (2006). *Marketing Research: An Applied Orientation*. (3rd Ed). Frenchs Forest: Pearson.

Miller, G., Hudson, S. & Turner, R. (2005). Applying the mystery shopping technique: The case of Lunn Poly. In Ritchie, B.W., Burns, P. & Palmer, C. (Eds.). *Tourism Research Methods – Integrating Theory with Practice*. Wallingford, Oxforshire: CABI Publishing, pp. 119-130.

Patton, M.Q. (2002). *Qualitative Research & Evaluation Methods*. (3rd Ed). Thousand Oaks: Sage.

Patton, M.Q. (2015). *Qualitative Research & Evaluation Methods*. (4th Ed). Thousand Oaks: Sage.

Pike, S. (2006). Destination decision sets: A longitudinal comparison of stated destination preferences and actual travel. *Journal of Vacation Marketing*. 12(4): 319-328.

Pike, S. & Larkin, I. (2010). Longitudinal evaluations of student satisfaction with a postgraduate unit using Importance-Performance Analysis. *Journal of Teaching in Travel & Tourism,* **10**(3): 215-231.

Stringham, B.B. & Gerdes, J. (2010). An analysis of word-of-mouse ratings and guest comments on online hotel distribution sites. *Journal of Hospitality Marketing & Management,* **19**(7): 773-796.

6 Designing Tourism Services and Experiences

Chapter outline

The tourism industry has long been about providing intangible services. *Service* is an interactive process of doing something for someone, which they value. Two major shifts in thinking by marketers about the service concept have been taking place in recent years. First, there has been a change to now regarding service value as something that is *co-created* by the customer in conjunction with the service provider. This has become known as service-dominant logic, and is contrary to the dominant paradigm that views service as something that is just provided by the business. In this regard, tourism is becoming increasingly based around the customer's involvement, which means tourism suppliers and consumers are engaging more closely at each stage of their relationship. Second, since Pine and Gilmore's (1998, 1999) treatise on the emergent *experience economy*, there has been increasing interest by firms in transitioning from providing services to staging memorable experiences. The challenge for tourism businesses in this new economy is to design an engaging experience that will be memorable for individual customers, and command a price premium for the business.

Learning aims

To enhance your understanding of:

- Service value as being co-created by the customer and the service provider
- The challenges in transitioning to the experience economy
- The key characteristics of memorable experiences

Key terms

Service
An interactive process of doing something for someone, which they value.

Service-dominant logic
A philosophy that views service value as being co-created by the service provider together with the customer.

The experience economy
A paradigm shift recognising the need to evolve from providing a service to staging an experience. The challenge in the *experience economy* is to design an engaging experience that represents a memorable event for the customer, and commands a price premium for the business.

Service-dominant logic

Service is an interactive process of doing something for someone, which they value. This goes beyond the moment the actual paid service is delivered and consumed. Service can also take place prior to purchase, such as providing information and advice. Service can also continue post-purchase consumption, such as offering a money back warranty, returning a lost property item, and keeping repeat customers updated with special offers and rewards programmes.

Providing intangible services has long been one of the key characteristics of the visitor industry. However, within the marketing field there is a paradigm shift away from thinking about service as being a product that is *provided* by a business. This product-dominant thinking is characteristic of an internal organisation orientation, which has a focus on production and promotion. What has emerged relatively recently, is service-dominant thinking, which has a more outward marketing orientation based on the needs of consumers.

Lean marketing: A personal touch and a free beer

A humble motel in the regional Queensland city of Mackay was the highest rated hotel in Australia for 2017 on the online booking site Hotels.com. The key to the success for the three year old property was free beer and a personal touch, according to the owner: "Our ranking on all those sites has been pretty high for quite a while and it's something we take a lot of pride in. We go the extra mile for our guests and show an interest in who they are and where they come from. We also offer them a free beer when they arrive, something for the weary traveller. It blows people away".

Source: Pierce (2017)

The critical concept underpinning service-dominant logic (S-D) is *value co-creation* (Vargo & Lusch, 2004, 2008). This goes beyond the world view of service as something that is provided to a customer, to one where service is co-created. Within S-D logic, service value is co-created, by the supplier's value proposition (see *7: Tourism Branding*) and the customer's consumption experience. What consumers generally value in a proposition, when comparing available offerings, will be on the basis of price or quality (e.g. cheaper, faster, or better). The customer decides whether value has been delivered, and this will depend on their individual expectations, previous experiences, the price they paid, and the extent they themselves take advantage of, and participate in, the consumption opportunities offered. A competitive edge can be gained by using operant resources (intangible skills and knowledge) to engage with consumers in a way that is superior to how competitors use their resources.

The importance of people in delivering service

To paraphrase the late management guru Peter Drucker, *culture eats strategy for breakfast*. The best laid marketing plans will come to nothing if staff are not motivated to deliver. It is important to remember that people are required to deliver tourism services. This seems like an obvious statement, and yet consider how many frontline staff are the lowest paid in hospitality businesses. Frontline staff who are engaging with customers really are *the stars of the show*. All workplaces have a culture, whether cultivated or not. Therefore it is critical to consider the type of collective purpose that will best deliver job satisfaction, customer satisfaction and return on investment; and then to lead, inspire and nurture this consistently over time. Perceptions about employment in the tourism industry are sometimes negative, and staff retention levels low, with key concerns including low wages, long hours, difficult customers, and few opportunities for career progression. This presents opportunities for businesses that develop a culture that makes for an attractive employer brand. Keep in mind the management axiom that if you get the workplace culture right, all the other stuff will take care of itself. Cultivating a service culture necessitates treating employees as internal customers, and empower them to *use their own best judgement* to solve customers' problems.

The customer is not always right, and they don't always know what they *want* to satisfy a *need*

The customer is not always right, and they don't always know what they *want* to satisfy a *need*. There is a fine balance between designing services based on consumers' *needs*, and understanding their *wants* might be limited by their imagination. Revolutionary new products such as the cell phone, jet ski, light bulb or ice cream cone, for argument sake, would not have eventuated if marketers only listened to consumers' wants. Indeed, successful new product ideas that were actually rejected in consumer focus groups have included ATM machines, the Sony Walkman, and Bailey's Irish Cream. Conversely, it is important to note that new product failure rates are estimated to be between 30% (Crawford, 1987) and 95% (Nobel, 2011) every year, even though many were supported in focus groups.

Activity 6.1: Design your perfect tourism subject

As a class of students, brainstorm ideas for designing a perfect tourism subject, such as *Tourism Marketing*. To begin, reach consensus on what is the *need* underpinning your enrolment. In other words, why are you studying, and what will this degree or diploma get you at the end of the day? Next, brainstorm how you would like the subject to operate, so that you would be satisfied at the end of the semester. Imagine that all suggestions would be accepted, on the basis of the customer (you) being right. Finally, assess the proposed new subject in terms of how it meets your *need* (reason for being enrolled).

Co-creation in tourism

Until recently there has been a failure by tourism researchers to engage with the concept of S-D (Shaw et al., 2011). Examples of co-creation in tourism, where there is a clear value proposition, include:

■ The business model of low cost airlines relies on the customer self-booking their own flights via the internet and then benefitting from discounted fares (see Mintel, 2005).

■ Travel itinerary management platforms, such as TripIt.com, which enable the user to consolidate different bookings into one master itinerary (see Applegate et al., 2008).

Another S-D approach is to work with customers in a way that seeks their advice to improve future service delivery. In this way the customer becomes an operant resource for the business as a source of expertise. A common example involves engaging with customers by seeking their feedback (e.g. guest surveys, online reviews) and then acting on their advice. Examples used by different hotels were reported by Shaw et al. (2011), who suggested, perhaps not surprisingly, that customers were more likely to be operant co-creators when there were experiential and economic benefits for them:

■ Repeated trial and error product testing and experimentation with a new in-room entertainment system in a few guestrooms. Undertaken with regular guests who were briefed on the initiative on arrival, and then subsequently interviewed at checkout.

■ Development of a multi-sensory dining experience, where guests are seated 'back stage' to witness the skill involved in preparing their menu. Guests are also able to interact with the kitchen staff, and subsequently offer suggestions.

■ Customer survey feedback is scrutinised, and then used to structure focus group meetings with key clients. Clients are given two nights' accommodation and wined and dined in return for four hours of focus group 'work'.

The experience economy

Tourism has become increasingly based around the customer's involvement, which means tourism suppliers and visitors are engaging more closely at each stage of their relationship (Shaw et al., 2011). Increasingly competitive markets crowded with tourism businesses offering similar features have led to the recognition of the need to evolve from providing a service to staging a memorable *experience*. An experience takes place when the business intentionally uses their services as a theatrical stage (Pine & Gilmore, 1998, 1999). While goods are tangible and services are intangible, experiences are memorable. The central challenge is to design an engaging experience that represents a memorable event for individual *guests,* and commands a price premium for the business.

The key characteristics of *experiences*

Pine and Gilmore (1998) modelled experiences on four realms across two dimensions, as shown in Figure 6.1.

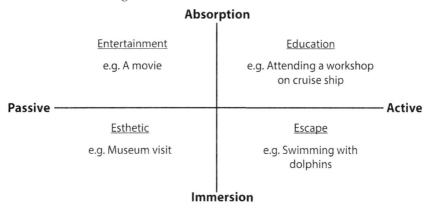

Figure 6.1: Four realms of experiences. Adapted from Pine and Gilmore (1998, p. 102).

The first dimension is *participation*, where there is a continuum from *passive* (e.g. watching a cultural performance) to *active*, where the guest is playing an important role in creating the experience (e.g. swimming with dolphins).

The second dimension is *connection* with the event or performance, and the continuum ranges from *absorption* to *immersion*. For example, those guests watching a major horse race from the grandstands will be absorbed in the spectacle, while those who are trackside are more immersed in the sounds, smells and sights around them. Experiences can be categorised into four realms, based on where they fit along both continuums. Watching a movie is an example of *entertainment* because it is absorbing and passive. Attending a workshop or receiving a ski lesson is *education*, given the experience is both absorbing and involves active participation. An *escapist* experience can be educational and/or entertaining, but involve more immersion such as in a bungy jump. An *aesthetic* experience occurs when the guest is immersed but has no direct effect on the outcome, such as visiting a traditional art gallery.

Tourism should be at the forefront of the experience economy, with travellers actively seeking involvement in memorable activities away from mundane everyday life (MacCannell, 1973; Dann, 1977). Indeed, the tourism industry has long been staging experiences for guests, arguably pioneered in the modern era by Walt Disney. Theme park experiences such as Disneyland were followed by the development of themed restaurants such as Hard Rock Café and Jimmy Buffet's Margaritaville, where the menu is a prop. There have also been attempts by airlines to differentiate based on a unique service culture, most notably Southwest Airlines in the USA; although this is a difficult sector to achieve price premiums, with most airlines competing on price. Today there are experiences being offered by businesses in every sector of travel and tourism, such as in film-induced tourism, corporate incentive travel, culinary tourism, trekking and mountaineering tourism, and cruise tourism.

Case 6.1: Cat poo coffee experience, Bali

Kopi luwak from Indonesia is one of the most expensive coffees in the world, selling at over US$300 a kilo. Luwak coffee is made from beans that have passed through the digestive system of cats. The civet cats, which are known in Indonesia as luwaks, feed on red coffee cherries. The beans ferment inside the cat's stomach, intact within their protective shell. The beans are extracted from the cat poo, removed from their shells and processed. On the holiday island of Bali, rural visitor attractions have been developed where guests can *experience* the unique taste of Kopi luwak. One of these small businesses is Lubak Bali, where guests are given a free individual guided tour of the coffee making process, from the berry garden, to the cats, to the cat poo extraction, to the coffee processing. The tour culminates with a personal tasting session of different coffees and teas in a rustic hut overlooking rice fields. Although the coffee and tea platter is free, there is a fee to experience a cup of luwak coffee. The exit is of course via the small gift shop, but it very much a soft sell. The attraction doesn't charge an admission fee for the overall experience (which they could and probably should). However, the cost to sample the luwak coffee is about the same as you would expect to pay for a coffee in many countries, which is about 10 times that of the local coffees. *Guests therefore pay a premium for the cat poo coffee experience.*

Discussion question

How is service value created in this experience?

In recent years many accommodation operators have been innovating with *experiences* that invite inclusion in anyone's bucket list. These include:

- **Kakslauttanen Artic Resort** in Saariselka, Finland
  Billed as one of the best places to view the Northern Lights and the Midnight Sun, this resort has developed glass igloo accommodation. Guests get to experience the Aurora all night while staying in this glamping style accommodation.

- **Per AQUUM Niyama**, Maldives
  This resort built the first underwater nightclub, Subsix. Also, there are 40 overwater villas of various sizes. That is, each of these villas is built on stilts in the water with direct access to the lagoon from a private sundeck and pool.

- **Hotel de Glace**, Canada
  This hotel is only open from January to March, because it is made of ice! Located only four kilometres from Quebec City, the hotel features over 40 rooms with different themes, all carved from ice.

- **Microluxe Hotel**, Australia
  The theme of this Melbourne accommodation is *rest and retail* where the room is curated as a gallery of items that guests can purchase. Stay the night and buy the furniture! This architect-designed hotel features only one room and is only bookable through Airbnb.

Disruption

Even though the term *disruption* has exploded onto the business scene in the Web 2.0 era, it is not a new phenomenon. History is full of examples where entire industries have been significantly disrupted by the development of new technology. For example, pianos were a dominant focus of family entertainment in many households during the 19th century, until the arrival of the gramophone. The gramophone industry, which decimated piano manufacturing, was eventually disrupted by the arrival of wireless radio, then audio cassettes, then CDs, then free online radio apps…... what next? Another example is the arrival of the automobile in the early 20th century, which wiped out an entire industry focused on manufacturing horse drawn carriages and buggy whips. Other historical revolutionary technological advancements are sometimes forgotten about in discussions about current disruptions, as if we are somehow living in more special times. Consider the massive impacts on society, business and tourism when the following new technologies were introduced: steam engines, railroads, electricity, and the telephone. What is different in the digital age is the rapid speed at which new technologies can lead to disruption.

Industry insight: Technology is not the real disruptor

- Amazon did not kill the retail industry. It did it to itself with bad customer service.
- Netflix did not kill Blockbuster. It did it to itself with ridiculous late fees.
- Uber did not kill the taxi business. It did it to itself with limited the number of taxis and fare control.
- Apple did not kill the music industry. It did it to itself by forcing people to buy full-length albums.
- Airbnb did not kill the hotel industry. It did it to itself with limited availability and pricing options.
- Technology by itself is not the real disruptor.
- Being non-customer centric is the biggest threat to any business.

Source: Alberto Brea, 2017,

https://www.linkedin.com/pulse/amazon-did-kill-retail-industry-alberto-brea.

Creative thinking is harder than critical thinking

Most of the innovative tourism service ideas seem simple in hindsight. What differentiates the developers of these ideas from the rest of the population was their creative ability to spot an opportunity in situations where others didn't. It is easy to use critical thinking to critique someone's creative ideas, but it is an altogether different challenge to come up with an innovation. For a review of the literature relating to innovation in tourism see Hjalager (2010). Innovation consultant Mark Payne (2014) provided the following ideas about creativity:

- An ideal innovation is one that will cause minimal disruption to the firm, but maximum disruption in the market.
- Creativity is a delicate process, so avoid any criticism during the brainstorming phase. Generate as many ideas at possible without judgement.
- Take the most glaring flaw facing you and flip it. Zipcar.com identified the processing required at rental car offices as the defining negative characteristic in that market, so their business model was based on removing the office from the hire process.
- Assume transformation is necessary, ask transformational questions (the hardest part of the process), and try to forget what you know (e.g. entrenched paradigms).
- Address the *how* as well as the *wow,* by thinking money and magic. Money focuses on the business questions to generate profit, while magic focuses on the needs of the customer.

Borrowing innovative ideas from those who came before us

Some successful tourism innovations have been based on spotting an opportunity to commercialise the ideas of other people.

The Big Mac

McDonalds didn't invent the Big Mac. Jim Delligatti was the McDonald's franchisee who developed the Big Mac, first served to his customers in Uniontown, Pennsylvania in 1967. Delligatti freely admitted the Big Mac was inspired by the double decker burgers being served up by his local competitors. "This wasn't like discovering the lightbulb. The lightbulb was already there", he told the *Los Angeles Times* in 1993, "All I did was screw it in the socket" (Source: *The Wall Street Journal*, 5 December, 2016: A10).

Bungy Jumping

A.J. Hackett may have been the first to commercialise bungy jumping, but he and business partner Henry van Ash didn't invent the concept. The pair noticed how a group of British university students had developed a rubber band imitation of the ancient vine jumping ceremony from the tiny pacific island nation of Vanuatu. While the students' technology was successful, they were only using it for fun, and didn't recognise the massive commercial opportunity seen by A.J. Hackett.

Backpacker hostels

Share accommodation wasn't a new idea, but the concept of commercial hostels for backpackers proved revolutionary. The idea was based on the model of shared accommodation offered around the world by the Youth Hostel Association (YHA). The YHA is a not-for-profit charitable organisation, which originated over 100 years ago, and dominated share accommodation for travellers with large dormitory rooms until the 1980s. The original YHA concept, which included an alcohol ban and the requirement for guests to undertake chores, proved too conservative for the backpacker market, which emerged in earnest during the 1970s hippy era.

Experiential coach touring

Popular international youth market travel company Contiki Tours reinvented coach touring holidays. Prior to the 1960s, coach tours were a rather staid and passive form of travel, mostly suited to older segments. Contiki Tours was the first to cater to the needs of youth travellers, with a new business model based on a more experiential, social and affordable offering. In the 1990s, Kiwi Experience introduced a new and innovative variant of the Contiki Tours model, by allowing travellers to hop on/hop off at any of the stops in the itinerary, rather than undertake the tour in one go with the same group of people.

Pop culture campervans

In many parts of the world the widespread introduction of campervan rentals during the 1980s represented a shift away from passive coach touring to more independent travel. In 2000, the campervan rentals model was then reinvented by Wicked Campers to better cater to the youth market. Using older beat up vehicles, spray painted with (often offensive) pop culture images, the company opened up a whole new market.

Case 6.2: Tamaki Maori Village, New Zealand

In the early 1960s a former Miss New Zealand, Maureen Waaka (nee Kingi), developed the first Maori (indigenous people) *hangi* and concert entertainment for visitors to the holiday town of Rotorua. With a high ratio of Maori in the population and the highest number of overseas visitors to a regional destination, Rotorua was a logical location. The hangi and concert experience was launched at the THC International Hotel, adjacent to the New Zealand Maori Arts and Crafts Institute and Whakarewarewa geothermal attraction. *Hangi* is a traditional Maori method of cooking meat and vegetables underground for hours on hot stones. The THC Hotel developed an adaptation using the underground geothermal energy, and packaged the meal with a Maori cultural performance by Maureen's concert group. The concert featured the male warrior *Haka* (war dance), made famous by the New Zealand All Blacks rugby team, singing, stick games, and *poi* twirling.

It didn't take long for other hotels in the city to imitate the idea. A number of local hotels provided an almost identical experience for almost 30 years until two young brothers revolutionised the concept. Mike and Doug Tamaki were from the small forestry town of Tokoroa, and had no tourism industry experience. From an outsider's perspective they saw an opportunity to present travellers with a better experience of Maori culture than just "a feed and a dance". So, in 1990 Mike convinced his brother to sell his prized Harley Davidson motorcycle to buy a second-hand 16-seater mini bus they would renovate, and start Tamaki Tours. The long term vision was to develop an authentic Maori village experience in an ancient forest. Without any willing financiers the brothers based their new experience at a series of existing Marae (traditional tribal meeting ground) for a number of years, until they could afford their own property. Tamaki Tours eventually became the most popular evening cultural experience in Rotorua, based on a more traditional and educational storytelling experience than was offered by the hotels. A major part of their success was the clever use of Maori humour and a more participative experience, which proved difficult for competitors to imitate. Today the original vision of Mike and his late brother Doug can be experienced at Tamaki Maori Village, in an ancient forest on the outskirts of Rotorua. The business is the best known and most commercially successful Maori tourism experience in New Zealand.

Discussion question

Why do you think two young men, who weren't from Rotorua and had no tourism industry experience, saw an opportunity that those providing the existing product didn't?

Industry insight: Airbnb, an innovative service start-up by accident

Airbnb started as a small business by accident in 2008, when the founders' rent in San Francisco was raised by 50%. Around the same time a major design fair was being staged in the city, and there were not enough hotels to house all the attendees. The innovative service idea was to pump up air beds, hence the name Airbnb, which were offered as accommodation on a basic website. Three guests stayed for one week, generating income of $1,000. Within a decade the company had become a business community with 2.5 million homes in 34,000 cities in 191 countries. While Airbnb is considered a *disruptor* in the business community, company management consider the operation to be a service *innovator*. Regional director Julian Persaud told the 2016 PATA Global Insights Conference: "If you are a consumer you don't look at the world and ask 'is this disruptive?', but 'is this useful to me?' 'Is it innovating and do I want to try this?'" An estimated one in three visitors to the 2016 Rio Olympics stayed in private homes.

Source: Inside Tourism (2016)

6

Innovative experience failures

Unfortunately, novel ideas don't necessarily guarantee a profitable business. One theory on why so many innovative ideas fail is that the creators put the *wow* before the *how* (see Payne, 2014). In other words, not enough thought is put into asking the tough business questions about how to get the practical details right. Examples of innovative experience failures, include:

Ocean Dome, Japan

The Ocean Dome was a state-of-the-art indoor beach, opened as part of the Sheraton Seagaia Resort in Miyazaki in 1993. The Dome had a Polynesian theme, and was 300 metres long with an air temperature of 30C (86F) and a water temperature of around 28C. Two innovative experiences were arguably the world's best fake surf pool, and unstickable sand! Unfortunately the Dome closed in 2007, due to a combination of high operating costs and the fact that its location was only 400 metres from a real beach!

Duds n' Suds, USA

The original Duds n' Suds chain was an innovative idea that combined a coin-operated laundromat with a bar. The rationale was: 1) a large portion of laundromat customers are singles, and 2) laundromat customers have to wait around while their clothes go through the wash/dry cycles. Why not throw in a bar where these singles can mingle with other singles over a drink or two while they wait for their washing? Unfortunately the chain went bust because the combination of the smells of phosphates and beer had a negative impact on the senses.

Designing memorable experiences

An experience firstly needs to be desirable to attract visitors, and then be memorable by surprising and delighting authentically, to retain them as loyal customers. Loyalty can be in the form of word of mouth recommendations to friends, as well as repeat visitation. Following Pine and Gilmore (1998:103-105), there are five key principles of experience design:

1. Theme the experience

There should be a clear, focused and compelling theme, which drives all the design elements and the staged events. This goes beyond just making a promise, such as in a brand's slogan. One small business example is CornEvil in rural New Zealand, which is a haunted horror maze. The horror themed experience takes place in the evenings during the summer, in a maze that has been carved out of a corn field. There are no snakes in New Zealand, and so this is an attraction that might not work safely in some parts of the world. The experience is similar in theme to indoor horror mazes, where costumed *scarers* leap out in front of visitors with roaring chainsaws and other props to surprise and scare them. The advantage of the outdoor location over a controlled indoor space is the heightened sense of authenticity.

Even cafes can feature a distinctive theme. One of the most novel in this regard was the world's first cat café, the Cat Garden, which opened in Taipei in 1998. The concept has been imitated and adapted around the world as a form of pet rental where customers pay an hourly rate to engage with cats. Other experiences around the world have been themed around an almost limitless range of possibilities such as dark tourism, medical tourism, food and wine tourism, special events, outlet shopping malls, nature and wildlife safaris, luxury, spirituality and pilgrimages, quirky/bad service, literary characters, fantasy, sports, unique locations, technology, story telling...

2. Harmonise impressions with positive cues

Impressions are what the guest takes away from the experience, and fulfil the theme. Visual or oral cues, supporting the theme, need to be introduced to the guest to affirm the nature of the experience. Step inside the Jane Austen Centre in Bath, England and you are greeted by staff in period costume who are passionate followers of one of the world's most famous novelists. The visitor attraction has been set up in an original Georgian townhouse, a few doors down from the identical home where Jane lived from 1801 to 1806. The costumed guides take small groups for a short guided tour of Austen memorabilia, some of which the visitors can engage with hands-on. This includes dressing up in clothing of the era, for the ubiquitous selfie. There is of course a small gift shop, but also a themed tea room. A feature of the experience is the way in which visitors engage with strangers who are like-minded avid Jane Austen fans.

Industry insight: Recreating celebrities' homes

Recreating the homes of celebrities gives fans an opportunity to experience some part of their idol's private life. Two innovative examples in Australia demonstrate how small towns that are off the main tourist routes can attract increased visitors.

The Margaret Olley Art Centre (MOAC) is an innovative wing inside the Tweed Regional Galley in the small New South Wales town of Murwillumbah. MOAC celebrates the life of and legacy of Australia's best known painter of still life and interiors. The centrepiece of MOAC is the re-creation of parts of Olley's home-based studio. Original doors, windows, fittings, and over 20,000 personal items were moved from Olley's home at Duxford Street, Sydney, to recreate her eccentric private studio. Visitors are able to gaze through open windows, as if walking around outside her house, and see objects and settings alongside some of the famous paintings in which they feature. The Tweed Regional Gallery (www.artgallery.tweed.nsw.gov.au) is an outstanding credit to the local community who envisioned a world class art exhibition centre in a rural setting. Dining on the deck overlooking the tranquil Tweed River Valley, visitors feel a million miles from civilisation; and yet are only 30 kilometres from the Gold Coast and 50 kilometres from Byron Bay.

On the outskirts of rural Bundaberg in Queensland is a unique tribute to local aviation pioneer Bert Hinkler, who was the first person to fly solo from England to Australia and the first to fly solo across the southern Atlantic Ocean. Hinkler died in 1933, aged 40, when he crashed near Florence, Italy. In 1925 Hinkler built a house in Southampton, England, where he lived until his death. Hinkler developed and tested the plane on the site. In 1983, the house was dismantled brick by brick and relocated to Bundaberg, his birthplace. The house sits in the local Botanical gardens overlooking the spot where Hinkler landed at the end of the historic 1928 flight from England to Australia. Visitors are able to walk the hallways and gaze at the private life of Bundaberg's most famous son. The popularity of the attraction has led to the addition of the Hinkler Hall of Aviation, containing flight simulators, old aircraft and interactive attractions (www.hinklerhallofaviation.com). As an aside, part of Hinkler's glider was on board the ill-fated 1998 Challenger space craft.

3. Eliminate negative cues

Eliminate anything that diminishes or distracts from the theme. This not only includes poor service, but other negative cues such as unnecessary messages/ signs. Consider the example of London bookshop Liberia; a bookshop that only sells books! That's right, no coffee, no gifts, no CDs or DVDS or other clutter that are so prominent in bookshops that feel forced to sell other products due to the competition from online bookstores. Liberia was architect-designed to be a space where visitors can immerse themselves in words and ideas, without distractions. This means electronic devices are also banned in this old fashioned book reading/ buying experience.

4. Mix in memorabilia

A memento of an experience sells for a premium over similar items, since the price point is related to the value the guest places on the experience rather than the cost of the item. T-shirts and other memorabilia at music concerts will always cost more, for example, because of the experience. This doesn't necessary mean mementos are always expensive, since they can be inexpensive but still cost more than would be usual. One example is at the outdoor Paris Christmas Markets, where stallholders offer you a warm mulled wine to ward off the cold. The price is only a little more than you would pay at a local café, but you get to keep the branded plastic cup as a souvenir. So it is a way of paying for a tangible reminder of a memorable intangible experience. It is common for themed attractions to ban the taking of personal photos, but offer photo/video packages of the guest's experience. Naturally, these offerings are at a price premium, but where else can you have a photo of your head on an executioner's chopping block such as at The London Dungeon, for example. Another common example is the selection of products on offer at the cellar door of boutique wineries. For example, the House of J. de Telmont, not far from Paris, offers a wine workshop experience where guests get to not only taste the wines but blend their own champagne to take home. In some cases a memento is designed to take advantage of the phenomenon of souvenir collecting, such as t-shirts, teaspoons and fridge magnets. Other types of mementos include: local artisan crafts, such as handbags made from cork in the Algarve region of Portugal; based on local flora or fauna such as seashells from Sanibel Island, Florida; based on special local food products such as Balsamic vinegar from Modena, Italy; gift shop souvenirs, such as a clip of decommissioned army rifle bullets from the Firing Line – Cardiff Castle Museum of the Welsh Soldier.

5. Engage the senses

The more senses, in relation to the theme, that are engaged, the more memorable the experience. It is important this begins with first impressions on arrival. One of the best examples of this *sense of arrival,* which goes beyond the all-important staff uniforms and welcome greetings, is at Las Vegas casinos where the accommodation check-in area is in the same space as the gambling floor. Guests are immediately immersed in the sights, smells and sounds of the gaming machines, bars and restaurants. Another theme that is explicitly focused on the senses is dark dining. Pitch black restaurants aim to provide sighted guests with the opportunity to experience blindness while dining. Having no visual cues at all means all the other senses become heightened, which can lead to greater enjoyment of the meal through touch and taste and smell. The concept was first set up in Switzerland in 1999, but variations now exist around the world. Dark dining involves eliminating all light, including smart phones, but in some cases involve blindfolds. Often, pitch black restaurants employ visually impaired serving staff who are able to work in the darkened environment, and teach guests how to feed themselves.

Critical point: Remember to focus on the *how* as well as the *wow*

Remember that it is critical to ask the tough business questions about the practical aspects of innovative ideas. Not only should the experience represent a memorable event for the individual guests, but it should command a price premium for the firm, even if it is a low cost ticket.

Key points

1: Service value is co-created by the service provider and the customer

Service is an interactive process of doing something for someone, which they value. However, there has been a revolutionary change to now regarding service value as something that is *co-created* by the customer in conjunction with the service provider. In this regard, tourism is becoming increasingly based around the customer's involvement, which means tourism suppliers and consumers are engaging more closely at each stage of their relationship.

2: The challenges in transitioning to the experience economy

There is increasing interest by firms in transitioning from providing services to staging memorable experiences. In crowded tourism markets, where consumers are spoilt for choice of available services, competitive advantage will be gained by developing and using the firm's intangible skills and knowledge to engage more effectively with the customer's consumption experience than rivals. The challenge for tourism businesses in this new economy is to design an engaging experience that will be memorable for individual customers, and command a price premium for the business.

3: The key characteristics of memorable experiences

An experience must be desirable to attract visitors, and memorable to retain them. There are five key principles to designing memorable experiences. There must be a clear, focussed and compelling theme. Positive cues supporting the theme need to be introduced to the guest to affirm the nature of the experience. Anything that diminishes or distracts from the theme should be removed. Mix in memorabilia, which for a memorable experience can sell for a premium. Finally, the more senses, in relation to the theme, that are engaged, the more memorable the experience.

Discussion questions

1. Why is it important for a firm to not base all future service and experience designs on what consumers say in focus group research?

2. Why do many creative new product ideas fail commercially?

3. While Pine and Gilmore suggested the transition from the service economy to the experience economy would be difficult, why might small tourism businesses hold an advantage over the big travel brands in this regard?

References

Applegate, L.M., Piccoli, G. & Brohman, K. (2008). *TripIt: The Traveler's Agent*. Boston: Harvard Business Publishing.

Crawford, C. M. (1987). New product failure rates: A reprise. *Research Management*, **30**(4): 20-24.

Dann, G. M. S. (1977). Anomie, ego-enhancement and tourism. *Annals of Tourism Research*, **4**: 184-194.

Hjalager, A.M. (2010). A review of innovation research in tourism. *Tourism Management*, **31**: 1-12.

Inside Tourism. (2016). Airbnb, from disruptor to innovator in eight short years... *Inside Tourism*. Issue 1,095. 11 October. pp. 1.

MacCannell, D. (1973). *The Tourist: A New Theory of the Leisure Class*. New York: Schocken.

Mintel. (2005). *No frills/low cost airlines*. Leisure Intelligence Report. London: Mintel.

Nobel, C. (2011). Clay Christensen's milkshake marketing. *Working Knowledge*. 14 February. http://hbswk.hbs.edu/item/clay-christensens-milkshake-marketing.

Payne, M. (2014). *How to Kill a Unicorn*. New York: Crown Publishing Group.

Pierce, J. (2017). Humble hotel's big splash – Top gong for beer and personal touch. *The Courier-Mail*, 13 April. pp. 22.

Pine, J.B. & Gilmore, J.H. (1998). Welcome to the experience economy. *Harvard Business Review*, **76**(4): 1-9.

Pine, B.J & Gilmore, J.H. (1999). *The Experience Economy: Work is Theatre and every Business is a Stage*. Boston: Harvard Business School Press.

Shaw, G., Bailey, A. & Williams, A. (2011). Aspects of service-dominant logic and its implications for tourism management: Examples from the hotel industry. *Tourism Management*, **32**(2): 207-214.

Vargo, S.L. & Lusch, R.F. (2004). Evolving to a new dominant logic for marketing. *Journal of Marketing*, **68**: 1-17.

Vargo, S.L. & Lusch, R.F. (2008). Service-dominant logic: continuing the evolution. *Journal of the Academy of Marketing Sciences*, **36**:1-10.

7 Tourism Branding

Chapter outline

For any tourism purchase decision, consumers are spoilt for choice of available services offering similar features and benefits. Owning a brand that stands out from the crowd and simplifies decision making for the consumer represents a source of competitive edge. Therefore, effective branding is mutually beneficial for both the organisation and the consumer. Branding is a co-creative process involving the organisation and consumers, a philosophy underpinned by the inter-related concepts of brand identity, brand image and brand positioning. The *brand identity* is the image aspired to in the market by the organisation. *Brand image* represents the actual perceptions held by target consumers, and might or might not be similar to that intended in the brand identity. *Brand positioning* is the attempt to achieve congruence between the brand identity and brand image, through a focused value proposition that is meaningful to consumers and differentiates the organisation from competitors. The chapter presents a seven-stage brand positioning process for small tourism businesses. Due to the challenges in developing and maintaining a differentiated position in crowded markets, branding needs to be a long term investment. This necessitates that all marketing communications reinforce the brand identity and brand position, and thata there is a consistency of message over time.

Learning aims

To enhance your understanding of:

- The role of branding in tourism marketing

- Branding as a co-creative process involving a brand identity, brand positioning and brand image

- The seven-stage brand positioning process.

Key terms

Brand identity
The desired brand image that differentiates the organisation from competitors. How the organisation aspires to be perceived in the market.

Brand image
How the organisation is actually perceived by consumers, which might or might not be similar to that intended in the brand identity.

Brand positioning
A set of marketing activities that attempt to achieve congruence between the actual brand image and the brand identity, through a focused value proposition that is meaningful to consumers.

Differentiation

The concept of branding products has been around for thousands of years, with evidence of identification marks on pottery from China, India and parts of Europe from as far back as 1300 BC (Keller, 2003). The purpose of these early identification marks was to differentiate the manufacturer's products from those of others, a philosophy that continues to support the rationale for branding today. Ever since the topic appeared in the psychology literature in the 1940s (e.g. Guest, 1942), there has been acknowledgment from marketers that branding provides firms with a process for achieving differentiation in markets crowded with *me too* type products. For every tourism purchase decision, consumers are spoiled for choice of services offering similar features and benefits. Therefore, owning a brand that can help the consumer simplify their decision making, reduce the perceived purchase risk, create expectations and deliver on them, represents a source of competitive edge.

Branding has also always been a key factor in the balance of power in manufacturer-distributor-consumer relationships (King, 1970). As is discussed in *13:Tourism Distribution*, travel trade intermediaries, such as tour wholesalers and travel agents, play a powerful role in influencing consumers' buyer behaviour. In this regard, the ultimate goal of individual tourism businesses seeking to attract customers via travel intermediaries is to develop a brand that will be in *demand* from target consumers. If there is not sufficient demand from customers, a tourism business will be regarded as a commodity where competing on price is the only differentiating factor. In other words, tourism marketers need to enhance the value of their brand in the mind of consumers, with the ensuing aim of increasing demand on travel intermediaries. This principle applies whether the target travel intermediary is a small local visitor information office or a multinational online travel agent.

Case 7.1: Kumazawa Brewing Company: Pioneer of Saké Tourism

Makoto Kanda, Faculty of Economics, Meiji Gakuin University, Japan
Rumintha Wickramasekera, QUT Business School, Australia

Saké is an integral part of the Japanese food culture, and the national alcoholic beverage. Like the wineries in France, saké breweries have a history dating back several millennia and have been an important constituent of the regions they are located in, many being family owned small businesses. Also, like wine, saké exhibits unique attributes and flavours based on the *toji's* (master brewer) skills, the brewery, and the region they are located. Regrettably, since 1945 the number of the saké breweries has steadily declined because of severe competition from other alcoholic beverages such as beer, whisky and liquors, and shrinking local market due to depopulation in regional areas.

Saké makers and their representative bodies have embarked on implementing branding strategies to ensure the survival and prosperity of the breweries and regions. The key strategy has been to develop differentiated high-quality saké that the market demands. Japan Saké and Shochu Makers Association (JSS) (http://www.japansake.or.jp/), the nationwide body of saké breweries have embarked on destination branding to promote the breweries and regions. In addition, the Japanese government started an initiative in 2013 named "Sakagura (Saké Brewery) Tourism" to promote saké producing regions and breweries as desirable destination for both local and international travellers.

A pioneer of destination branding and saké tourism is Kumazawa Brewing Company (KBC) (http://www.kumazawa.jp/). KBC was established in 1872 at Chigasaki city in Kanagawa prefecture about an hour's drive from Tokyo. In the 1980s, like many other small brewers, KBC was languishing in obscurity and struggling to survive. Mokichi Kumazawa, became the sixth president of the company in 1993. He began implementing changes to the corporate strategy to ensure the survival and growth of the firm while keeping the company firmly rooted in its rural settings. Kumazawa – san was aware that KBC was a local saké brewery with little brand power, and relying on the regional market had little prospects for growth. Therefore, he implemented a strategy focused on a higher-quality, premium price niche marketing with smaller volumes. To achieve success he: reduced production by two thirds to minimize inventory carrying costs; recruited a young graduate specializing in *zymurgy* (fermentation process) from Tokyo University of Agriculture; and recruited a master brewer from Nada, the most famous place in Japan for its long lived saké breweries. New sake, branded *Tensei* (sky blue) was developed after five years of experimentation. It won acclaim and accolades from professionals and saké lovers. The company opened a restaurant named after its new saké brand adjoining the brewery in 2002.

Saké production takes place during the winter months, leaving many of the workers underutilized during summer. To offset this downtime and to tap into the craft beer market that was gaining popularity in Japan, KBC established a beer brewery. In keeping with his philosophy of maintaining quality, Kumazawa – san sent an engineer to learn the science and craft behind the age-old German beer-making practices. The result was the now renowned *Shonan Beer* brand, named after the nearby surf capital of Japan. Since its introduction, the beer has won many accolades, including a gold medal prize at the World Beer Cup in 2008. KBC is now a successful brand and thriving business, and the only surviving saké brewery within the region.

Discussion question

Discuss some of the reasons for keeping sales limited to the brewery and a small number of local restaurants (even after becoming successful)?

Brand equity

The ultimate commercial power of successful branding is brand equity, which is the financial valuation. For tourism businesses, brand equity is an estimated intangible asset value on the balance sheet, also referred to as the *goodwill* value. This is a premium that would have to be paid in a purchase of the business, over and above the value of the tangible assets. Brand equity is based on an accounting formula of the net present value of future earnings, where future earnings for a well-known brand will be greater than for a competing commodity product. Any financial valuation of brand equity will be based on consumer perceptions (e.g. level of intent to purchase), and so in *14:Tourism Marketing Performance Measurement*, the concept of consumer-based brand equity (CBBE) is discussed in detail. CBBE provides measures of past marketing performance as well as indicators of future performance. For some organisations, such as not-for-profits (e.g. museums) and DMOs, a financial brand equity is not usually relevant as the organisation is unlikely to ever be offered for sale. In these situations CBBE is a practical performance measure of brand *salience*, brand *associations* and brand *loyalty*.

Given the importance of CBBE and financial brand equity, the marketing budget should be regarded as an *investment* in consumers' perceptions of the brand. To support this investment, all marketing communications must reinforce the brand, in ways that link the organisation's service features to consumers' wants. The aim is for the brand to be *associated* with a given purchase situation. There are two theories in particular that have practical implications in this regard. Decision Set Theory holds that for any major purchase decision, a consumer will only seriously consider the merits of 4 +/- 2 brands in decision making (Howard & Sheth, 1969; Pike & Ryan, 2004). Associative Network Theory suggests an individual's memory consists of nodes with links to a range of other nodes (Anderson, 1983). A node represents stored information about a concept, and activation of links between nodes is sparked by processing external information when retrieving information from memory. An important implication of this is that when a purchase situation (node) is being considered, there should be a link to the brand (node) in memory that is recalled in the decision set. The second implication for tourism marketers is the strength and favourability of associations for the brand (e.g. a restaurant) with attributes (e.g. great food, fast service) and benefits (e.g. relaxing atmosphere) that are salient during decision making in a purchase situation (e.g. family dinner) in the mind of the consumer. Therefore, there are two main aims of branding:

1   The brand is top of mind when consumers are considering a purchase situation

2   When the brand comes to mind, there will be favourable associations with the features and benefits desired in the purchase situation

Activity 7.1: What first comes to mind when I mention this brand?

Pick a small local tourism brand, such as a visitor attraction or café. Then ask your friends what thoughts first come to mind when you mention this brand? Their responses will be representative of any *associations* they have with the brand in their mind. If they haven't heard of the brand then clearly there are no associations. What are the implications of the responses for marketers?

7

Branding as a co-creative process

While there is no universal agreement on the definition of a brand, most are typically a variation of the following:

> A name, logo, and slogan designed to differentiate a specific product or service from competitors.

However, branding is much more complex than designing a name, logo and slogan, even though these are fundamental to the success of the brand. Following Berthon et al. (1999), Keller (2003), and Blain et al. (2005), tourism branding is described as the set of marketing activities designed to:

■   Support the design of a name, logo and slogan, which identify and differentiate a tourism service from competitors,

■   Reduce the level of perceived financial and emotional risk for consumers, and

■   Create expectations of, and deliver, a memorable experience.

This perspective acknowledges both the marketer and the consumer as being involved in co-creating the brand, remembering that any measure of brand equity is based on market perceptions. With this in mind, it is useful to consider branding as comprising the three key elements of brand identity, brand image, and brand positioning, as highlighted in Figure 7.1. The *brand identity* is the image aspired to by the organisation in the market place. *Brand image* is the actual perceptions held of the brand by consumers, which might or might not be similar to that intended in the brand identity. *Brand positioning* is the attempt by marketers to achieve congruence between the brand identity and the brand image.

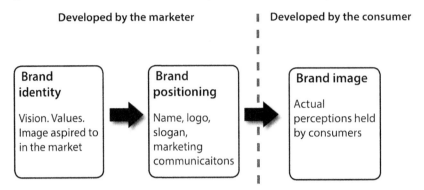

Figure 7.1: Three elements of tourism branding co-creation

Brand identity

The first stage in branding is the development of a brand identity that will differentiate the business from competitors. This is the image aspired to in the market; how the organisation wants to be perceived by consumers and travel intermediaries. Developing the brand identity is underpinned by the findings from the situation analysis, which was discussed in *4: Tourism Marketing Planning*. Key questions for consideration in the brand identity development stage typically include:

- What is our vision for the brand?
- What are the brand's core values?
- Does the brand have a particular personality?
- What are the key features and benefits offered?
- Who is the target audience?
- What is our source of competitive edge?
- On what basis should the brand be differentiated from competitors?

The answers to these questions can be used to develop a succinct brand charter, culminating in the articulation of the vision, core values and a brand promise or mantra. Keller (2003) suggested that to be memorable the mantra should only be up to five words long, such as *Fun family entertainment* in the case of Disney, and Las Vegas' *Adult playground*. The purpose of the vision, values and mantra is to motivate staff, but will not necessarily be explicit in marketing communications. These dimensions underpin the design of the name, logo and slogan, which provide a focus for all marketing communications. The brand charter would also provide guidelines for the use of the name, logo and slogan.

Brand image

Brand image represents the actual market perceptions held of the organisation, regardless of what is intended in the brand identity. The actual brand image in the market might or might not be similar to the brand identity, or might even be non-existent. The perceptions of consumers play a major role in their tourism purchase decisions, even if they are wrong. It has long been recognised that perceptions held of a brand might only have a tenuous relationship to the facts (Gardner & Levy, 1955: 35):

> Sometimes the notions people have about a brand do not even seem very sensible or relevant to those who know what the product is 'really' like. But they all contribute to the customer's deciding whether or not the brand is the one for me.

Critical point: Perception is reality

One of the best known marketing axioms is *perception is reality*. This is based on near century old theory Thomas & Thomas, 1928, in Patton, 2002), which proposed what people believe to be true will be real in its consequences. That is, whether an individual's perceptions are right or wrong about a brand, they influence their purchase decisions.

Brand image is the sum of the knowledge of, and attitude towards, the brand. As discussed in *3:Tourism Consumer Behaviour*, there are two sources of stimuli that lead to image formation (Gunn, 1988), and the level of influence of the marketer varies between the two. Organic (natural) image formation occurs through an individual's everyday assimilation of sensory information, such as media editorial content, movies and word of mouth. Induced (forced) image formation on the other hand is stimulated through the efforts of marketers through advertising. Organic images are considered more influential in consumer decision making.

Intangibility and risk

In Chapter 1, intangibility, variability and risk were introduced as key characteristics of tourism services. This has important implications in branding. To recap, most tourism offerings are in the form of *intangible* services. This means the consumer cannot usually try before they buy, and in many situations the purchase takes place from a distance, in advance of the service consumption experience. Therefore, if they have not previously sampled the service, their decisions will be reliant on their perceptions. This means there is an element of risk inherent in all service purchases. Types of risk include financial, physical, social, and performance satisfaction. Since there will usually be a wide range of competitors offering similar features and benefits, most tourism services are *substitutable* in the consumer's mind, and so product switching can occur between brands in their decision set. Even if they have purchased the service previously, the issue of *variability* means there is no guarantee the experience will be exactly the same on another day or time, and so a level of risk still exists. A consumer can easily switch preferences for one brand over another, either on the basis of perceived risk, or a better value deal, and perceive they will still enjoy the features and benefits desired. Remember also, the difficulty in patenting a tourism service means that novel ideas can be quickly imitated. Hence, two of the core aims of branding are to reduce the level of perceived risk for consumers, and reduce potential product switching for the organisation (brand loyalty).

Brand positioning

Brand positioning represents the attempt to achieve congruence between the image aspired to in the brand identity and the actual perceptions held in the market (brand image). An effective position is one that successfully differentiates the brand in the minds of target consumers, on the basis of features and/or benefits that *determine* their purchase intent. On this basis, brand positioning is recognised as being mutually beneficial for both the organisation and the consumer. From the supply perspective, effective positioning helps the brand to stand out in markets crowded with the noise of competitors offering similar features and benefits, and is therefore a source of competitive edge. From the demand perspective, effective positioning simplifies decision making for the consumer, by catering to their needs and reducing the level of information searching and purchase risk. The brand position is the part of the brand identity to be actively communicated to the target market, through a focused value proposition that is meaningful to the consumer and differentiates the organisation from competitors.

As discussed in *4: Tourism Marketing Planning*, the marketing strategy aims to maximise strengths to take advantage of opportunities. A competitive edge is gained when consumers perceive a performance capability gap (strength), the organisation has over competitors, which will endure over time. This must be based on an attribute that represents an important purchase criterion. However, not all attributes that differentiate an organisation from competitors will be important to the consumer, and not all attributes that are important will be used in the purchase decision process. Figure 7.2 is used to demonstrate the distinction between attribute importance, salience and determinance, in the context of a 4-star hotel stay. When considering such an accommodation purchase there will be a range of attributes that are *important*. However, since it is assumed all competing 4-star hotels will provide some of the important attributes (e.g. cleaniness, private bathroom etc), these will not all be considered during decision making. Rather, there will be a subset of important attributes that are *salient* (top of mind) in the decision process (e.g. car parking, good view). Of these attributes that come to mind, there will be one or at most a few attributes that will ultimately **determine** product choice (e.g. price, location). Therefore it is important to be positioned favourably on the basis of a determinant attribute:

> Attitudes toward features which are most closely related to preference or to actual purchase decisions are said to be determinant; the remaining features or attitudes - no matter how favourable - are not determinant (Myers & Alpert, 1968:13).

Figure 7.2: Attribute importance, salience and determinance

Critical point: Identifying determinant attributes

A practical research tool for identifying determinant attributes is Importance-Performance Analysis (IPA), introduced by Martilla and James (1977). IPA is discussed in more detail in *14: Tourism Marketing Performance Measurement*. A questionnaire is used to ask participants to rate the importance of a list of attributes, and then to rate the perceived performance of an organisation and key competitors, across the same list of attributes. This identifies those attributes that are the most important, and where the organisation is perceived to perform strongly (or not) relative to competitors. The graphical nature of the output is easily understood by tourism operators who have no research training, and is useful for justifying to stakeholders the rationale for categorising a resource as a strength (see also Pike 2002, 2009, 2016, 2017).

7

The brand positioning process

The role of branding is to help guide consumers through the purchase decision process highlighted in Figure 7.3, with the aims commonly related to the following:

■ Stimulating consumers' needs recognition

■ Creating a new image

■ Correcting a negative image

■ Reinforcing positive images

■ Stimulating intent to (re)purchase

Figure 7.3: Purchase decision process

In general, the three key objectives in tourism branding can be summarised as:

- Increasing awareness
- Increasing positive perceptions
- Stimulating intent to purchase, repurchase, and recommend to others

These practical objectives are shown in Table 7.1, in relation to the cognition/affect/conation process, Hierarchy of Effects (AIDA) mode) that seeks to guide the consumer through **A**wareness, **I**nterest, **D**esire to **A**ction (Lavidge & Steiner, 1961), and the hierarchy of Consumer-based Brand Equity (CBBE) (Aaker 1991, 1996, Keller 2003).

Table 7.1: Branding objectives. Adapted from Pike & Page (2014)

Brand objectives	Hierarchy of effects	Types of images	CBBE
1. To increase awareness	Awareness	Cognition	Brand salience
2. To increase positive perceptions	Interest Desire	Affect	Brand associations
3. To stimulate intent to (re)purchase	Action	Conation	Brand loyalty

There are seven stages in brand positioning:

1. Define the target market

Segmentation and branding are inseparable, since a marketing orientation dictates all marketing decisions are made with the target consumers in mind. This requires an understanding of the needs of target consumers, and of how to deliver satisfaction more effectively than rivals. A small tourism business cannot appeal to, nor satisfy, everyone in the market, and any attempt at mass marketing represents a shotgun approach where all consumers are treated as one. So trade-offs must be made in terms of identifying realistic target segments. It is a more effective use of the marketing budget to divide the market into groups of people with similar needs so that the marketing mix can be tailored to cater to them. As well as needing to ensure the organisation can cater to the segment needs, the SPASM criteria should be considered. That is, the target market should be:

- Substantial
- Profitable
- Accessible
- Sustainable
- Measurable

When more than one segment is targeted it is important the different segments are compatible with each other. The main approaches to segmenting a market are:

- **Geographic segmentation:** This is a common and simple means of dividing the population based on the consumers' place of origin (e.g. country, state, city), or the catchment area (e.g. hotel guests within a certain radius of a theme park).

- **Demographic segmentation:** Also a common approach, demographics can be used to divide the population on the basis of characteristics such as gender, age, marital status, family life-cycle stage, education levels, income, religion and language.

- **Behaviour segmentation:** This approach is used to group consumers on the basis of behaviour in relation to the product. Options include: travel purpose (e.g. visiting friends and relatives), travel situation/context (e.g. short break holiday), and frequency of purchase (e.g. repeat customers).

- **Psychographic segmentation:** This is a more complex and challenging segmentation approach for small tourism businesses, due to the difficulty in identifying members of a population with the characteristics of interest, such as: motivations, learning styles, personalities and attitudes.

- **Benefits segmentation:** This approach recognises the product features/attributes represent a bundle of benefits. The different categories of benefits sought by different groups include: adventure, excitement, fun, romance, spiritual growth, education, and relaxation.

- **Values segmentation:** Although not a common approach, consumers can also be grouped according to their personal values. These are a small set of enduring traits that guide an individual's information processing, decision making and behaviour. Examples of personal values relating to travel include: healthy lifestyle, happiness, family safety/security, status, ambition, self-fulfilment, achievement, dignity, loyalty, empowerment, respect, equality, and environmental sustainability.

- **Socialgraphics segmentation:** A relatively new approach to segmentation is by grouping consumers according to their social media habits (Pan & Crotts, 2012). These include understanding what type of blogs, social media and websites consumers use in travel planning, their social behaviour online, and the type of online information they rely on.

2. Identify the competitive set of brands

One of the fundamentals of brand positioning is that the organisation does not need to be the best on the planet. Rather, the brand should differentiate from the competitors in a given purchase situation. This should be examined from the perspective of the consumer, by identifying the brands that comprise the decision set (usually ranging from two to six).

3. Identify the salient attributes/benefits for the purchase situation

Again, from the consumer's perspective it is critical to understand the range of attributes and/or benefits that will be salient to the target segment in decision making. See *5: Tourism Marketing Research.*

4. Identify perceptions of the strengths and weaknesses of each of the competitive set of brands

Using a research technique such as Importance-Performance Analysis (Martilla & James, 1977; Pike, 2002), enables the identification of how the organisation and its competitors are perceived to perform across the range of salient attributes.

5. Identify a differentiated positioning proposition focused on a capability gap based on attribute determinance

A brand positioning theme must represent a point of difference, which competitors can't currently match, on the basis of an attribute and/or benefit that determine the purchase choice. In the case of Importance-Performance Analysis this will be an attribute that is rated most important, and where the brand is perceived to perform strongly relative to competitors. This technique is discussed more fully in *14: Tourism Marketing Performance Measurement.*

6. Select and implement the position proposition

Developing the value proposition is the greatest challenge in branding (Gilmore, 2002). The key term in this regard is *focus*. Once the potential determinant attributes are known, a key decision must be made about which should be used as the focus of the brand positioning. To gain cut-through in crowded markets necessitates a succinct and meaningful message, a seven word single-minded value proposition that reinforces the brand identity.

Lean marketing: Online lists of slogans

Google the term *tourism slogans*, and you will see links to a range of sites that offer opinions on the positives and negatives on different tourism slogans from around the world. While most of these relate to destination slogans, you should get a feel for (i) what makes a good one, and (ii) the challenge of finding one that is unique and cannot be imitated.

For more discussion about accountability criteria for tourism slogans see Pike (2004). As well as differentiating the brand from competitors, the following are key criteria of good slogans:

- **Propositional**: The message must be proposing something to the target consumer.
- **Meaningful**: What is being proposed should be of value to the target consumer.
- **Truthful**: Today's sophisticated consumers demand truthful advertising.
- **Deliverable**: Staff must be able to meet the expectations created.

Activity 7.2: What's the proposition?

The following are actual slogans that have been used in the tourism industry. What is the proposition in each of them?

- Get wrecked on Great Keppel Island
- Hawkes Bay – Wine country
- Prince of Wales Hotel – We treat everyone like royalty!
- Cartier Place Suite Hotel – Location, hospitality, value
- Hans Brinker Budget Hotel – The hostel that couldn't care less, but we will try
- Norman Hotel – Brisbane's worst vegetarian restaurant
- Bulgaria – A discovery to share
- Belgium – The place to Be

The other two main elements in brand positioning are the brand name and brand symbol/logo. Thus the name, logo and slogan should succinctly encapsulate the brand identity. This succinct focus is so important, because rarely does the marketer get consumers' attention for long enough to tell the whole story. In markets crowded with the messages of competing and substitute products, *attention is in short supply out there*, but it is gettable. So, think of brand positioning as an arrow that cuts through the clutter of the market noise and gets noticed by target consumers for something meaningful to them. Note also that the symbol used in brand positioning might not be a logo. Alternatives include: the type of script used for the brand name and/or slogan (e.g. Virgin), a patented sound (e.g. Harley Davidson), a patented colour (e.g. Cadbury), the founder (e.g. Colonel Sanders' KFC), packaging (e.g. Bombay Saphire Gin), architecture (e.g. Gaudi), a character (e.g. Mickey Mouse) or a celebrity (e.g. Jamie Oliver).

Activity 7.3: What image on the billboard or postcard?

Imagine you have been commissioned to design a roadside billboard for the city or town in which you live, along with an identical souvenir postcard. Remember, to catch people's attention with these you don't have time to tell the whole story of the destination. What one image would you have as the focus, to attract attention and appeal to target visitor markets? What is the proposition that would be of value to target consumers?

7. Monitor the performance of the positioning strategy over time

This issue is discussed in detail in *14:Tourism Marketing Performance Measurement*. An important point to make here however is the need to benchmark the existing position at the beginning of any new brand positioning. This enables comparisons at future points in time to track the success or otherwise of the campaign (Pike, 2017, Pike et al., 2017).

Branding consistency over time

To reiterate, the following key issues are inherent in branding:

- It is difficult to stand out in crowded markets.
- Attention is in short supply out there.
- It is difficult to change people's perceptions.
- Branding is a long term investment.

Therefore, branding is underpinned by three fundamental principles. First, all marketing communications should reinforce the brand identity and brand proposition. Second, brand positioning must be regarded as a long term strategy. The world's best known brands understand the time it takes to gain traction in the market and the need for consistency of message over a long period. If the research leading to the development of the brand positioning strategy was sound, as it should be, avoid the temptation to tamper with the proposition. This can occur with the appointment of a new marketing manager or new media agency, who might wish to use change as a mark of their innovation. Third, focus on reinforcing positively held perceptions rather than trying to change negative images.

Repositioning

Repositioning is the attempt to create a new and different position in the market. Given the challenging and long term effort and cost of trying to change market perceptions, examples of successful repositioning for small tourism businesses are rare in the academic literature.

The brand name

Most small business owners and marketers undertake branding with an existing organisation name. The business name is in effect the brand name, and will have established equity, both in the form of an intangible financial value on the balance sheet, and in terms of market perceptions. In this regard, any decision to change the brand name must be cognisant of the costs versus the benefits of doing so.

Key points

1: The role of branding in tourism marketing

For any tourism purchase decision consumers are spoilt by choice of available products offering similar features and benefits. Owning a brand that stands out from the crowd and simplifies decision making for the consumer represents a source of competitive advantage. Effective branding is mutually beneficial for both the organisation and the consumer.

2: Branding as a co-creative process involving a brand identity, brand positioning and brand image

Tourism branding is a co-creative process involving the organisation and consumers, a philosophy underpinned by the inter-related concepts of brand identity, brand positioning and brand image. The *brand identity* represents the image aspired to in the market by the organisation. *Brand image* represents the actual perceptions held by target consumers, and might or might not be similar to that intended in the brand identity. *Brand positioning* is the marketing activities that attempt to achieve congruence between the brand identity and brand image.

3: The seven stage brand positioning process

The chapter presented a seven-stage brand positioning process for small tourism businesses. Due to the challenges in developing and maintaining a differentiated position in crowded markets, underpinning the process is the understanding that it needs to be a long term investment. This necessitates that (i) all marketing communications reinforce the brand identity and brand position, and (ii) there is a consistency of message over a long period of time.

Discussion questions

1. Why is it argued branding is a co-creative process involving both the organisation and consumers?

2. Why does brand salience represent a source of competitive edge?

3. Why is it preferable to focus marketing communications on promoting positively held perceptions of the brand, rather than trying to reverse a negative image?

7

References

Aaker, D.A. (1991). *Managing Brand Equity*. New York: Free Press.

Aaker, D.A. (1996). *Building Strong Brands*. New York: Free Press.

Anderson, J.R. (1983). *The Architecture of Cognition,* Harvard University Press, Cambridge, MA.

Berthon, P., Hulbert, J.M. & Pitt, L.F. (1999). Brand management prognostications. *Sloan Management Review*, **40**(2): 53-65.

Blain, C., Levy, S.E. & Ritchie, J.R.B. (2005). Destination branding: Insights and practices from destination management organizations. *Journal of Travel Research*, **43**:328-338.

Gardner, B. B. & Levy, S. J. (1955). The product and the brand. *Harvard Business Review*. March-April: 33-39.

Gilmore, F. (2002). Branding for success. In Morgan, N., Pritchard, A. & Pride, R. (Eds). *Destination Branding*. Oxford: Butterworth-Heinemann, pp. 57-65.

Guest, L.P. (1942). The genesis of brand awareness. *Journal of Applied Psychology*, **26**: 800-808.

Gunn, C. (1988). *Vacationscape: Designing Tourist Regions*. (2nd Ed). Austin: Bureau of Business Research, University of Texas.

Howard, J. A., & Sheth, J. N. (1969). *The Theory of Buyer Behavior*. New York: John Wiley & Sons.

Keller, K.L. (2003). *Strategic Brand Management*. Upper Saddle River, NJ: Prentice Hall.

King, S. (1970). Development of the brand. *Advertising Quarterly*, Summer: 6-14.

Lavidge, R.E., & Steiner, G.A. (1961). A model for predictive measurements of advertising effectiveness. *Journal of Marketing*, **25**: 59-62.

Martilla, J., & James, J. (1977). Importance-Performance Analysis. *Journal of Marketing* **41**(1), 77-79.

Myers, J. H., & Alpert, M.I. (1968). Determinant buying attitudes: meaning and measurement. *Journal of Marketing*, **32**:13-20.

Pan, B. & Crotts, J.C. (2012). Theoretical models of social media, marketing implications, and future research directions. In Sigala, M., Christou, E. & Gretzel, U. (Eds). *Social Media in Travel, Tourism and Hospitality: Theory, Practices and Cases*. Farnham, Surrey: Ashgate Publishing Limited, pp. 73-86.

Patton, M.Q. (2002). *Qualitative Research & Evaluation Methods*. (3rd Ed). Thousand Oaks: Sage.

Pike, S. (2002). The use of Importance-Performance Analysis to identify determinant short break destination attributes in New Zealand. *Pacific Tourism Review.(Tourism Review International)*, **6**(2): 23-33.

Pike, S. (2004). Destination brand positioning slogans – towards the development of a set of accountability criteria. *Acta Turistica*, **16**(2): 102-124.

Pike, S. (2009). Destination brand positions of a competitive set of near-home destinations. *Tourism Management*, **30**(6): 857-866.

Pike, S. (2016). Destination image: identifying baseline perceptions of Brazil, Argentina and Chile in the nascent Australian long haul travel market. *Journal of Destination Marketing & Management*, **5**(2): 164-170.

Pike, S. (2017). Destination image temporality – Tracking perceived strengths and weaknesses over time. *Journal of Hospitality & Tourism Management*, **31**: 126-133.

Pike, S., Gentle, J., Kelly, L., & Beatson, A. (2017). Tracking brand positioning for an emerging destination during the advent of the social media era: 2003 to 2015. *Tourism and Hospitality Research*. (In press).

Pike, S. & Page, S. (2014). Destination Marketing Organizations and destination marketing: A narrative analysis of the literature. *Tourism Management*, **41**:202-227.

Pike, S. & Ryan, C. (2004). Destination positioning analysis through a comparison of ognitive, affective and conative perceptions. *Journal of Travel Research*, **42**(4): 333-342.

8 Pricing Tourism Services

Chapter outline

Price plays a major role in consumers' perceptions of value, and consequently their purchase decisions. A price is what a consumer agrees to exchange in return for a service they perceive as good value, both in terms of a desired benefit to meet a want, as well as monetary worth. Therefore, pricing is a marketing function, because the exchange taking place must reflect a mutually beneficial relationship, and because pricing is influenced by other elements in the marketing mix such as the costs of promotion and distribution. For tourism service providers, pricing is one of the most flexible elements in the marketing mix. Indeed, tourism businesses are increasingly using dynamic pricing to meet fluctuating levels of consumer demand, and to maximise yield. Since pricing is a function of supply and demand, the chapter discusses key internal factors and external forces influencing decisions about price setting. A range of different pricing options are presented, which represent both strategic and tactical opportunities. A key message in the chapter is that ultimately, pricing decisions must be both consistent with the brand identity and market positioning value proposition, as well as enhance the return on investment in the fixed costs of the business.

Learning aims

To enhance your understanding of:

- Pricing as a marketing function
- The key internal factors and external forces influencing pricing decisions
- The use of dynamic pricing for effective yield management.

Key terms

Value
Value is co-created by the service provider, who offers a value proposition, and the customer, who decides the extent to which the service is providing a benefit to meet a need.

Price
Price is the foundation in the relationship between supply and demand, and is what is exchanged by the customer in return for a product or service that offers perceived value.

Yield management
Dynamic (constantly changing) markets necessitate pricing decision making that is flexible to meet fluctuating levels of demand and to maximise yield (return on investment).

Value

As discussed in *6: Designing Tourism Services and Experiences*, service value is co-created by the provider in conjunction with the customer. The service provider offers a value proposition, and as discussed in *7:Tourism Branding*, what consumers generally value in such a proposition, when comparing offerings, will be on the basis of price and quality (e.g. cheaper, faster, or better). Ultimately the customer decides whether the service was good value for money, and this will depend on:

- Their individual wants and expectations,
- The extent to which they themselves take advantage of, and participate in, the consumption opportunities offered,
- Their level of satisfaction, in terms of whether the benefits promised met their wants, and
- The price they paid.

The marketer is pricing to sell value, in keeping with the brand's value proposition. It is important to note that regardless of whether consumers are considering a luxury purchase or a cheaper category, they still expect to get value for money.

Critical point: People will pay top dollar for a special experience

Any business owner offering an outstanding experience that is valued by consumers should not be afraid to charge a high price, particularly when it is a relatively small part of the total travel cost. Many people will happy in the knowledge they are paying top dollar for a special experience. For example, witness the number of high priced shows that play to sell-out crowds night after night at New York's Broadway theatre district, London's West End, the Las Vegas casinos, and at Paris' Moulin Rouge. While the admission ticket is usually expensive, as are the refreshments and souvenir programmes, the cost of the experience is small relative to the travel costs to get there.

Pricing

In competitive tourism markets, price plays a major role in consumers' perceptions of value for money, and consequently their purchase decisions. A price is what a consumer agrees to exchange in return for a service they perceive as good value, both in terms of a desired benefit to meet a want, and as a monetary worth. Pricing can be challenging for marketers. If the price is too high, demand will be soft, but if the price is too low there won't be a sufficient contribution towards fixed costs. If the price is the same as those of the competitors, there is the risk of substitutability. Each of these scenarios can affect business survival. Therefore pricing is a strategic function, which goes beyond an internal accounting analysis to understand the minimum price needed to cover costs (the price floor). What is also needed is an external marketing orientation to understand consumer behaviour in terms of what the target market will bear financially (the price ceiling) and what benefits consumers value in terms of their wants (market position).

Critical point: Develop an interest in numbers

If you are going to be involved in operating or marketing a small business, you will need to understand the principles of basic accounting, as well as marketing research. Otherwise, to what extent will you be able to trust your accountant or marketing researcher, if you don't understand the strengths and weaknesses of different options they recommend to you? Also, the level of understanding needed of financial and research data only increases the more successful the business becomes. The more successful the business the harder the decisions, and decision making is reliant on analysis of data. Putting aside a fear of numbers and being prepared to engage with data can lead to a better understanding of what constitutes *good information*, and therefore a competitive edge in the marketplace (and the job market) over those who shy away from numerical data.

8

For tourism service providers, pricing is one of the most flexible elements in the marketing mix. Every business' pricing decisions will be a function of supply and demand, and can be influenced by a range of internal factors unique to their operation, and external forces over which they have no control. From the *supply* perspective, the range of influences on the pricing decisions for a service include:

Internal factors unique to the business - Financial

- The business' current financial situation
- The current occupancy rate relative to the level of capacity
- The fixed costs of the business
- The variable costs of providing the service
- The distribution methods and commission levels
- Brand equity value, particularly in terms of customer loyalty.

Internal factors unique to the business - Strategy

- The market positioning strategy and value proposition
- The marketing objectives
- The product life-cycle stage.

External forces over which the business has no control

- The level of market demand
- The intensity of the competition
- The prices of competitors in the decision set being considered by the consumer
- The extent of substitutability of competing businesses, based on consumers' perceptions of value
- The current *going rate* price for the service category
- The competitiveness of the destination at the time (e.G. For importance of price as a destination attractiveness variable see pike 2016, 2017; pike & bianchi, 2016)
- Current macro-environment forces, particularly economic conditions such as bank interest rates, currency exchange rates, and consumer confidence levels
- The potential for retaliation by competitors
- Seasonality and the timing of the offer.

From the consumer *demand* perspective, the range of issues affecting the attractiveness of a price offering includes:

- The travel situation
- The relative size of the purchase in their overall holiday experience or package bundle
- Their level of experience with the service category
- The importance of the purchase decision for them
- The benefit(s) they seek to meet their wants
- Their current capacity to pay (e.G. Business travellers versus families, international versus domestic visitors)
- The level of perceived risk
- Their life-cycle stage
- Their perceptions of the value propositions of the brands being considered in their decision set.

Substitutability

As discussed in Chapter 1, one of the characteristics of intangible tourism services is the difficulty to protect against imitators. In free market economies it is not usually possible to patent an innovative service idea. As a result most tourism markets are crowded with *me too* services that all offer similar features and benefits.

This environment means that in so many purchase situations one tourism service provider is easily *substitutable* for another in the mind of the consumer. When service offerings are substitutable they are become commodities that can only compete on price and volume. Hence the importance, highlighted in *7: Tourism Branding*, of developing a differentiated market position with a distinctive value proposition that is meaningful to the target market. Importantly, pricing decisions need to be consistent with this branding strategy.

Also, it must always be remembered that tourism as an activity is generally substitutable in consumers' minds. This is because so much travel and tourism activity represents discretionary spending, which is only an option after taking care of more mandatory day to day living expenses, health and education costs, and emergency repairs. For example, the need replace a costly household item such as the family car, the home's carpet, or a laptop, might outweigh the want of a holiday, and so a desired travel situation might be delayed.

Pricing objectives and options

The most common objectives related to pricing decisions include:

- **To generate immediate cash flow**, in situations where the business' financial survival is at risk due to external forces such as economic recession or a natural disaster at the destination.
- **To achieve market share**, which is particularly important for new businesses.
- **To a achieve product-quality leadership position**, particularly in luxury markets
- **To maximise current profit**, which has a focus on short term return on investment.

Depending on the external forces and internal factors, tourism businesses have a range of pricing options available.

Break-even analysis for pricing decisions

The key terms used in break-even analysis are fixed costs, contribution, proposed price, and the variable cost. The break-even point is a function of the fixed costs divided by the contribution, which is the proposed selling price less the variable cost per sale, as shown in Figure 8.1. Scenario analyses can be undertaken on a spreadsheet to test the outcome of different input levels of proposed price and variable cost, and to estimate sales/price ratios to achieve a desired level of return on investment.

$$\frac{\text{Fixed costs}}{\text{Contribution (Selling price – variable cost) per sale}}$$

Figure 8.1: Break-even point formula

Many tourism businesses have high *fixed costs* from the investment in buildings, vehicles and/or equipment. Ongoing fixed costs (finance, rent, depreciation, salaries, maintenance, advertising and promotion, printing of menus, etc) are incurred regardless of the number of customers or sales volume. Even if there are no sales, the fixed costs are still incurred.

Lean marketing: Sponsorship from suppliers

For hospitality businesses it is common practice for major suppliers of products and ingredients, such as wine and coffee beans, to help offset some of the fixed costs by contributing to the cost of signage, the printing of menus and promotional material, advertising, beer glasses, ashtrays etc. There are opportunities to gain sponsorship from suppliers who benefit most from having the tourism business as a trade customer.

Each sale should make a *contribution* towards paying for the fixed costs of the business. The contribution per sale is the margin of difference when the variable cost of the sale is deducted from the proposed selling price. The *variable cost* is that incurred in the production of each service, and so the total amount of variable costs for the firm will fluctuate depending on the level of production. Examples include: raw materials for meals; production labour such as non-salaried casual staff; packaging such as gift wrapping and takeaway coffee cups; cleaning costs for bedsheets; disposables such as napkins and shower soaps; energy such as fuel for a jet boat ride; and distribution costs such as commissions for travel trade intermediaries and credit card sales.

Case 8.1: Pricing the motel

A small Western Australian country motel, situated on a remote part of the Eyre Highway in the Nullabor Desert, is on the market for AU$400,000. This price includes the land, buildings and business. This is one of the lowest priced motels on the market in the state, and represents an affordable opportunity for new entrants to the industry. The current owners have run into financial difficulties and are looking for a quick sale. Given that banks may only lend 50% of the purchase price of a motel, the equity required from a purchaser will be $200,000. The motel has seven self-contained one-bedroom units, each with its own kitchenette, bathroom and car park. Two-bedroom owner's accommodation and a communal spa pool is also included. The motel does not offer cable television or Wi-Fi due to the isolated location. The location is adjacent to the only service station for 100 kilometres in either direction, and is a brick building, built 15 years ago. The accommodation is ideal for weary travellers who are often driving thousands of kilometres between Western Australia and the eastern states. Cars are warned to not drive between dusk and dawn on this highway due to the danger of kangaroos crossing the road in the dark at speed, and so these small motels dotted along the highway are a necessity.

Approximate annual costs

Depreciation	6,600
Government taxes	5,000
Gas heating	12,400
Insurance	5,000
Advertising	10,000
Printing/stationery	3,000
Cleaner	35,000
Repairs	15,000
Power	12,500
Phone	2,500
Bank interest	15,000
TOTAL	**$122,000**

Current tariff:

$100 per unit per night

Variable costs include: dry-cleaning of sheets, travel agents' commission and credit card commission. These have been estimated at combined 20% of the nightly tariff per room.

1. What level of sales, in terms of a) total unit nights and b) total sales revenue, is needed to break even?

2. What average occupancy rate is required to break even, and does this leave room to make a profit?

8

Cost-plus pricing

The simplest pricing approach is to add a mark up to the cost of producing the service. While this might appear to provide certainty of covering costs, the approach doesn't take into account the level of competition and consumer demand. This might be a viable option in the case of the introduction of a new innovative product where demand is likely to exceed supply. However, in most other competitive markets this strategy is not recommended.

Going-rate pricing

Another simple approach is to set a price based on what the competition is doing. While this avoids a price war, the strategy doesn't take into account the level of consumer demand, nor the business' costs. This can be an option for new entrants to a market, based on the assumption that the collective wisdom of the existing suppliers has worked out the appropriate price.

Auction prices

A relatively new pricing option is where consumers are offered the opportunity to place bids in an auction style sale. This approach is usually offered at short notice, in an effort to fill excess capacity. For example, some airlines use intermittent last minute auctions asking economy class passengers to make an offer for an upgrade to business class, particularly when there is low demand for business class and high demand for economy class on a particular service.

Yield management and dynamic pricing

Pricing needs to be dynamic, because the external environment in which businesses operate is dynamic (constantly changing). Pricing can be dynamic, because it is one of the most flexible aspects in marketing. However it is also one of the most complex marketing activities, dealing with trade-offs between occupancy and yield. Yield represents the return on investment (ROI), or gross profit. Lowering prices can help increase use of the assets (e.g. increased occupancy rate) but not increase yield compared to what could be generated by higher prices and lower occupancy. Dynamic pricing to achieve optimum yield management at a hotel involves allocating different rates to different numbers of rooms at different times, based on projected levels of demand and current occupancy rates. While history is no predictor of future sales, a yield management system is reliant on analysis of data from historical booking patterns. For more detailed discussion on the complexities of revenue management in tourism see books by Burgess (2014), Dopson and Hayes (2009), Yeoman and McMahon-Beattie (2004), and the journal special issues listed in Table 8.1.

Table 8.1: Journal special issues related to pricing in tourism

Journal	Issue	Topic
International Journal of Revenue Management	2016, Vol 9, Issues 2/3	Pricing and revenue management in the international hospitality industry
Journal of Travel & Tourism Marketing	2015, Vol34, Issue 7	Revenue management for tourism and hospitality

Perishability

Pricing decisions need to be made regularly to adapt to market conditions, and to help ensure maximum use of the business' assets to minimise the effects of perishability. As discussed in Chapter 1, perishability means that any services not sold today cannot be stored for sale on another day, as is possible for tangible products such as souvenirs. Underutilized assets in the form of unsold services each day are regarded as perished, much in the same way unsold fruit and vegetables perish for the grocery business. Airbnb is useful example of an initiative enabling better use of underutilized accommodation assets. Dynamic pricing can result in different prices at different times of the year due to the effects of seasonality of demand, different days of the week, and different times during the day (e.g. happy hour at a bar). For example Hotel Maruyama in one of Tokyo's red light districts offers rooms at a *rest* tariff for two hours and a *stay* tariff for up to nine hours. Limes Hotel in Brisbane, Australia offers a midnight *play and stay* rate, where any unsold rooms at that time are offered at a third of the rack rate.

Discounting

There has often been criticism that the performance of tourism operators globally has been one of *profitless volume*, through discounting and price-based competition. In many countries, the government tourism policy is driven by the pursuit of growth, such as increased visitors and increased visitor nights, which are the most measurable performance indicators. However, in free market economies, where there are low barriers to entry, higher volumes often yield low average returns due to intensifying competition and recession affected markets.

Industry insight: The growth trap

The result of the growth trap, which is the pursuit of growth as the strategy, is ultimately less profit. An example of this was given to me a few years ago by the CEO of a major tourism company that had a portfolio of investments. One of the company's recent investments was a popular wildlife sanctuary with over 350,000 visitors per year, who all exited through a large gift shop. The CEO lamented their growth strategy was problematic, because they had been discounting retail souvenir prices by 27% to secure group tour business from Asia. With a retail gross profit margin of 46% and staff costs of 10%, only 9% was left to cover operating costs, before any contribution to yield. The CEO suggested this was an example of a situation where fewer visitors, with less discounting, could have generated more yield.

Yield is more important than growth in numbers, for both the wider destination economy and for small businesses. While discounting can fill a hotel during tough economic times, a study involving data from 6,000 hotels over a three year period found hotels with lower prices, relative to the competitive set of brands, did capture market share but achieved a lower yield (see Enz et al., 2004). This suggested when the market is heavily discounting, a hotel that keeps prices constant will lose occupancy but can achieve a higher yield than competitors.

Activity 8.1: Discounting the motel to increase occupancy

Use the information from *Case 8.1: Pricing the motel*. A friend suggests you could increase the occupancy rate dramatically by reducing the nightly tariff to $70, which would still enable you to cover costs. Undertake a break even analysis using this tariff. What do you think of the discounting idea?

Discounting can be used as both a long term strategy, in keeping with value proposition, and as a short term promotional tactic to counter perishability. One of the most common types of strategic discounting is for trade customers, based on larger volumes of sale. For example, conference organisers and meeting planners bring large groups to hotels and expect a volume discount. Another common example of a long term discount policy is where visitor attractions offer a reduced admission price to local residents, and where restaurants offer a discounted meal for a visitor celebrating a birthday, if they are accompanied by paying guests.

Lean marketing: Discounts for locals

For some visitor attractions, offering free or discounted admission to local residents is a strategic decision to enhance long term loyalty through word of mouth recommendations. At many destinations there will be a proportion of visitors who don't stay at traditional commercial accommodation, but stay at the homes of friends/relatives or at hosted Airbnb rentals. Since these local hosts are often unofficial tour guides with a strong influence on their guests' local itineraries it can often make sense for local visitor attractions to make sure they have good product knowledge. At Brutrint National Park, one of Albania's best known historic sites, the publicly displayed prices at the ticket office show a 60% discount for locals. At the Agrodome, New Zealand's most visited sheep show, local residents can apply for a pass that gives them free admission when they are accompanied by paying visitors. At Australia's Gold Coast, locals can purchase a heavily discounted pass giving unlimited entry for a year to major theme parks. The historic Driving Creek Railway in New Zealand's Coromandel region offers a frequent passenger ticket, where every second trip is free.

Short term discounting tactics can be an effective way to stimulate demand for perishable services during off-peak periods and generate tomorrow's much needed cash flow to offset fixed costs, or to rebuild business following a disaster at the destination. These *sales promotions* are typically in the form of a discount coupons, across a range of different media, including online using discount portal sites such as Scoopon.com. Given this is a short term tactic, the offer is limited to a specific level of sales. One of the key advantages of the use of coupons is the ease with which the effectiveness can be tracked, relative to other forms of promotions. A major disadvantage of discounting is that prevalent use can train consumers in a given situation to wait for such sales promotions before making a purchase. Similar consumer training occurs at motels and hotels in holiday areas where unpublicised discounts are offered for unsold rooms at a certain point in the late afternoon; much in the way that a baker or butcher might discount late in the day to offload goods about to perish. They are not usually advertised but word gets around, and savvy travellers learn to wait until this time to approach these operators for accommodation for the evening.

Loss leaders are offerings that are discounted below their market costs, and therefore each sale makes a loss. However, this approach is designed to attract customers to purchase other more profitable products or services. While commonly used by new entrants to a market, this is regarded as an aggressive strategy with a risk of starting a pricing war with competitors, which is ultimately counterproductive to the financial bottom line.

Psychological pricing

This strategy has a number of options to base prices on the likely psychological impact on target consumers. Boachie (2016) succinctly summarised five key psychological pricing strategies:

1   Charm pricing: Reducing the left digits by one
Our brain processes $3.00 and $2.99 differently, but not in the case of $3.60 and $3.59. Hence the strong psychological influence of left digit reduction.

2   Prestige pricing
The opposite to charm pricing, this approach rounds number up, from $99 to $100. This is suitable for upmarket brand positioning of product categories where the consumer is make a decision based on emotional feelings rather than practical costing. For example a bottle of champagne is more attractive at a price of $40 than $39.72 or $40.28.

3   Buy one, get one free
The psychology here is related to greed, where logic goes out the window in the pursuit of a free item. However because this practice is now so common, businesses need to be more creative with the offers, such as 'buy one and get 25% off your next purchase'.

4   Comparative pricing
This involves promoting two similar products simultaneously, but where the price of one is much more attractive than the other.

5   Visually highlight the different prices
A new sale price is more attractive when offered side by side with the previous price, particularly when the sale price has a different font size and colour.

Market penetration pricing

This is a low-price strategy aimed at undercutting the competition and quickly achieving a deep market penetration, usually for a new product. The goal of a high market share must be economically viable over the longer term, necessitating a low cost structure that competitors can't easily match, in a price sensitive market where a large number of consumers will value the cheaper option.

Market skimming pricing

Completely opposite penetration pricing, this strategy aims to skim a small and profitable share of the market through a high price. This will only be effective when targeting a segment that is not price sensitive, and where demand exceeds supply; such as during peak periods for existing products or the introduction on a revolutionary new offering.

8

Industry insight: A James Bond Martini Experience

Legend has it that Dukes Bar in London's upmarket Mayfair provided author Ian Fleming with the inspiration for the famous James Bond request that his martini should be "shaken, not stirred". Dukes Hotel has taken great care to ensure that visitors to the bar are treated to an experience befitting Agent 007. The small bar, serving a limited number of tables, has a quiet conservative British atmosphere, where the speciality is billed as the best martini in the world. There is a certain brag-value to securing a table here and experiencing the drink made famous by James Bond, and this comes at a price. A martini at Dukes Bar meets all the conditions for a prestige pricing strategy. For a glimpse inside see this brief YouTube clip: https://www.youtube.com/watch?v=kLQW6nGUON8

Package pricing

At the nexus of pricing and distribution is the concept of packaging tourism services. Packaging involves bundling a set of products/services for purchase at a lower price for the consumer than would be available if each service was purchased individually. Packages can be in the form of horizontal integration or vertical integration. As is discussed in *13: Distributing Tourism Services,* horizontal integration is when a group of suppliers combine at the same level, most commonly visitor attractions and activities. Vertical integration involves businesses at different levels of the supply chain between the tourism experience and the customer (e.g. hotel/wholesaler/retail travel agent). An increasingly common example of horizontally integrated packages are pre-paid discount cards:

- CityPASS San Fransisco (USA) is a nine-day pass that includes unlimited cable car rides and visits to four of the top local attractions. CityPASS is available at a number of other major cities in the USA and Canada.

- The Edinburgh Pass (Scotland) offers admission to over 30 attractions in the city, as well as the airport bus service, for up to three days. The Pass is also offered in major cities in the USA.

- The Go Boston Card (USA) is a multi-attraction pass, which for a one-off price includes unlimited free admission to over 40 attractions for various time periods between one and seven days. The Go Card also operates in a number of other major cities in the USA and also in London (UK).

Packages are attractive to the travel trade, particularly when it is uneconomic to sell the products individually. For example, there is a greater incentive for a travel agent to sell a $100 package of local attractions for commission, than a number of individual $10 admission tickets. Clearly for the package to generate demand, it must also represent value to the consumer through either a lower overall price or convenience such as time-saving. For the same reasons individual businesses can also bundle their own services in a package offering, such as a banquet of selected items on a restaurant menu. A further advantage of packages is they mask the price of each individual component. In some cases a hotel, for example, might need to offload a lot of capacity at short notice, due to the cancellation of a large group booking, at a heavily reduced price. This might cause damage to the hotel brand if advertised as an individual product. However, if the capacity was offered to an airline for inclusion in a bundle with an airfare, the package price would mask the individual hotel room price component.

Pricing mistakes

There is a range of common pricing mistakes:

- Prices are too internally cost-oriented rather than based on what the market will bear. A business with inefficient operating costs cannot expect to pass these on to customers.

- Prices are not sufficiently cost-oriented, such as not factoring in costs for repairs and maintenance of plant and equipment.

- Being too slow to adapt and react to changing market conditions and demand levels, which might necessitate a competitive price reduction or present an opportunity to test a price increase.

- Being overly greedy with price increases for a future peak period, such as during a major event, when actual demand might not meet projections.

- Pricing is not congruent with the market positioning strategy, such as in the case of a high quality position competing on price.

- A lack of understanding of tourism distribution channels and the need to factor in provision for different commission costs payable to travel trade intermediaries.

8

Key points

1: Pricing is a marketing function

Price plays a major role in consumers' perceptions of value, and consequently their purchase decisions. A price is what a consumer agrees to exchange in return for a service they perceive as good value, both in terms of a desired benefit to meet a want, as well as monetary worth. Therefore, pricing is a marketing function, because the exchange taking place must reflect a mutually beneficial relationship, and because pricing is influenced by other elements in the marketing mix such as the costs of promotion and distribution.

2: Internal factors and external forces influencing pricing decisions

Every business' pricing decisions will be a function of supply and demand, and can be influenced by a range of internal factors unique to their operation, as well as external forces over which the firm has no control. Ultimately however, pricing decisions must be both consistent with the brand identity and market positioning value proposition, as well as enhance the return on investment in the fixed costs of the business.

3: Dynamic pricing is increasingly being used for more effective yield management

Pricing is one of the most flexible elements in the marketing mix. Dynamic (constantly changing) markets necessitate pricing decision making that is flexible to meet fluctuating levels of demand and to maximise yield (return on investment). Lowering prices can help increase use of the assets (e.g. increased occupancy rate) but not increase yield compared to what could be generated by higher prices and lower occupancy. While history is no predictor of future sales, a yield management system is reliant on analysis of data from historical booking patterns.

Discussion questions

1. Summarise the key advantage and disadvantage for an accommodation supplier considering using an online travel agency specialising in last minute discounts.

2. Why is yield a more important marketing focus than growth in numbers of visitors?

3. On what basis will a customer decide whether a tourism service price represented good value?

References

Boachie, P. (2016). 5 strategies of psychological pricing. www.entrepreneur.com/article/279464. Accessed 27/6/17.

Burgess, C. (2014). *Essential Financial Techniques for Hospitality Managers*. Oxford: Goodfellow Publishers.

Dopson, L.R. & Hayes, D.K. (2009). *Managerial Accounting for the Hospitality Industry*. Hoboken, NJ: John Wiley & Sons.

Enz, C.A., Canina, L. & Lomanno, M. (2004). Why discounting doesn't work: The dynamics of rising occupancy and falling revenue among competitors. *Cornell Hospitality Report*, **4**(7): 6-25.

Pike, S. (2016). Destination image: identifying baseline perceptions of Brazil, Argentina and Chile in the nascent Australian long haul travel market. *Journal of Destination Marketing & Management*, **5**(2): 164-170.

Pike, S. (2017). Destination image temporality – Tracking perceived strengths and weaknesses over time. *Journal of Hospitality & Tourism Management*, **31**: 126-133.

Pike, S. & Bianchi, C. (2016). Destination brand equity for Australia: testing a model of CBBE in short haul and long haul markets. *Journal of Hospitality & Tourism Research*. **40**(1): 114-134.

Yeoman, I., & McMahon-Beattie, U. (2004). *Revenue Management and Pricing: Case Studies and Applications*. London: Thomson.

9 Promoting Tourism Services to Consumers

Chapter outline

The role of promotion is to stimulate demand and generate customers (sales), through the three key goals of *informing* consumers, and then *persuading* and *reminding* them to act. Promotion is the most creative and most visible element in the marketing process, and there is no shortage of media with which to promote a tourism service. Effective marketing communications require the creative promotional ideas to be developed from the critical objective setting undertaken in the marketing planning stage. This means all promotions should support the brand identity (the desired image in the market), in ways that address specific marketing objectives. The chapter presents a six-step marketing communication process, which involves 1) selecting the marketing objective, 2) specifying the target segment(s), 3) determining the desired response from consumers, 4) designing the message content, 5) selecting the type of promotion/media, and 6) monitoring the impact. The main approaches used in promoting tourism services to consumers discussed in this chapter are: advertising, sales promotions, personal selling, direct (e) mail, point of sale, brochures, consumer expos, experiential, and collaborative. Internet promotion is discussed in *10: Social Media in Tourism*, followed by publicity seeking in *11: Tourism Public Relations and Publicity*, promotion to existing customers in *12: Customer Relationship Management in Tourism*, and promoting to the travel trade in *13: Tourism Distribution*.

Learning aims

To enhance your understanding of:

■ The role of promotion in the marketing plan

■ The six-step marketing communications process

■ The main approaches used in promoting tourism services to consumers.

Key terms

Promotion
Promotions are communications in the market, aimed at stimulating demand to generate customers (sales). The type of promotion used will vary depending on the marketing plan objectives.

Marketing communications
Also referred to as *MarComs* or *Comms*, and often used interchangeably with the term promotion, this represents the integration of the *message* and the *media* used in the promotional mix to communicate with *target consumers*.

Hierarchy of Needs/AIDA
The Hierarchy of Needs is a theory proposing advertising should lead consumers through a process from reminding them of their needs though to making a purchase. A variation of this is the AIDA model of enhancing **A**wareness, stimulating **I**nterest, creating a **D**esire, which leads to **A**ction (purchase).

The role of promotion

Ultimately, the role of promotion is to stimulate demand and generate customers (sales), through the three key goals of *informing* consumers, and then *persuading* and *reminding* them to act. To do so requires more than just creative ideas, which while important, need to be based on the critical objective setting undertaken in the marketing planning process. Since a marketing orientation dictates all marketing decisions are made with the consumer in mind, promotion is more than just pushing a message about how great the tourism service is; it should be meaningful to the consumer and ideally stimulate purposeful dialogue. This is known as *marketing communications*, which acknowledges the needs of the target consumer, the message content, as well as the promotional media used. All marketing communications should consistently reinforce the brand identity (desired image in the market). Attention is in short supply out there, but it is gettable, and so the challenge is to cut through the clutter of the noise of competitors and substitute products (e.g. consumer goods brands such as fashion, electronics, cars etc), and be noticed by the target consumers who we seek to influence through a process of increasing awareness, interest, desire, and then action (purchase).

Setting the promotion budget

Small tourism businesses and not-for-profit organisations, such as museums, operate with scarce resources. The promotional budget must generate a measurable return on investment, and small tourism businesses have to look for ways to execute well planned promotions at low cost. While the size of the promotion budget does not in itself guarantee success in the absence of effective tactics, a key challenge is setting the amount allocated for promotions, and allowing for flexibility to adapt to changing market conditions. Muddying the budget setting process is the difficulty in actually measuring the return on investment. There is an old adage used in the advertising industry, which states "I know half of my advertising is working, I just don't know which half". Also, every business is different, and so there is no single budget model that will fit all situations. Examples of circumstances that can influence the size of the promotion budget are summarised in Table 9.1.

Table 9.1: Circumstances influencing the size of the promotion budget

Internal factors unique to the firm	External forces not controlled by the firm
Business size	Seasonality on demand
Location, relative to target segment(s)	Number of competing firms
Staff marketing experience	Competitors' promotions
Business network	Macro-environment forces at the time
Type of service category	• Socio-cultural
Life-cycle stage of the business	• Technological
Cost structure	• Economic
Sources of competitive advantage	• Political
Current financial situation	
Marketing objectives	
Pricing strategy	
Customer relationship management	
Sophistication of performance metrics	

There are four common approaches to setting the promotion budget:

1   **Affordability**. The simplest approach is to set a budget based on what the business can afford. Most small tourism businesses operate with an uncertain future cash flow and so this approach does actually represent reality rather than what might be ideal.

    The disadvantages to this method are potentially underspending or over-spending relative to the marketing objectives, and a short term focus rather than a long term strategy.

2   **Industry average**. This approach results in a promotion budget based on analysis of what competitors are spending. Similar to *going rate* pricing, where prices are set to match the competition, the assumption is there is a collective wisdom within the sector. However, since every individual business faces different circumstances, setting a budget based on average industry spend is difficult to justify.

3   **Ratio of sales**. This is based on a percentage of past or projected sales, and might be flexible to adjust to actual sales on a monthly basis for example. In this way promotion budget levels are a result of sales, as well as the cause. A

9

disadvantage of this approach is that when there is an unforeseen event that impacts negatively on sales, such as inclement weather, or if there is a general decline in consumer demand, the promotion budget ratio declines accordingly, at the very time more promotion is needed.

4 **Marketing objectives**. An assessment is made of the range of initiatives best suited to achieve the objectives, and these are then costed. If there are clear performance measures, this approach makes the most sense, particularly in terms of justifying the budget rationale to stakeholders such as financiers and investors.

The marketing communication process

There are six stages in the marketing communication process:

1. Select the marketing objective being addressed

In *4: Tourism Marketing Planning*, a framework was presented that provides the rationale for the development of promotional tactics. The situation analysis (where are we now?) enables the development of the marketing objectives (where do we want to get to?). Therefore the first step in designing a specific promotion is to determine which of these marketing objectives is being addressed.

2. Specify the target segment

Most businesses cater to more than one segment, which by definition means groups of consumers sharing similar needs and/or characteristics. The differences between segments influence the type of message to be communicated, and the media to be used. For a small tourism business, one promotion might be directed at the full target market, while another will be aimed at a niche segment.

3. Determine the desired response

The overall aim of promotion is to stimulate demand to generate sales. However, different objectives might be related to leading different segments through varying stages of a process based on the Hierarchy of Needs theory (Lavidge & Steiner, 1961):

- **Stimulating recognition of their needs**, to create a *want* for our type of service.
- **Increasing brand salience**, which represents top of mind awareness of our service when a tourism situation is being considered to satisfy a want.
- **Enhancing the brand image**, so they develop a favourable attitude towards our service, relative to competitors.
- **Stimulating intent to purchase,** through a call to action.

These stages are often referred to as the AIDA model of creating **A**wareness, stimulating **I**nterest, creating a **D**esire, which leads to **A**ction (purchase). So the desired response to any promotion will be related to the marketing objective.

4. Design the message

All marketing communications should be aimed at stimulating *purposeful dialogue* with the target consumers. Therefore the message must be *meaningful* to them, by communicating a *value proposition* that addresses their *needs* and *wants*. To *cut through the clutter* of the noise of competing tourism services and substitute products means messages must be *distinctive,* and *focused* on stimulating the *desired response*. The message also needs to be *easily understandable*. Critically, given the increasing level of sophistication among consumers experienced with receiving more marketing communications in their lifetime than previous generations, the message must be realistic and therefore *believable*. No matter how incredible the offer, if it's not backed by a good service at a good price it's not going to work in the long term.

5. Select the type of promotion

Different objectives related to the AIDA process require different promotional tactics and media. For example, advertising can be effective in enhancing awareness, whereas personal selling is more effective at closing a sale. The key advantages and disadvantages for the following range of promotional approaches are discussed in the next section:

- Advertising
- Sales promotions
- Personal selling
- Direct (e)mail
- Point of sale
- Brochures
- Consumer expos
- Experiential
- Collaborative

9

Internet promotion is discussed in *10: Digital and Social Media in Tourism*, followed by publicity seeking in *11:Tourism Public Relations and Publicity*, promotion to existing customers in *12: Customer Relationship Management in Tourism*, and promoting to the travel trade in *13: Tourism Distribution*.

6. Monitor the impact

One of the greatest challenges with tourism promotions is quantifying the impact made, and so it is important this final step is taken into account when designing the message and selecting the media. How will we know if we have achieved the objective? The results of some types of promotions (eg coupons) are easier to monitor than others (eg roadside billboard). This topic is discussed fully in *14: Tourism Marketing Performance Measurement*.

Types of consumer promotion

The *promotional mix* will comprise a range of approaches, each of which has advantages and disadvantages, selected to achieve specific objectives.

Advertising

Advertising, which is paid media placement of a message designed to influence people, has advantages and disadvantages. These are summarised in Table 9.2.

Table 9.2: Potential advantages and disadvantages of advertising

Potential advantages	Potential disadvantages
High reach at a low cost per reader	Lower credibility and believability
Enables visual creativity	Easy for consumers to not pay attention
Useful for enhancing brand salience and brand image	Difficult to get noticed in the advertising clutter
Opportunity to reach new consumers	
Opportunity to include a call for action	Difficult to close a sale
Non-invasive contact	Difficult to measure effectiveness
Many available media formats	High wastage
Ability to target segments through niche media	High cost of prime media space
Short lead times possible	Short life span

One big idea

Regardless of the type of media used, all advertisements should have one attention grabbing idea, which also translates as a meaningful value proposition for the target consumer. An ad can be memorable, but not necessarily effective if it doesn't elicit the desired response. There have been plenty of ads that have won creativity awards for the advertising agency, but were not effective in generating sales.

Reinforce the brand identity

Remembering that messages should reinforce the brand identity the business is investing resources in, ensure visual and/audio cues, such as the logo, slogan and contact website contact, are linked to the brand, not necessarily waiting until the end. After all it's not a mystery novel.

Well scripted

Whatever the opportunities and constraints of the type of media selected, the message needs to be well worded, whether it's a *seven word single minded proposition* on a roadside billboard or a 30 second radio ad, the message needs to be to the point, short and snappy. As master communicator Sir Winston Churchill once advised, "Short words are best and the old words when short, are best of all". Keep it simple, in the language of the target recipient, and with a message specifically tailored to them.

Call to action

The message should always have a call to action, in the right spot. This doesn't always mean at the end of the radio or television ad, but rather at the point in the ad when you have attracted the most attention with your big idea. Put careful thought into how the call to action can be tracked to monitor the effectiveness of the ad.

Television advertising

Television offers arguably the most high profile non-online advertising opportunities, with potential to achieve a high reach. The combined visual and audio format can also have high persuasive impact. While television advertising is expensive, there are opportunities to leverage geographic and demographic selectivity, by day of the week and time of the day for affordable advertising packages. However, there is a high level of wastage since the clutter of television advertising makes it hard to get noticed and gain attention. Viewers are not a captive audience, and are easily distracted. This means the audio content is important so the ad can be heard from another room in the home. Also, emerging ad-skipping technology enables the viewer to record programmes and potentially automatically fast forward through the ads. The traditional 15/30 second formats mean the ad has a short life span and also can't include detailed information. Contact details can be difficult to get noticed. In addition to the relatively high costs of media placement, television ads can also be the most expensive to produce.

Lean marketing tips: TV ads

- Check out the low rates for off peak timeslots, where audience characteristics might be of interest. For example, lunchtime soaps have audiences of stay-at-home mums and dads, who are often the family travel influencer/organiser, along with retirees.
- Consider using a package of 10 second or 15 second ads, rather than the traditional 30 seconds.
- Shop around for a professional production company offering an affordable deal, rather than cut corners by doing it yourself. Quality is critical in television, and remember the segment can also be reused in other digital media, such as a website and social media.

Newspaper advertising

Although there has been massive disruption to the traditional newspaper format, there are still many high circulation daily tabloids offering high reach. Newspapers have relatively little competition in terms of directly competing tabloids, and so while advertising costs can be high there is a low cost per circulation contact. Newspaper ads are tangible and able to be cut out and stored by the reader, particularly is a coupon is involved. There are opportunities for geographic targeting such as the major daily newspaper in a big city, or a free small regional community publication. Usually a short lead-in time is possible, with options to target specific sections of the publication, on different days of the week. Detailed information can be communicated. Newspaper readership is also higher than the circulation sales as this form of publication is often shared by the buyer/subscriber with family or work colleagues. There is the opportunity to provide contact details. However, advertising clutter is a challenge and so it can be difficult for small ads to get noticed. Relative to some other forms of media, hard copy newspapers have poorer reproduction quality. Newspapers advertisements also have a short shelf life.

Lean marketing tips: Newspaper ads

- Make sure your ad placement is for the outside of the right hand page, which grabs more attention than ads on the left page or close to the centre fold.

- Seek out the newspaper section that will most likely be read by your target consumers. Not all readers look at all sections of the paper.

- Use a catchy headline, in the form of a short sentence of up to seven words, to grab attention.

- Making use of white space, particularly around the border of the ad, will help make it stand out from the clutter, even though this is paying the newspaper to not print anything in that space.

- Increased online advertising has reduced the clutter of many newspaper classified advertising sections. Consider trialling a small regular classified.

- Newspapers are one of the best outlets for providing detailed information in a large display ad. The key is to hook the reader into getting involved with the ad.

Activity 9.1: Which travel advertisement grabs your attention

Imagine you have in the back of your mind the need for a holiday. Get hold of a local newspaper and skim through the pages and look out for travel advertisements. Which ad most appeals to you, and why? Is it clear who the target market is? Is it clear whether the ad seeks to achieve in terms of the AIDA process? What is the call to action?

Radio advertising

Radio advertising can be relatively low cost with a high reach, through high frequency of ad placements. Short lead in times are possible, and placements can target different times of the day and days of the week. Many popular shows have loyal followers who don't switch stations during ad breaks. Different segments can be targeted by stations catering to different age groups, religions and lifestyles. However, ads are relatively short, contain no visual clues, and can be challenging to communicate contact details. Radio ads also have a short life span and so need high frequency air time to gain traction.

Lean marketing tips: Radio ads

- Buy timeslots for a show that appeals to your segment's demographics, rather than a run of station schedule.

- Give listeners a reason to respond to the call to action in terms of a phone call or website visit. The ad should offer something of potential value such as a free trial, free information or a special price. Keep the offer limited to a time period, because a human trait is to not want to miss out. The time frame also helps measuring the ad's effectiveness.

- The call to action should use a phone number or website URL or street address that is easy for the listener to remember (eg 1800 – COFFEE).

- Investigate the possibility of a contra deal, to provide in-kind (free) services to a local station for use as prizes, in return for free or discounted advertising.

- Keep the message simple. Radio is not the ideal format for trying to communicate detailed information.

- Script the ad for the listener's ear, rather than their eyes. Aim to grab attention to your big idea immediately, to lessen the chance the listener will switch to another station. This is particularly so for music shows, rather than talk shows, where an ad is more of an interruption.

- Consider referring the brand name at the beginning, the middle and end of the ad. Tell them what you are going to tell them, tell them, then tell them what you told them.

9

Magazine advertising

The diversity and specialised nature of magazines provide opportunities to target niche segments, such as travel, motoring, fishing, food, and fitness, for example. Such specialised media, with high production quality, often has a higher credibility than mainstream television and newspapers. Relative to other media, magazines have a long shelf life, and readership often extends beyond the original buyer/subscriber. Magazine advertising can include: detailed information, graphic imagery, and call to action/contact details. However, this form of advertising is relatively expensive with a high cost per contact, can involve high production costs, and requires longer lead-in planning time. This advertising is also not suitable if consumer attention during a particular time of day or day of the week is sought.

Lean marketing tips: Magazine ads

- Consider an ongoing small classified ad in a niche magazine that appeals to your segments' needs and characteristics. One example is automobile club magazines, in regions within a comfortable travel time to the business.

- Take advantage of the glossy presentation format by using four colours, which while more expensive than black and white imagery enhance credibility and are usually more cost-effective in terms of gaining attention and ultimately generating a response.

- Having a photo and/or brand imagery enhances the professional look and appeal of the ad.

- Don't sign up for more than one ad over time. If the initial ad doesn't generate a response why continue in that publication?

Outdoor advertising

Outdoor advertising has the potential for high reach in high profile locations. A long life span is possible. Relative to other forms of media, in some areas there is less clutter competing for consumer attention. Outdoor also has the potential for high visual impact though size and creativity. However, detailed messages are not practical as consumer attention is usually fleeting as they pass by. Also, it is difficult to measure effectiveness outdoor advertising. Outdoor has a longer lead in planning time, and design and placement can be expensive.

Lean marketing tips: Outdoor advertising

- Passers-by notice movement. An pavement noticeboard outside a business gets noticed more if there are balloons or similar attached, which move in the breeze.

- Pedestrians look down as they walk, so consider placing interesting chalk messages on the pavement near the business entrance.

- Drivers and cyclists stopped at red lights notice more of their surroundings, so look for economical ways to have a message at a strategic high profile commuter location(s).

- Walking human billboards are relatively inexpensive, particularly when used in short bursts in peak hour commuter routes, and do stand out from other forms of outdoor advertising. Consider creating a presence outside places where large numbers of people congregate for special events such as music concerts and sports matches.

- Ask a major supplier of disposables, such as menu ingredients, to supply/sponsor the pavement noticeboard.

- If the business has a vehicle, even it's the family car, don't waste the opportunity for signage, in any form.

Activity 9.2: Funny captions

Some businesses attract attention by having funny captions or interesting facts, written on chalk boards on the pavement. Bringing a smile to someone's day could enamour them towards the business. For example, a funny caption outside a café could be: *My yoga teacher told me to touch my toes, but I said no that would be a bit of a stretch for me!* A message about an interesting fact outside a bar could read: *Celebrate the birthday of (INSERT CELEBRITY NAME) today with a special happy hour glass of your favourite.* What guidelines would you provide the staff member responsible for the chalkboard captions?

Sales promotions

Sales promotions are essentially sales incentives, which are used when there is a short term need for a quick increase in sales. This typically occurs with the introduction of a new product, when urgent cash flow is needed, and when there is a temporary need to offload excess capacity/inventory. Incentives include discounts, giveaways and competitions. The main advantages are the relative cost-effectiveness compared to other media, and the ability to measure responses. This is a short term tactic, and not suitable for long term brand loyalty development. If used over the longer term the disadvantages are potential price wars and the training of consumers to wait for the next special offer from the business and its competitors.

Lean marketing tips: Sales promotions

- Using *buy more/save more* sales incentives provides more of a win/win by psychologically justifying the consumer's rationale for spending money, and selling more of the business capacity/stock for the business than a one-off purchase discount.

- Competitions are ideal for new businesses to generate a mailing list of prospective customers for direct (e)mail promotions, and for the sake of only one prize can create a lot of awareness and interest.

- For free giveaways with a purchase, which most people love, consider using small mementos that are branded with the business name and slogan.

- Distributing promotional coupons featuring an incentive with a deadline, are tangible, inexpensive to print, and one of the easiest forms of promotion to measure response levels.

Personal selling

Personal selling is the most effective means to build trust, reduce purchase risk and close a sale, through personalised contact. The art of selling is to take the fear out of saying 'yes'.

Other advantages include the opportunity to hold the consumer's attention longer, and for two-way dialogue that provides instant feedback. However, this is the most expensive form of promotion, particularly if using non-commission sales representatives, and is best suited where there is a high level of involvement in the consumer's decision making. The negative reputation of telemarketers has also led to the establishment of 'do not call' registers in some jurisdictions, which makes it illegal to phone. 'Do not knock' legislation is also in forces in some places due to the annoying behaviour of door-to-door sales people. Consumer expos are a particularly valuable opportunities for personal selling, which can relatively less threatening and more credible sales environments for many consumers

Lean marketing tips: Personal selling

- Give individual staff (who have good phone communication skills) a list of prospective customers, from entries to a competition for example, to contact with a special offer. This can be an add-on to their usual duties, and performed when there is a lull in demand. Incentivise the initiative by rewarding staff for sales. Opt for a friendly soft-sell approach.

- Look for options to improve staff selling skills, such as shorts courses offered by polytechnics, local business organisations, e.g. the Chamber of Commerce, and online MOOCs (Massive Online Open Courses).

- Give each staff member their own business card to hand out to new contacts at social and networking events.

- Personal selling is not always cold calling. Encourage front line staff to *upsell* when taking orders. As well as increasing cash flow, upselling creates the opportunity for increasing the customer's satisfaction when they purchase a higher quality product or service.

Direct (e)mail

Direct marketing involves communicating directly with consumers through personal selling by phone, or messages via text, email or post. Don't underestimate the power of old fashioned direct mail approaches, which still outperform digital channels (Haskel, 2015). This type of promotion enables high audience selectivity by targeting specific consumer characteristics through contact members of a list, which can be developed as a database of customers in-house (see *12:Customer Relationship Management* for database marketing to existing customers). Direct marketing communications can be tailored to target the characteristics of the target segment, and can provide more detailed information than many other forms of promotion. This is particularly useful for following up on leads from other promotions such as competitions, and for distributing catalogues and brochures. As discussed in regard to personal selling there have been unethical practices used by some that have led to increased resistance from consumers for direct contact methods, and increasing attention to developing legislation that inhibits bad practices. Also, direct (e)mail is so prevalent that it can be very difficult to stand out from the clutter of the (e)mail box. For this reason response rates are typically relatively low compared to the high reach possibilities, but direct responses mean it is relatively easy to measure effectiveness.

Direct (e)mail approaches can be expensive when contact lists need to be purchased. Be prepared for low response rates initially. Haskel (2015) cited a report by the Direct Marketing Association, which estimated oversized envelopes can achieve a response rate of 5%, followed by postcards (4.25%), dimensional (4%), catelogs (3.9%), and standard DLE envelopes (3.5%).

Lean marketing tips: Direct mail

- There are proven techniques for effective direct mail, which can be grasped quickly through publications such as by Stevenson (2009), Simpson & Kenney (2014) and Perry (2016).

- Personalised letters are more effective. Pay a casual to handwrite names and address on oversized envelopes. Considering inserting a small sweet to make the envelope appear lumpy to attract the target's curiosity.

- Make use of any leads generated through other promotions, such as competitions, coupon responses, and from email enquiries, to develop a database of potential customers.

- Make it easy for the contact to respond, by offering multiple alternative means such as by free phone, email, as well as links to social media and website.

- Direct mail must be permission-based. Always allow contacts to *opt out/unsubscribe* from future communications, to avoid generating negative perceptions about the brand. In some parts of the world, this is required by law.

- Be very targeted by contacting only those consumers with the potential characteristics and needs that will suit your offering. Tailoring messages that appeal to them personally will have a higher chance of response than from a larger random list.

- Headlines are everything. Be creative to capture attention and avoid relegation to the junk mail folder. Build a file of direct marketing materials from others that appeal to you.

- Don't limit the campaign to one mail out. Sequential letters, mentioning the previous letter, are more effective.

Point of sale

Point of sale promotions take place where on-site payments are taken from customers, and are particularly suitable for small tourism businesses. This can be either at the cash register or another part of the business where a staff member collects payment, such as at a café tables. This invariably involves a sale promotion offer, such as a giveaway, discount or prize draw. Some products lend themselves to this type of promotion more than others. For example, when Parker Pens recognised they were in the gift-giving business, rather than the pen business, and that many gift purchase decisions were made spontaneously in-store, the brand developed point of sale displays at retail outlets as a priority strategy. One popular approach at hospitality businesses is to offer a special deal at certain times of the day, week or year, usually at off-peak times. Examples include a happy hour specials noticeboard at a bar/restaurant, or an early bird coffee and cake deal at a café. The key advantage of point of sale promotions is they generate extra sales through impulse buying. Also, well designed inexpensive cardboard displays can be effective, and can be discarded after the promotion is finished.

Lean marketing tips: Point of sale

- In a retail situation such as a souvenir or gift shop, seek out a supplier to pay for the privilege of a point of sale promotion, such as a product display cabinet.
- Similarly, offer a key supplier the opportunity to supply a poster offering a buy more/ save more incentive near the diner's table (e.g. a bucket of beers at a reduced price, which they supply at a lower cost).
- Place an unobtrusive offer, in the form of a coupon or an advertisement, in a place where every customer will notice, such as in a ticket wallet, with the condiments on a table, on the bedside table etc.

Brochures

In the digital online era hard copy brochures still have their place as a tangible part of tourism decision making, and as a memento of an experience that can be passed on to others. For most small businesses DLE size (trifold A4) is the most practical, and can be used in conjunction with other approaches in the promotional mix. DLE fits inside a standard envelope, most brochure display racks, as well travellers' handbags and jeans back pockets. Brochures, including catalogues, are particularly useful at events where consumers can be engaged with in conversation such as consumer expos. Brochures can also be mailed out in response to contact from other types of promotion, such as from phone requests for information and competition entries, and used in direct mail campaigns.

Lean marketing tips: Brochures

- A brochure can be as simple as an envelope size card with two-sided printing, which are inexpensive to produce. Engage a graphic design professional to set up the artwork design and layout.

- When your brochure is to be displayed at an external location such as a visitor information centre or hotel lobby, spent some time analysing in person which brochures on display grab your attention, such as by colour, imagery, headline, and position in the rack.

- While specialist companies can be hired to manage brochure distribution far and wide, maintain a personal presence at high profile venues, such as the local visitor information office. Have one of your team regularly visit the venue to top up the brochure rack. This is an opportunity to gradually build rapport with the office staff.

- Never ever interfere in anyway with another business' brochures in a rack.

Flyers

Flyers are simple one page leaflest, which are inexpensive to print and can be handed out at promotional expos, public places, and outside the venues of special events. Also look for opportunities to pin a flyer to noticeboards at venues with high traffic and/or captive audiences, such at university campuses and in the lifts of large apartment complexes. Special offers should include a code number that must be quoted when redeemed, to enable monitoring of results.

Consumer expos

9

Consumer expos combine personal selling with other forms of promotion such as coupons, brochures, outdoor advertising and competitions. In major centres there will usually be a wide range of consumer expo opportunities, many of which enable targeting specific segments because of the specialised event theme. These include:

- **Travel expos**, which are a feature on the event calendar of all major cities
- **Specialist lifestyle expos**, such as boating and fishing, automobiles, food & wine, caravan, home and garden
- **Cultural food/dance festivals**, such as when different nationalities celebrate their national day
- **Major sports events and sporting festivals**, such as the New York marathon and Air New Zealand's series of Golden Oldies tournaments, usually have an expo as part of the program

Although participation at major consumer expos is expensive there are many smaller affordable options, including regional community events such as swap meets, festivals and farmers markets, Consumer expos can provide excellent opportunities to have two-way dialogue with consumers and develop potential sales leads. These events also enable product demonstrations (e.g. video display), and can feature tangible examples of products (e.g. campervan hire, wine tasting). However, a disadvantage is there are many visitors to these events who can be time wasters because they have already made their purchase decision or are never going to actually purchase. For some people a visit to an expo is just for a social/entertainment outing. It is also difficult to measure the overall effectiveness of participation, outside of counting visitor numbers. Even though trackable promotional coupons can be effective, there are intangible benefits of participation that will be difficult to measure, such as increasing brand awareness, brand image, word of mouth referrals and future sales.

Lean marketing tips: Expos

- Display space at major consumer expos can be very expensive, but does present opportunities for a collaborative presence by a group of businesses, such as a local tourism association or local accommodation association, where costs are shared.

- Always have a special offer in the form of a tangible coupon or flyer, which can be in a simple and inexpensive two colour format, so that the resultant response can be monitored.

- A competition is an effective way to get noticed in the crowd, engage in conversations with visitors, and collect personal contact details that can be used in future direct mail promotions. The competition only needs to have one prize, and so is not necessarily a high cost initiative.

- Have a good supply of business cards on display.

Experiential

Also referred to as events marketing and engagement marketing, experiential promotions involve staging promotional events in high traffic areas, where passers-by are encouraged to participate in an activity. The aim is to develop a relationship between the brand and people by enabling them to get a sense of *experiencing* the brand. This is a form of *co-creative* promotion where consumers actively engage with brand representatives, rather than passively receive messages. This interaction helps counter intangibility of tourism services. Clearly this type of promotion will not appeal to all consumers, and might even be perceived as annoying, and so needs to be effectively targeted at the right audience. These events take place in targeted public locations such as at a shopping mall, transport centres such as airports and rail stations, a weekend market, a sporting event, or a university campus, for example, depending on the target segment. Part of the rationale is its easier to gain access to a public space where people frequent, that try to lure them somewhere where they wouldn't normally go. Creative experiential promotions offer the opportunity to attract news media attention and generate additional free publicity, a topic discussed more fully in *11: Tourism Public Relations and Publicity*. Examples of the pop-up events include:

■ Taking farm animals into an urban public place frequented by families

■ Setting up a mock adventure activity (e.g. the Zorb) in a city business district

■ Setting up virtual reality activities

■ Food and wine tasting, with giveaway samples

■ Hiring a local celebrity to host a competition or provide giveaways

■ Prizes draws for purchasing a product in a bar, where participants are involved in their own prize selection through spinning a wheel or tossing a coin

Lean marketing tips: Experiential promotion

■ Ensure the audience clearly knows who you are and what you are offering. Have a call to action, and tell them how to respond.

■ Make sure there is a great photo opportunity for participants and passers-by, and create a hashtag they can share on social media. Experiential can create a lot of social media attention.

■ Collaborate with another brand to share costs and create a bigger experience.

■ Make it fun, and really engage with participants.

Networking, collaboration, and cooperating to compete

9

Integral to the success of destinations is the philosophy of stakeholders cooperating to compete, to create a bigger impact in the marketplace than could be achieved by individual businesses working in isolation. The key advantages for small tourism firms collaborating include (Fyall, 2008:334):

■ The opportunity to collectively brand a product theme in a geographic area

■ The pooling of resources such as finance and human resources

■ Conducting joint marketing research

■ Reducing individual risk and uncertainty through information sharing

■ The opportunity to distribute the group product through more complex distribution channels

■ Raising the profile of individual businesses through wider reach of joint promotions

■ Stronger collective representation with tourism industry and political bodies.

However, Fyall also warned of the potential pitfalls in collaborative arrangements (p. 335):

■ Mutual distrust between businesses with contrasting visitor numbers

■ Possible apathy due to the tension between competing and collaborating

■ Inertia due to the failure of partners to advance at the same pace

■ Conflict between the various ownership styles and objectives

■ Unease over loss of control of decision making

■ Non-achievement due to lack of expertise, time or finance.

The tourism industry offers many opportunities to network with potential collaborative partners, such as at: conferences, seminars, and awards events co-ordinated by the local tourism industry associations, DMO, and Chamber of Commerce. Most small businesses don't take advantage of these opportunities. For example, there are an estimated 40,000 tourism-related businesses in the state of Queensland, Australia, and yet less than 10% are members of the Queensland Tourism Industry Council. Opportunities to work with the local DMO and other businesses were discussed in summarised in Table 2.1 in *2: Destination Marketing Organisations* (see also Pike, 2016). Opportunities to work with the travel trade are discussed in *13: Tourism Distribution*.

Lean marketing tips: Networking and collaboration

■ Look for opportunities for the business to have a regular presence at local industry networking events.

■ Look for options to partner with other businesses, locally and/or along a popular touring route, by displaying each other's brochures.

■ Consider forming a cooperative alliance with a small number of compatible local businesses, to develop cooperative advertising and participation at travel trade events and consumer expos.

■ Many university business schools and tourism schools offer seminars that are open to industry, where they showcase the real world relevance of their research. It's usually simply a matter of subscribing to their industry/alumni database. Most also seek industry guest speakers to meet with students and discuss real world issues. Today's students are tomorrow's potential industry network.

Digital and social media

The dynamic (ever changing) world of online promotion, such as through digital advertising and social media is presented in *10: Digital and Social Media in Tourism*.

Publicity seeking

Opportunities for working with the media, in a mutually beneficial manner, to generate free publicity are discussed in *11: Tourism Public Relations and Publicity*.

Customer relationship management

For many small tourism businesses, keeping in touch with previous customers, in a meaningful way, represents an efficient and powerful opportunity to enhance brand loyalty through repeat visitation and word-of-mouth recommendations. This is the topic of *12: Customer Relationship Management in Tourism*.

Travel trade promotion

The range of approaches used to promote tourism services to travel trade intermediaries, such as travel agents and tour wholesalers is presented in *13: Tourism Distribution*.

Case 9.1: The oldest pub in town

The Red Lion is a historic British pub in a prime position in the high street in Southampton, England. The location in a busy foot traffic area is a source of competitive parity as there are other pubs nearby, including a Weatherspoon a few doors away. Weatherspoon is a chain of over 900 pubs across the UK, which has a business model based on low cost drinks and meals. The Red Lion can't compete on price, but has a strength that can't be imitated by larger rivals. Dating back to 1140, the Red Lion is the second oldest pub in England, where most of the exterior and interior remains authentically similar to how it looked in the pre-Tudor period. Part of the unique history here is that King Henry V held court in the Red Lion before leading his army to France and the Battle of Agincourt in 1415, one of the most legendary victories of the 100 year war between England and France. During his stay King Henry held a famous trial, in the same space in the Red Lion where you can enjoy a beer or a meal today, of three noblemen who had plotted to assassinate him. The three conspirators were found guilty and executed in public nearby. The pub is also said to be home to over 20 ghosts, and so as well as visitors interested in English history, the Red Lion also attracts media and others interested in the paranormal.

As an aside, the pub features in Jane Austen's novel *Pride and Prejudice*. Miss Austen lived for a while at the nearby Dolphin Hotel, where she celebrated her 18th birthday. The Dolphin now has a *Jane Austen Suite* to commemorate the author's time there. The Red Lion is not a large pub, and so the meal service and small bar area quickly become full during peak hours. As with any hospitality business with a limited capacity, a major challenge is levelling out the demand during the week so that the resources are being used effectively during time that are traditionally slow for high street pubs. This style of building is rare in downtown Southampton, in comparison to more historic English cities such as Bath, Oxford and York, due to the heavy bombing the city endured during *the Blitz* in World War II.

Discussion question

What low cost promotion initiatives would you recommend to capitalise on the Red Lion's unique history, to even out demand during the week?

Key points

1: The role of promotion in the marketing plan

Ultimately, the role of promotion is to stimulate demand and generate sales, through the three key goals of *informing* consumers, and then *persuading* and *reminding* them to act. While promotion is the most creative and most visible element in the marketing process, creative promotional ideas need to be developed from the critical objective setting undertaken in the marketing planning stage, and focused on achieving a marketing objective.

2: The six-step marketing communication process

The chapter presented a six-step marketing communication process, which involves 1) selecting the marketing objective, 2) specifying the target segment(s), 3) determining the desired response from consumers, 4) designing the message content, 5) selecting the type of promotion/media, and 6) monitoring the impact.

3: The main approaches used in promoting tourism services to consumers

Different marketing objectives require different promotional tactics and media. For example, advertising can be effective in enhancing awareness, whereas personal selling is more effective at closing a sale. The key advantages and disadvantages for the following range of promotional approaches were discussed: advertising, sales promotions, personal selling, direct (e)mail, point of sale, brochures, consumer expos, experiential, and collaborative.

Discussion questions

1. What is the purpose of promotion?

2. What is the difference in meaning between the terms *promotion* and *marketing*, and why is promotion sometimes incorrectly referred to as marketing?

3. With so many different forms of promotion and types of media channels, on what basis should a particular approach be selected?

References

Fyall, A. (2008). Marketing visitor attractions: A collaborative approach. In Fyall, A., Garrod, B., Leask, A. & Wanhill, S. (Eds). *Managing Visitor Attractions*. (2nd Ed). Abingdon, Oxfordshire: Routledge, pp. 331-346.

Haskel, D. (2015). *2015 DMA response rate report: Direct mail outperforms all digital channels combined by 600%*. IWCO.Com. 14 April. Accessed at https://www.iwco.com/blog/2015/04/14/dma-response-rate-report-and-direct-mail/

Lavidge, R.E. & Steiner, G.A. (1961). A model for predictive measurements of advertising effectiveness. *Journal of Marketing*, **25**: 59-62.

Pike, S. (2016). *Destination Marketing Essentials*. (2nd Ed). Abingdon, Oxon: Routledge.

Perry, G. (2016). *The Ultimate Direct Marketing, Copywriting & Advertising Bible*. MakeRight Publishing.

Simpson, C. & Kennedy, D. (2014). *The Direct Mail Solution: A Business Owner's Guide to Building a Lead-Generating, Sales-Driving, Money-Making Direct-Mail Campaign*. Entrepreneur Press.

Stevenson, S.C. (2009). *Profitable Direct Mail Appeals: Planning, Implementing and Maximising Results*. Stevenson, Inc.

9

.

10 Digital and Social Media in Tourism

Chapter outline

The opportunity to digitise media content has transformed the way in which small tourism businesses' promotional material can be made available across different internet-based platforms. Over half of the world's population are internet users, and we are now witnessing the most technologically savvy consumers in history. The emergence of Web 2.0 in 2004 enabled co-creation of content on social media, which has democratised the internet. User-generated content (UGC) on social media, related to tourism, has reached levels that now swamp the marketing communications of the global travel industry. For small tourism businesses, digital and social media offer the benefits of lower costs and greater efficiency than traditional marketing approaches, and provide opportunities to enhance the visitor experience and relationships with customers. The chapter discusses how travellers use various digital and social media, both creating and being influenced by online content, during the three stages of travel planning, travel, and post-travel; and presents different types of opportunities for small tourism businesses to engage with consumers through digital and social media. The chapter does not attempt a technical discussion on how to design and manage digital platforms, as the technology will have changed since the time of writing. Management of the digitisation and placement of media can be efficiently outsourced. The focus here is on the need to have a plan for engaging with consumers online. What is required is a clear focus on *social* engagement, rather than simply *media* placement.

Learning aims

To enhance your understanding of:

- The influence of digital and social media in tourism
- How travellers are using digital and social media
- Opportunities for small businesses to use digital and social media.

Key terms

Digital media
Media content such as text, photos, graphics, audio and video, which are encoded into machine readable formats (digitised), and able to be transferred to other devices, sent across the internet, and used across a business' various online promotional platforms.

Web 2.0
The internet platform facilitating content and applications to be continuously modified by all users in a collaborative way.

Social media
The activities of virtual communities who share information, knowledge and opinions, using Web-based applications that enable ease of creating and modifying content.

The digital media era

The commercial digitisation of media content evolved in earnest during the late-1990s, following the widespread adoption of the internet. Prior to this development, traditional media (e.g. brochures, advertising material) were difficult to transfer to other people, devices and locations. In the early 1990s for example, print media generally had to be photocopied and shared by floppy disc or sent by facsimile. Audio content was stored on cassettes, which had to be physically distributed to another location, as were video and film. Advertising material therefore had a limited shelf life and limited range of usage. Now, all forms of media content, such as text, photos, graphics, audio and video, can be encoded into machine readable formats (digitised), and made available to other people and devices, sent across the internet, and used across a business' various online promotional platforms.

The internet e-commerce era started in 1995 with the launch of Amazon.com and eBay.com (Kaplan & Haelein, 2009). As highlighted in Table 10.1, by 2017 half the world's population had become internet users, with the highest population penetration in North America (88.1%), and the highest number of users in Asia (almost 2 billion). Worldwide, the number of internet users grew by nearly 1000% during the period 2000-2017. Furthermore, the number of mobile-only internet users is now over 15% of adults (Mander, 2016). By 2014, mobile apps generated more revenue than Hollywood's movie industry (The Courier-Mail, 2015), with the TripAdvisor App reaching 100 million downloads (Pike, 2016). By 2020 it has been estimated there will be over 30 billion devices connected to the internet and most of these will be mobile (Gartner, 2013, in Trendwatching, 2014).

Table 10.1: World internet users as at June 2017. Adapted from Internet World Stats (2017)

	Internet users Dec 2000 (Millions)	Internet users June 2017 (Millions)	Penetration of population	Growth 2000-2017
Asia	114,304	1,938,076	46.7%	1,595%
Europe	105,096	659,634	80.2%	528%
Latin America/ Caribbean	18,069	404,269	62.4%	2,137%
Africa	4,514	388,376	31.2%	8,501%
North America	108,096	320,059	88.1%	8%
Middle East	3,284	146,972	58.7%	4,374%
Oceania/ Australia	7,620	28,180	69.6%	1%
World Total	360,985	3,885,567	51.7%	976%

The rise in influence of social media in tourism

During the Web 1.0 era, the internet was used predominantly to push static information in one direction, in what was a *read-only* format; which didn't facilitate any interaction with, or between, other users (Borges, 2009). However, in 2004 the emergence of Web 2.0 enabled user generated content (UGC) to be uploaded. Web 2.0 was used at that time as a term to describe a platform enabling content and applications to be continuously modified by all users in a collaborative way (Kaplan & Haenlein, 2009). This development didn't represent a sudden upgrade of the internet, but rather the availability of a new group of programmes such as Adobe Flash, RSS, and Javascript, which radically changed the way information could be created, disseminated and viewed by any internet user (Sigala, 2012).

TIME Magazine named its 2006 person of the year as **You,** the internet user, to acknowledge the democratising power of social media. By 2013, engaging with social media had become the most popular activity on the internet (GWI, 2014 in Oliveira & Panyik, 2015). Social media is defined as (Brake & Safko, 2009:6):

> *activities, practices, and behaviours among communities of people who gather online to share information, knowledge, and opinions using conversational media. Conversational media are Web-based applications that make it possible to create and easily transmit content in the form of words, pictures, videos, and audios.*

The volume of UGC on social media, related to tourism, now swamps the marketing communications of the global travel industry. Furthermore, traffic to the world's top two web sites, facebook.com and youtube.com, dwarfs that of traditional mass media sites such as cnn.com, nytimes.com, bbc.co.uk, and espn.go.com (Pan & Crotts, 2012). This shift in power from corporate organisations to internet users and virtual communities has occurred in a short space of time, and the global tourism industry is being forced to adapt quickly to the digital and social media phenomenon (Pike, 2016:79):

10

- The internet has emerged as a dominant medium for travel bookings, both through travel trade intermediaries and through disintermediation.

- Many travel situations involve high levels of information seeking in the planning stages, with the internet a primary source.

- Tourism offerings are mostly intangible services with many types of risk, and UGC is regarded as credible form of word of mouth advice.

- Increasing influence of travellers' online reviews of destinations and tourism services.

- Increasing use of mobile social media applications and portable navigation devices (PND) during travel.

- Increasing *free Wi-Fi* available for visitors and residents at destinations.

- High levels of *brag value* UGC in virtual social networks during travel.

- Unlike any other brand category, travellers are spoilt for choice of an almost unlimited number of destinations with an online presence.

How travellers use digital and social media

Leung et. al. (2013) reported that the number of academic journal articles published about tourism social media activity increased from only two in 2007 to 22 in 2011. The number of publications has increased exponentially since then. The first journal special issue on tourism social media was by the *Journal of Travel & Tourism Marketing* in 2013 (Volume 30, Issue 1-2), the first academic book was by Sigala, Christou and Gretzel (2012), while the first academic book related to travellers' mobile sociality was by Molz (2012). The general reasons travellers participate in virtual communities include: entertainment, bragging, following, information provision/seeking, social and professional networking, and sense of belonging (Pike, 2016). More specifically, in relation to users of TripAdvisor, Mkono and Tribe (2017) identified the following roles:

- **Trolls**, who gain pleasure from deceiving other users, and should therefore be separated from genuine users

- **Activists**, who encourage others to take action to support a cause, such as a critical issue facing the tourism industry

- **Socialites,** who seek status, and whose online behaviours provide insights into tourism consumption fads and trends

- **Social critics**, engage with other users to articulate sociocultural and political issues

- **Information seekers,** who solicit advice from other users, and in the process highlight information gaps for the tourism industry

Mkono and Tribe suggested knowledge of these roles will help tourism managers better understand the different online travel-related gratifications sought by consumers, which in turn enables them to devise more meaningful and "suitably nuanced online community engagement strategies and responses" (p. 296).

Travellers now use digital and social media in many ways, shaping content and/or using content, during each of the three stages of travel planning, travel, and post-travel.

Travel planning

It has been suggested that over 85% of travellers use the internet during travel planning (Torres 2012, in Leung et al., 2013). Indeed, increasing numbers of consumers prefer to engage with a business, such as asking questions, on social media rather than by phone for example (Hootsuite, 2017). As shown in Table 10.2, Europeans' use of the internet for travel bookings increased from 13% to 76% in the decade between 2003 and 2013, while their use of travel agents decreased from 65% to 18% (Oliveira & Panyik, 2015).

Table 10.2: Changes in booking methods: Europe. Adapted from Oliveira and Panyik (2015)

	2003	2013
Travel agent	65%	18%
Phone	22%	5%
Internet	13%	76%

Leung et. al's (2013) literature review found social media was used mostly during travel planning, where a key factor in decision making was trust. UGC represents online *word of mouth* (WoM), which is also known as *word of mouse* (Gelb & Sundaram, 2002), and eWoM. The European Travel Commission found online recommendations from significant others was the most frequently used source of trip planning information (56%), followed by websites (46%), personal experience with a destination (34%), travel agents and tourism offices (21%) and tourism brochures (11%) (Oliveira & Panyik, 2015). As such, UGC is a form of organic image development (see *3: Tourism Consumer Behaviour*), which has higher believability for consumers, and therefore more credibility than advertising. As an example, one in four Australians have booked a trip after seeing a friend's photos online, with *social media envy* being a particularly strong travel motivator for Gen Y (MX, 2015). Indeed, an estimated 75% of purchase decisions for this demographic are influenced by recommendations on social media (Hootsuite, 2017). For a review of the literature published about tourism eWoM see Luo and Zhong (2015), who found travel-related eWOM communications via social media relied strongly on existing social relationships.

10

During travel

Digital and social media are used for a variety of reasons during travel, such as keeping in touch with friends (e.g. Facebook and messenger), sharing experiences (e.g. Instagram, Twitter), providing reviews and searching for information (e.g. Tripadvisor.com, Lonelyplanet.com), onward bookings (e.g. Expedia.com, Hotels.com), and even online dating (e.g. PlentyofFish.com, RSVP.com). Travel-related apps include trip organisers (e.g. Google Trips), maps (e.g. Maps.me), language translations (e.g. Duolingo), ride sharing (e.g. Uber), destination guides (e.g. City Souks, Dubai), flight status (e.g. App in the Air), airport terminal guides (e.g. Flight Stats), food delivery (e.g. Grubhub), currency conversions (e.g. XE Currency), bill splitting (e.g. Splittr), weather (e.g. Weather), music streaming (e.g. Spotify), caravanning (e.g. Grey Nomads), social games (e.g. Words with friends), sun safety (e.g. Wolfram Sun Exposure), dating (e.g. Happn), and travel journals (e.g. LiveTrekker).

Engaging with social media while travelling can influence activities under-taken at destinations, as well as onward travel planning. Increasing numbers of travellers actively seek recommendations from virtual communities, and deviate from their original plans based on information on digital and social media. For a review of the academic literature about the use of social media during travel see Parra-Lopez et al. (2012).

Post-travel

Sharing post-trip experiences with friends, and providing online travel reviews for other travellers, are common and potentially influential forms of UGC. LeadSift (2013) found 76% of Twitter travellers shared information about their holiday on social media after they arrived home. Further, 55% *liked* Facebook pages or Twitter accounts related to a recent holiday, 46% posted hotel reviews and 40% posted restaurant reviews. Tripadvisor's annual lists of top destinations, hotels, restaurants, and things to do are based on travellers' reviews. An algorithm fac-tors in the quantity and quality of reviews and ratings over a year for various service categories.

Opportunities to use digital and social media

There are opportunities for small tourism businesses to actively try to engage with travellers online at each of the three stages of travel planning, travel, and post-travel. We live in an age of digital disruption, where changes in technology are continuous, but also discontinuous. That is to say, constant change is the new normal, but the changes are disruptive rather than incremental improvements on the previous system. In this time of continuous discontinuous change, it is impossible for most small businesses to stay on top of the continual technologi-cal changes to digital and social media. The key is to focus on developing clear and manageable objectives, rather than trying to stay technically proficient. The technology aspects can then be outsourced to achieve the marketing aims. After all, we don't need to understand how an automobile or a computer works, to be able to use them. When there is a technology issue we can outsource the servicing.

Lean marketing: Outsourcing the digitisation and placement of media

Small tourism businesses can efficiently outsource the digitisation of media content, as well as the targeted placement of content on the internet and social media. There are numerous companies that will host a business' internet domain for a minimal annual fee, with many offering free set up of the website design and content. This frees up time for the business operator to focus on the marketing objectives rather than the technical set up. Once the website has been established, it can be easily managed and updated in-house. Specialist agencies can also be hired to place digitised media ads on targeted search engines, third party websites, and social media sites. These can be placed relatively inexpensively compared to traditional media, and tracked for impact. It is usually a far more efficient and effective use of resources for a small business to outsource technical expertise, and focus on marketing planning and service delivery.

The need for clear and manageable objectives

It is not sufficient to have a digital and social media presence, "to appear to be keeping up with the times" since inept implementation could be counterproductive (Hays, 2011:10, in Hays et al., 2013). It is essential to have a clear vision and objectives for the investment. As shown in Table 10.3, Gunelius (2011, in Shao et al., 2012: 91) proposed 10 laws of social media marketing, which guide the development of goals and objectives.

Table 10.3: Ten laws of social media marketing. Adapted from Gunelius (2011, in Shao et al., 2012)

1	Listen	Learn how your customers and target consumers engage with social media, and understand what is important to them
2	Focus	Focus on the social media of most relevance to the business, rather than attempt a presence on everything
3	Quality	Connect and engage with a small group of influential customers, rather than try to reach everyone
4	Patience	Ensure you make a long term commitment to the strategy
5	Compounding	Consumers share quality content, which will virally increase the reach
6	Influence	Identify those customers and target consumers who have the greatest influence in virtual communities
7	Value	Followers will value your content if it is interesting and trustworthy
8	Acknowledgement	Acknowledge those customers and consumers who reach out to establish a relationship with you
9	Accessibility	Always be available to respond to your followers
10	Reciprocity	Share content that has been published by others in your network

10

Website

While different types of businesses will require different website designs, there are a number of uniform success factors to consider:

- **Minimalism**. Use the least amount of text and graphics as possible to make the site user-friendly and easy to navigate. Having a site that is visually attractive, clean, easy on the eye, and yet still conveying a strong message, is essential for first impressions. It can take less than one second for a viewer to decide the site doesn't appeal.

- **Responsive design**. The ever increasing use of mobile devices by consumers, means the site needs to be viewable on different devices (e.g. laptop, cell phone, and tablet).

- **Modular design**. Provide easy navigation for the viewer by using simple blocks, which when clicked, lead the viewer to specific content. Each block is distinguished from the others by size or colour, and are purposefully positioned. The focus of each block is a theme tailored to different needs of consumers, rather than simply pushing business information. Remember the viewer is only interested in *what's in it for me*.

- **High quality images**. Professional photos and graphics are essential. Include real customers where possible, rather than produce staged scenes using actors. Ensure the images reinforce the brand identity and brand positioning theme, and are therefore relevant to the needs of target consumers.

- **Updated content**. Don't let the site become stale. Consistently keep content up to date.

- **Call to action**. As with any promotional media, there should be a call for the viewer to act. The site is not just an image building exercise, but a means to stimulate consumers to act, to engage with the business in some way.

Search engine optimisation (SEO)

Search engine optimisation (SEO) involves designing website content to gain high rankings on internet search engines, for popular travel search terms. With 90% global market share, Google is the dominant search engine, and those listing on the first page of a Google search result get by far the most click-throughs. What is required then is an understanding of common search terms being used. Also, there is paid search engine marketing, where a bidding process is used to allocate advertising space at the top of search engine results (usually the first four listings). However, in Rowett's (2017) explanation of the mechanics of SEO, it is suggested from travel related searches, less than 3% of click-throughs are for the paid listings. Rowett therefore recommended investing in SEO to try and achieve a page one organic listing.

Using digital and social media to enhance the customer experience

There are many ways for small tourism businesses to use technology in ways that enhance the customer experience. One option is to introduce a 'click and collect' process on the website, which enables customers to pay for service (eg theatre admission ticket) and/or an item (eg intermission drinks package) online. This then saves the customer time, by avoiding queues. Other options include supplying experiential devices, which is discussed below.

Case 10.1: MONA's experiential devices

Dr Caroline Wilson-Barnao, University of Queensland, Australia

The Museum of Old and New Art (MONA) is a privately owned gallery located in the island state of Tasmania, Australia. Opened in 2011, MONA combines art and artefacts with bar and lounge areas, a small vineyard, a microbrewery, and boutique hotel. MONA plays a central role in the DMO's attempt to position Hobart, the state capital, as a cultural tourism destination.

A feature of the visitor experience is MONA's 'O' system, which is an iPod Touch with custom-made software that tracks visitor movement using geolocation technology. What is particularly interesting about the 'O' is that it extracts the visitor's content and spatial data back to an onsite system, which pushes information back about different artefacts in the proximity. By clicking on the screen, the visitor receives a list of nearby works, which can then be selected for more information. Similar to the 'Like' button on Facebook the visitor can also vote to 'love' or 'hate' each artefact. The 'O' will even advise how many other people agree or disagree with the visitor's judgment. There is also an 'Artwank' section providing more formal curatorial style information, and a 'Gonzo' button for the owner's own views and ideas. The visitor has an option to listen to music that is matched to the object, or a recording of the artist talking about it. After looking at a number of works, the visitor can enter their email, and save their personalised tour for later online access.

While there are a number of key contemporary approaches to understanding museum visitors, there has been a clear distinction between visitor studies and the enjoyment of audiences in museums. In the past, visitors to the institution might take part in an exit interview or respond to a post visit survey.

The first museum hand-held devices to inform visitors about different artefacts were introduced during the early 1950s. The purpose of these early devices was to engage the visitor and their senses in the overall experience of the institution. However, systems such as the MONA 'O' differ from the early tour systems because rather than pushing information to the visitor in a static state, it is interactive and relies upon the visitor to

10

activate monitoring. Rather than in a traditional mode where the curator selects and presents what should be 'seen' by the visitor, it becomes more akin to an archive that holds a number of objects that stimulate a response. Key issues for not-for-profit museums and galleries are 1) how to fund these types of systems, and 2) how to use available data to draw visitor attention to specific content.

Discussion question

Explain how the MONA 'O' system represents disruption to the traditional museum or gallery experience.

Virtual reality

As discussed in *4:Tourism Marketing Planning*, virtual reality (VR) is not new technology, having been around in various forms since the 1980s. The relatively recent introduction of high quality mobile viewing devices has led to increased adoption by consumers, particularly gamers. However, the cost of recording VR content has been prohibitive for small businesses, and at the time of writing was predominantly being introduced to the websites of DMOs and large corporate travel brands. As the prices of technology continue to fall, the uptake of virtual reality by small businesses will increase, and so it warrants following the continuing development of VR for potential future implementation. In other words, watch this space.

Lean marketing: 360 degree, and live, videos

Creating a 360 degree video is quick and easy using an iOS or Android device, with either the built in camera or by using an app such as Google Camera or Street View. Adding a good quality 360 degree video to the business website is a way of countering the intangibility of a tourism service. A restaurant, for example, is better able to portray the atmosphere of the dining experience, than can be achieved by photos, and in a quicker way than a standard video. The recent introduction of live video services such as Periscope and Facebook Live provide opportunities to encourage interaction with social media followers, particularly during special occasions, celebrations, and events staged by the business.

Engaging with influencers

In digital and social media there can be a blurring between what is an organic (natural, such as word of mouth) source and what is an induced (forced, such as advertising) source. For example, consider a post by American actor Vin Diesel on his personal Facebook page on February 1st, 2011. With a photo of the Great Sphynx of Giza as a backdrop, Diesel wrote:

> *I have long dreamed of going to a place as sacred as Egypt, I was always, like everyone, fascinated by its rich history...one that both predates and has shaped our collective history. A year ago I was blessed with the opportunity to travel to Egypt...the experience changed me.*

Diesel's words look scripted, and was possibly some form of paid celebrity endorsement for the Egypt DMO. At the time, the actor had over one million Facebook followers, and therefore considered an *influencer*. An influencer is anyone who wields "the ability to cause or contribute to another person taking action or changing opinion/behaviour" (WOMMA, 2017:7). Influencer marketing is identifying and engaging influencers to share information with their network, to achieve a business objective. Most consumers trust recommendations from other consumers they respect and admire, over advertisements or content published by a business. Also, given that many consumers now book travel online, increasingly marketers are turning to influencer marketing to reach their consumers. This can result in reaching large numbers of targeted consumers, through influencers' networks. While small tourism businesses don't have the resources to pay famous celebrities to post endorsements online, a little creativity can come up plenty of inexpensive tactics to engage different types of *influencers,* such as bloggers, Instagrammers and YouTubers. Hootsuite (2017) estimated micro-influencers, who are local hometown heroes with 1000 – 10,000 followers, drive 87% of posting volume for hotels, bars and restaurants. Key advantages of engaging micro-influencers, relative to the celebrity and top tier influencers with over 100,000 followers, are: easily accessible with low barrier to contact, lower compensation demanded, more amenable to a partnership (WOMMA, 2017).

Activity 10.1: Meetup.com

Meetup.com is a global online social networking site and app, which facilitates social meetings. Anyone can start a meetup social group, which people with a common interest can join. Each group can schedule events (e.g. a bush walk, a guitar jam, a pub crawl etc), which members can rsvp to indicate intention to attend. Group members can communicate with others through the site. Other members can see who is attending, and most groups post photos at the event. Some of the larger groups have over 10,000 members, and so each of the organisers can be regarded as an *influencer* of consumer behaviour. Therefore, Meetup.com represents an opportunity for many small tourism businesses. Groups can be targeted by size, location and special interests, and then the organisers can be contacted with a pitch for their business. For an investigation into the experiences and preferences of members of a Meetup.com theme park social see Torres and Orlowski (2017). What opportunities are there for a new hospitality (e.g. café, restaurant, bar) business in your area to take advantage of local Meetup.com *influencers*?

10

Recruiting customers as influencers

Since (e)word-of-mouth recommendations represent a powerful source of favourable organic image building, it makes sense to try to recruit satisfied customers to act as influencers. Engage with these customers by monitoring and acknowledging any online contribution.

Encourage customer reviews

Offer an incentive for visitors to post a review on sites used for the service category, such as Tripadvisor. Ask for honest reviews and where suitable provide a reward such as a discount of added value for their next visit.

Encourage sharing

Encourage followers to share posts made by the business (e.g. on Facebook), by using a hook such as a competition, a special offer with a discount code, or value added for booking direct. Encourage sharing of the on-site experience, clearly signposting the venue with the icons for the business' social media accounts, and then engaging with customers at the venue to guide customers' purchases.

Many small tourism businesses overlook this opportunity. In Australia, for example, 4.5 times more customers location tag a hospitality venue than mention it, and yet only 4% of these businesses engage with customers who are on their location tag (Hootsuite, 2017). One option is to design a creative photo opportunity. Providing free wifi, where affordable, makes on-site sharing more likely for some visitors.

Social media platforms

In his 2017 annual survey of marketers across different industries, Stelzner (2017) reported the most popular social platform used for businesses was Facebook (94%), followed by Twitter (68%), LinkedIn (56%), Instagram (54%), YouTube (45%), Pinterest (30%), and Snapchat (7%). It is more efficient and effective for a small tourism business to be active on one or two social media sites, than attempt to have a presence on everything. Ensure the icons for these sites are promoted on all promotional collateral and signposted on-site. Social media marketing consultants, *TourismTribe.com*, advise the following mix to maximise engagement on a business' social media pages.

- **30% about the business**, such as the information provided in the 'About us' section of the website. What makes the business special?
- **30% educational**, of relevance to the reader, such as interesting facts about the area, local events, local hidden treasures, and other complimentary local business that provide excellent service.
- **30% entertaining or inspirational**, again of relevance to readers, which might brighten their day.

- **only 10% sales oriented**, so you need to make it count with special offers that have a sense of urgency, with added bonuses that only apply when a special code is used when booking.

TourismTribe.com suggested posting three to four times a week on a regular basis, to best manage the balance. However, a recent nationwide study of Australian hospitality businesses found 65% were publishing content less than once a week, and a similar ratio not engaging with their social media followers (Hootsuite, 2017).

Critical point: Focus on *social* engagement, rather than simply *media* placement

The key to effectiveness of social media in generating increased business is developing a plan to encourage engagement between staff and customers, and between customers and other consumers, rather than simply publishing content. Adopt a philosophy of *less is more*, in terms of the number of social media platforms used, and focus on publishing regular quality content on one or two sites. The aim is to attract and engage with a small number of active influencers rather than simply attempt to attract as many followers as possible.

Key points

1: The influence of digital and social media in tourism

Over half of the world's population are internet users, and we are now witnessing the most technologically savvy consumers in history. The emergence of Web 2.0 in 2004 led to the co-creation of content on social media, which has democratised the internet. User-generated content (UGC) on social media, related to tourism, has reached levels that now swamp the marketing communications of the global travel industry.

2: How travellers are using digital and social media

Travellers use various digital and social media, both creating and being influenced by online content, during the three stages of travel planning, travel, and post-travel. The reasons travellers participate in virtual communities include: entertainment, bragging, following, information provision/seeking, social and professional networking, and sense of belonging.

3: Opportunities for small businesses to use digital and social media

The opportunity to digitise media content has transformed the way in which promotional material can be made available across different platforms. For small tourism businesses, the internet and social media offer the benefits of lower costs and greater efficiency than traditional marketing approaches, as well as provid-

10

ing opportunities to enhance relationships with customers, and improve the consumption experience. The chapter did not attempt a technical discussion on how to design and manage digital platforms, as the focus is on the need to have clear and manageable objectives for engaging with consumers. What is required is a focus on *social* engagement, rather than simply *media* placement. Management of the digitisation and placement of media can be efficiently outsourced.

Discussion questions

1. What are some of the key reasons why most small tourism businesses shouldn't ignore the need to engage with consumers through digital and social media?

2. Why can it be a more efficient use of resources for a small tourism business to outsource digital and social media technical expertise?

3. What are two key ways in which satisfied customers could be recruited as online influencers for a small tourism business?

References

Borges, B. (2009). *Marketing 2.0: Bridging the gap between Seller and Buyer through Social Media Marketing.* Tucson, AZ: Wheatmark.

Brake, N. & Safko, L. (2009). *The Social Media Bible.* Hoboken, NJ: John Wiley & Sons.

Gelb, B.D. & Sundaram, S. (2002). Adapting to "word of mouse". *Business Horizons,* **45**(4): 21-25.

Hays, S., Page, S. .J. & Buhalis, D. (2013) Social media as a destination marketing tool: its use by national tourism organisations. *Current Issues in Tourism,* **16**(3): 211-239.

Hootsuite. (2017). *The Connected Consumer: Rethinking the Social Customer Journey in Australia's Hospitality and Tourism Industry.* Hootsuite.com. March.

Internet World Stats. (2017). *Internet Usage Statistics: The Internet Big Picture,* June 30. Accessed online at: http://www.internetworldstats.com/stats.htm

Kaplan, A.M. & Haenlein, M. (2009). Users of the world unite! The challenges and opportunities of social media. *Business Horizons,* **53**: 59-68.

Leadsift. (2013). *The Future of Social Media & Destination Marketing.* Infographic viewed online. http://leadsift.com/future-social-media-destination-marketing-infographic/

Leung, D., Law, R. van Hoof, H. & Buhalis, D. (2013). Social media in tourism and hospitality: A literature review. *Journal of Travel & Tourism Marketing,* **30**(1/2): 3-22.

Luo, Q. & Zhong, D. (2015). Using social network analysis to explain communication characteristics of travel-related electronic word-of-mouth on social media networking sites. *Tourism Management,* **46**: 274-282.

Mander, J. (2016). 15% of Internet Users are Mobile-only. Globalwebindex. 5 December. Accessed at: http://blog.globalwebindex.net/chart-of-the-day/15-of-internet-users-are-mobile-only/

Mkono, M. & Tribe, J. (2017). Beyond reviewing: Uncovering the multiple roles of tourism social media users. *Journal of Travel Research*, **56**(3): 287-298.

Molz, J.G. (2012). *Travel Connections: Tourism, Technology and Togetherness in a Mobile World World*. New York, NY: Routledge.

MX. (2015). Bookings rush – Tripped up by holiday envy. *MX*. 25 February. p. 2.

Oliveira, E. & Panyik, E. (2015). Content, context and co-creation: Digital challenges in destination branding with references to Portugal as a tourist destination. *Journal of Vacation Marketing*, **21**(1): 53-74.

Pan, B. & Crotts, J.C. (2012). Theoretical models of social media, marketing implications, and future research directions. In Sigala, M., Christou, E. & Gretzel, U. (Eds). *Social Media in Travel, Tourism and Hospitality: Theory, Practice and Cases*. Farnham, Surrey: Ashgate Publishing Limited. pp. 73-86.

Parra-Lopez, E., Gutierrez-Tano, D., Diaz-Armas, R.J. & Bulchand-Gidumal, J. (2012). Travellers 2.0: Motivation, opportunity and ability to use social media. In Sigala, M., Christou, E. & Gretzel, U. (Eds). *Social Media in Travel, Tourism and Hospitality: Theory, Practice and Cases*. Farnham, Surrey: Ashgate Publishing. pp. 171-187.

Pike, S. (2016). *Destination Marketing Essentials*. (2nd Ed). Abingdon, Oxon: Routledge.

Rowett, P. (2017). SEO 101: *What is Search Engine Optimisation + Why it's important for Tourism Brands*. TourismeSchool.com. Accessed at: https://tourismeschool.com/what-is-search-engine-optimisation-tourism-brands/. 9 March.

Shao, J., Rodriguez, M.A.D. & Gretzel, U. (2012). Riding the social media wave: Strategies of DMOs who successfully engage in social media marketing. In Sigala, M., Christou, E. & Gretzel, U. (Eds). *Social Media in Travel, Tourism and Hospitality: Theory, Practice and Cases*. Farnham, Surrey: Ashgate Publishing Limited.

Sigala, M. (2012). Introduction to Part 1. In Sigala, M., Christou, E. & Gretzel, U. (Eds). *Social Media in Travel, Tourism and Hospitality: Theory, Practice and Cases*. Farnham, Surrey: Ashgate Publishing Limited, pp. 7-10.

Sigala, M., Christou, E. & Gretzel, U. (Eds). *Social Media in Travel, Tourism and Hospitality: Theory, Practice and Cases*. Farnham, Surrey: Ashgate Publishing Limited.

Stelzner, M.A. (2017). *2017 Social Media Marketing Industry Report: How Marketers are Using Social Media to Grow their Business*. Social Media Examiner. May.

The Courier-Mail. (2015). Bigger than Hollywood – Apps earnings a blockbuster. *The Courier-Mail*. 25 January, pp. 33.

Torres, E.N., & Orlowski, M. (2017). Let's 'Meetup' at the theme park. *Journal of Vacation Marketing*, **23**(2): 159-171.

Trendwatching. (2014). *Internet of Caring Things*. April. Accessed at: http://trendwatching.com/trends/internet-of-caring-things/

WOMMA. (2017). *The WOMMA Guide to Influencer Marketing*. Word of Mouth Marketing Association.

10

11 Tourism Public Relations and Publicity

Chapter outline

The focus of this chapter is exploring opportunities for small businesses to gain free media publicity. Public relations (PR) is however more than just publicity seeking, which is a common misconception. PR is a strategic process of managing an organisation's relationships with its various publics (stakeholders). This is a planned effort to evaluate public attitudes, and develop two-way communications that foster mutually beneficial understanding and acceptance. Seeking media publicity is one component of PR, but for small tourism businesses will be the main PR activity. The key appealing factors of media editorial coverage, relative to other marketing communications, are greater cost-efficiency and higher public credibility. These make publicity attractive to small businesses with limited resources, and are therefore a key component in the marketing plan. The three main publicity seeking approaches for small tourism businesses discussed in the chapter are: media releases; the DMO's visiting media programme; and public stunts. Is any publicity good publicity? What is critical is developing an interesting story angle that both captures the attention of the target media, as being of appeal to their audience, as well as supporting the business' desired brand image, so that the ensuing editorial content generates the *right message for the right audience*.

Learning aims

To enhance your understanding of:

- The distinction between the roles of *public relations* and *publicity seeking*
- The key advantages of media publicity
- Publicity seeking opportunities for small tourism businesses.

Key terms

Public relations

A strategic two-way communication process to enhance the relationships between an organisation and its various publics (stakeholders).

Publicity

Publicity seeking is one aspect of public relations, involving non-paid communications aimed at achieving positive media editorial for the organisation, in a way that reaches the right people with the right message.

Story angle

Publicity seeking necessitates having an interesting story angle. The story angle is the main idea to be conveyed, which will attract the media's attention as being of interest to their audience.

Public relations (PR)

Public relations (PR) is more than just seeking free publicity in the media, which is a common misconception. However, PR has historically been challenging to define. For example, Tench and Yeomans (2014) cited a study by Harlow (1976) that identified 476 different definitions used between 1900 and 1976. One of the most cited definitions of PR in the academic literature is by Broom (2009: 25):

> *Public relations is the management function that establishes and maintains mutually beneficial relationships between an organization and the publics on whom its success or failure depends.*

The Public Relations Institute of Australia goes further to describe PR as:

> *The deliberate, planned and sustained effort to establish and maintain mutual understanding between an organisation (or individual) and its (or their) publics. The management function which evaluates public attitudes, identifies the policies and procedures of an individual or an organisation with the public interest, and plans and executes a programme of action to earn public understanding and acceptance.*

Explicit in this description is relationships with *publics*, in addition to customers, who are important to the organisation. Governments, large tourism brands and industry associations employ PR professionals to manage the communication process with their different publics, which are otherwise referred to as audiences and stakeholders. Just as a marketing plan addresses the needs of different market segments, the strategic PR plan is concerned with developing communications and dialogue tailored to different publics. PR practitioners need to understand both the needs of the organisation and the needs of their publics, who in tourism typically include: shareholders, media, politicians, government policy advisors, travel intermediaries, developers, conservationists, local businesses, financiers, customers, and the host community.

It is not commonly appreciated that PR is more than simply disseminating information for the purposes of influencing the behaviour of stakeholders or generating free media publicity. Two-way symmetrical PR uses research and open dialogue to improve relationships, where both the stakeholders and the organisation can be convinced of the need to change. For a review of the tourism PR literature see L'Etang et al. (2007).

While small tourism businesses will have fewer publics than larger organisations, clearly there is still a case for maintaining positive and mutually beneficial relationships with staff, customers, and the local community. This is often an informal process involving a common sense approach to fostering positive relationships, to be recognised as, a good employer, good neighbour, and good corporate citizen.

Lean marketing: Networking in the local community

Depending on the skills and experience of the small business owner/manager there are opportunities to engage with the local community for mutual benefit. This might not be seen as a practical option for time-poor managers, and yet there is a cost/benefit consideration; the more effort, the greater the long term benefit. The purpose of networking is to grow a network of relationships, which foster mutual information sharing, advice, support and referrals. Small businesses need to consider the range of contacts in the community with potential for mutual benefit; adopting a long term view rather than seeking short term gain. An owner can join local business groups, such as the Chamber of Commerce or SKAL international (for travel industry professionals), as well as develop their own network. There are many possibilities to engage with the range of potential stakeholders in the local community, including:

- Sponsorship of some aspect of the local school, in a way that fits the business. For example a café could link with the canteen, a hotel could support a travelling sports team, while any business could be one of the school newsletter supporters.

- Asking the local government representative if there is a personal cause that the business could support.

- Set up a monthly networking and brainstorming breakfast or lunch with nearby businesses.

- Develop a monthly newsletter of what's happening in neighbourhood (and of course the business). This can be paper-based, available at the door for passers-by, as well as emailed to the network.

11

- Join a local service club such as Rotary, and get involved in their community events.

- Discuss opportunities to provide contra prizes to a local radio station, television channel or newspaper for their competitions.

Critical point

The key to successful networking in the long term is to seek to benefit someone else first.

Media publicity

Is any publicity good publicity? As with any marketing communications, publicity should reinforce the desired brand image by *reaching the right people with the right message*. This form of promotion is different to advertising, where space is being purchased to present a controlled message. With this PR tactic there isn't any certainty about 1) whether there will actually be any resultant publicity, 2) when it might occur, 3) whether it will be positive, and 4) whether it is actually noticed by the target audience (Pike, 2016). However, there are two key advantages of non-paid media exposure, relative to other forms of marketing communications discussed in *9: Promoting Tourism Services to Consumers*, which make publicity seeking an attractive and realistic option for small tourism businesses; greater cost-efficiency and higher credibility.

Greater cost-efficiency

Publicity seeking has potential to achieve media coverage at little or no cost, compared to what the same editorial space would command for paid advertising. It is important to keep in mind that publicity seeking needs to be undertaken in a spirt of mutual benefit for the business and the media outlet. News stories are oxygen to the media, which are continuously open to hearing about new story angles that will be of interest to their audience. A business with something to offer the media shouldn't wait for the media to come knocking, but be proactive by using tactics that will gain their attention and interest.

The traditional media industry has been confronted with major disruption in recent years. The mass of free online content available via the internet has severely impacted on the revenues of broadcast and print media, which have been forced to cut costs to remain competitive. A major impact of this cost cutting has been a drastic reduction in the number of investigative journalists. This has led an increased reliance by the media on press releases and syndicated sources of information. A well-crafted press release, with an interesting story angle has the potential to gain editorial exposure at no cost to the business.

Lean marketing: Establish yourself as a voice for tourism with local media

Busy media news desks save a lot of time when they have *go-to* people they can call up to comment on topical issues in their field. There are opportunities to become a voice for tourism in the local community who reporters can rely on to help them develop a story. Identify which reporters cover tourism-related stories, make yourself known to them by sending quality media releases, and contacting them to let them know you have an interest in helping contribute to stories where you have experience/knowledge.

Higher credibility of media

News media editorial content has a higher credibility than advertising in the minds of consumers, because it is regarded as more believable. As news media editorial is perceived to be written by an independent source it can be a powerful endorsement for a business. As discussed in *3: Tourism Consumer Behaviour*, there are two sources of stimuli that lead to image formation, and the level of influence of the marketer varies between the two. Organic (natural) image formation occurs through an individual's everyday assimilation of information, such as media editorial content, movies, social media and word of mouth for example. Induced (forced) image formation on the other hand is attempted by marketers through advertising. Organic images are considered more influential in consumer decision making. It has been suggested six times as many people read an average news article as read the average advertisement, and so "advertising is what you pay for…editorial is what you pray for!" (Trout & Rivkin, 1995).

The story angle

Regardless of the type of publicity seeking, there must be a compelling story angle that will attract the attention of the media. How is it *news*? The story angle is the main idea to be conveyed, and needs to be able to *hook* the intended audience's interest. The communicator must cater to the needs of the journalist, and so the story must appeal as being relevant to their audience. Barry (2002, in Pike, 2004) suggested the starting point for developing a successful relationship with the media was understanding the three Ws:

- *Why* is what we have to say of interest to the media?
- *When* is their deadline for accepting a media release?
- *What* format does the media require?

11

Lean marketing: Read the papers!

The best way to understand what makes a good story angle is to read newspapers and travel industry newsletters. The headline and the first sentence of the first paragraph are written to grab the reader's attention. So skim read the publication by reading the headline and first sentence to get a feel for how they are trying to hook the audience.

Story angle opportunities

There are many different story angle opportunities for small tourism businesses to consider. This will of course depend on the type of business and the nature of the resources the firm controls.

A unique offering

Is there anything the business offers that is rare, and would attract media interest because of novelty value?

Activity 11.1: What do we offer that no one else does?

A keynote speaker at a Travel and Tourism Research Association conference I once attended in New Orleans posed an excellent real world story angle question to the audience. Well known to US television audiences for his popular show, *The Travel Detective*, Peter Greenburgh shared the one question he asks marketers when they pitch to host him at their business or destination: "What have you got, that I can't get anywhere else?" So, imagine you work for your local DMO, and answer that question about your destination. What is the unique story angle about your town or city that might attract the interest The Travel Detective?

Being the first

The offering of a new type of tourism experience is an opportune time to target media publicity.

Industry insight: The world's smallest museum

The community of Warley in the English county of West Yorkshire came up with an innovative idea to enter the *Guinness Book of Records,* and stimulate publicity with a unique story angle. The local community association turned a disused traditional red telephone box into the world's smallest museum. The museum, decorated with local historical artefacts, is so small that only one person can enter at a time. The artefacts are changed every three weeks, making the museum a popular attraction for locals and visitors alike. A number of other museums around the world have since laid claim to the *smallest,* which highlights the difficulty of protecting a creative service idea from imitators. These include the New York's M Museum housed in an elevator shaft, a converted shed in the town of Superior in Arizona, and a sidewalk museum in Somerville, Massachusetts measuring 61.5 inches x 20 inches x 8 inches.

An eccentric character

Most media audiences can't resist quirky characters who are different to everyone else. Eccentric characters are those who think differently, and/or are not afraid to speak their mind. Think of who gets your attention in your own consumption of media news and entertainment, and which ones do people in your social or business circle talk/gossip about? Donald Trump? Reality TV personalities? Sports personalities? The crazy TV advertising salesman? Like them or loathe them they got your attention and have become memorable. Tourism lends itself well to eccentric characters because of the entertainment, experiential and escapism characteristics of the industry. Well known examples have included New York city's naked cowboy, New Zealand's Christchurch Wizard, and British town criers. Small tourism businesses can take advantage of the personal relationships with customers, such as by the Mad Hatter café owner in Margate, England, who dresses like his namesake and provides witty banter for his customers.

Industry insight: Australia Zoo's Steve Irwin

In the 1970s and 1980s, Bob Irwin's *Beerwah Reptile and Fauna Park* was a modest family run business; of novelty value for visitors wanting to see crocodiles in small fenced ponds. The business has since developed into the 100 acre *Australia Zoo*, one of Australia's most popular themed attractions, employing hundreds of staff. Ultimately, the key to the success of this business was the publicity seeking eccentricity of Bob's son Steve, who became known as the Crocodile Hunter to television audiences around the world. Although Steve Irwin was tragically killed by a stingray in 2006, his wife and children have continued his legacy as wildlife warriors, and regularly appear in the media around the world, including regular appearances on the top rating US Tonight Show.

11

A *different* event

Not-for-profit organisations, such as festivals, museums and galleries, are suited to using novelty events to attract publicity. For example, the introduction of a wild cow milking contest at the Rerewhakaaitu Rodeo, was mentioned in the newsletter of my RTO and this resulted in the visit of a television film crew from Japan, who told me "this type of event appeals to the Japanese sense of humour".

An unusual type of service

Thinking outside the box can result in different approaches to providing what is usually expected of a particular service. For example, the Hans Brinkler Hostel,

in Amsterdam, has gained notoriety among backpackers through the brand positioning slogans such as *"It cant get any worse but we'll do our best"*, and *"The Hostel
that couldn't care less, but we will try"*. The hostel promotes a no-frills *get what you
pay* for stay without great service.

Industry insight: Restaurants that take pride in being rude to their customers (Language warning!)

Going against the hospitality mantra that *the customer is always right*, are a number of
restaurants where the philosophy is along the lines of "the customer is stupid and fat and
ugly and should leave immediately" (Gentile, 2013). For example, at The Weiner's Circle
in Chicago staff don't ask what you would like to order...they yell "what the f*ck do you
want, bitch?" At Shopsin's in New York, belligerent staff will throw you out if you take too
long to order, or if they don't like the look of you. Staff at Wong Kei in London will throw
the menu at you, talk rudely about you in Cantonese, and scream at you if you don't pay
immediately after finishing your meal. One of the most YouTube'd eateries of this bad
service genre is Dick's Last Resort, where abuse from serving staff is legendary

An interesting slice of history

Does the business or location have a link to an interesting historical event? Most
significant are locations linked to famous events. Obviously not every place can
boast a link to famous historical event such as the pilgrims landing at Plymouth
Rock in the US, or a movie setting such as Hobbiton in Matamata, New Zealand,
or a television series such as *Home and Away* in the northern beaches of Sydney,
or be part of a famous literary trail such as Jane Austen's Hampshire in England
for example. However, a little research might unearth a little known gem of local
history.

Media releases

A well-crafted media release, with an interesting story angle, can result in valuable free editorial coverage. The key outlets for distributing media releases are:

- **Traditional broadcast and print media** such as newspapers, television, magazine and radio, at national and local community levels.
- **DMOs** at NTO, STO and RTO levels are always interested in unique story
angles from their stakeholders, which can be forwarded on to their database of
media outlets and travel writers.
- **Travel trade media**, which range from free international online industry
newsletters such as Skift.com, Travelandtourworld.com and Travelmole.com,
to subscription-based local newsletters such as Insidetourism.com in New
Zealand.

Case 11.1: Inside Tourism (iT), a small PR business success story

Inside Tourism (www.insidetourism.com) has been the leading source of news about New Zealand's tourism industry for over 20 years. The brainchild of travel writer and former NTO journalist Nigel Coventry, Inside Tourism (iT) was launched in 1994 to fill a void in the market for an industry newsletter; providing inside information on industry events and developments on a weekly basis. iT has become a small business success story, because of a low-cost business model, great networking, and a vision of a newsletter that would be by the industry, for the industry. The benefits for New Zealand's tourism stakeholders are twofold. First, iT has become established as the most credible source of news about what's happening in the industry. For example, one Minister of Tourism was heard to say at a conference that "it must be true because I read it in iT". Second, the newsletter is an outlet for tourism businesses to have any updates about innovations in their operation to be read by the wider industry, which can result in new business opportunities or wider news media publicity. For example, the 6,000 subscribers to iT, in New Zealand and overseas, include inbound tour wholesalers, government Ministers, DMOs, banks, airlines, hotel chains, business consultants, universities, transport companies, and travel industry associations such as the Pacific Asia Travel Association (PATA). PATA has members on 40 countries and in 1995 named Nigel as Journalist of the Year. iT has a bias towards helping new businesses, particularly SMEs, because Nigel knows only too well what it is like starting up a new venture.

Amazingly, the only advertising cost incurred by iT in over 20 years was $300 for the personalized car registration plate: 2RIZM. The business has been built up by below-the-line promotional approaches such as networking at many tourism trade events, and word-of-mouth referrals. Nigel started with a trial in 1994 by faxing iT to 300 tourism operators he knew personally. He ran the trial every week for three months, at the end of which he gauged interest on an annual subscription of under $300 ($298.69). The newsletter became commercially successful very quickly, to the extent that Nigel was asked to accept advertising spots in the newsletter, and thus another revenue stream, the first by Qantas.

iT is seen as working for the industry. Controversial stories are covered, but in a cautious and non-sensational way. iT wants to be seen, not as the voice of the industry, but rather the source of useful news, views and information. Nigel's views are NOT published, even though he is often asked what he thinks about certain issues, as he does not believe that is his role. Subscribers find iT authoritative, up-to-date, reliable and easy to read. What do subscribers gain in return for their money? At the same time every week they are presented with news they can use, be it what competitors are doing, what's happening in overseas markets, what the NTO, airlines, airports and others are planning so operators can be kept alert to leverage opportunities. iT also covers most industry conferences and trade shows in detail, which many also find very useful. All stories are researched

11

and written by Nigel, although he does monitor other media outlets, to save his readers having to do so, and a number of industry associations write a commentary on a regular basis. One column, entitled *Speaker's Corner*, is where individuals are free to say what they want – provided it isn't libellous! With news stories, Nigel endeavours to gain comment from anyone who may be affected by its use, especially if there is criticism of that person or organisation. But with *Speaker's Corner*, partly because it has been in use for more than 15 years, it is accepted the writer can vent their spleen without fear of being gagged.

Discussion question

In terms of the opportunity to gain free publicity by being mentioned in iT, what type of information from a small tourism business would be of interest to wider readership, including the broadcast media, and therefore appeal to Nigel?

Lean marketing: Tips for an effective media release

- MEDIA RELEASE should be printed boldly at the top. Include the date.

- Think about a short creative headline that will stand out from all the other media releases the reporter will receive that day.

- Hook the reader in the most important first paragraph, with a succinct (around 30 words) summary of why this is *news* (if it's not news it wont be used), stating the who, what, where, how and why.

- Keep the release to one page, using short sentences and short paragraphs (remember however that a paragraph is more than one sentence).

- Make use of white space, so it is easy on the reader's eye.

- Write in the third person, as you would envisage it in the publication. Make it easy for the reporter to not have to edit much.

- Offer a few "quotes" the media can use, to humanise the story.

- The release should have a professional appearance. Avoid using unnecessary symbols such as '!!!', graphics such as smiley faces ☺, abbreviations, and industry jargon.

- Be truthful, and not make wild claims that can't be supported.

- Proofread. No typos or grammar errors.

- End the release with details of whom the media can contact for further information.

- When emailing the release, paste it into the body of the message rather than send as an attachment.

The DMO's visiting media programme

As discussed in *2: The Destination Marketing Organisation*, there are many opportunities for small tourism businesses to get involved with the local DMO for mutual benefit. In terms of publicity seeking, the DMO's *visiting media programme* is a key pillar of destination marketing. Most DMOs proactively target, invite, and host visiting media at the destination, the aim of which is to generate positive media editorial content in key markets (see also Pike, 2016). The DMO's visiting media programme is heavily reliant on local tourism businesses hosting the visiting media's travel arrangements and experiences at the destination. The programme would not be financially viable without such industry support. Typically the resultant travel articles are positive about the destination experience, given the journalist's visit was sponsored by the DMO, travel intermediaries, transport, accommodation and sightseeing businesses. However, some travel writers do tell it as they find it, so hosting visiting media is not without some degree of risk of negative publicity for individual businesses and the destination.

The following URL links to the visiting media programmes of DMOs at the national, state and local levels, give an indication of the range and commonality of activities involved:

■ Visit Britain's Media Centre: https://media.visitbritain.com/au/en

■ Ontario Tourism Marketing Partnership Corporation's Media Relations Team: https://www.tourismpartners.com/en/media-relations

■ NYC & Company's Global Communications Division: http://www.nycand-company.org/press

■ Destination Queenstown's Media Centre: https://www.queenstownnz.co.nz/media/

Industry insight: A guide to working with the media

Some larger DMOs provide free online guides that help their tourism stakeholders better understand how to work with the media. For example, Tourism Australia publishes *Making a Splash - A Practical Guide for Working with the Media* at: http://www.tourism.australia.com/content/dam/assets/document/1/6/x/3/2/2002430.pdf

11

As well as offering the DMO possible participation in hosting visiting media, the key opportunities for small tourism businesses to get involved with the DMO's Visiting Media Programme are summarised in Table 11.1.

Table 11.1: Summary of opportunities with DMO visiting media programmes

Newsletter	DMOs send a regular newsletter of story angles and product and event updates to a database of travel writers and news media agencies.	Quebec City and Area provides an archive of previous newsletters (http://www.quebecregion.com/en/travel-trade/services/travel-news-archives/)
Product database	A digital database of local tourism information, enabling businesses to list their services.	The Australian Tourism Data Warehouse has over 40,000 product listings, which are freely accessible by the media (www.atdw.au).
Digital library	A collection of story angles and high quality images and videos for free use by the travel trade to promote the destination.	Tourism New Zealand (http://visuals.newzealand.com/#/)
Contra prizes	DMO partnering with a TV or radio network to offer a competition for consumers with a travel prize to the destination.	Tourism and Events Queensland's Best Job in the World Campaign (see Belch, Belch, Kerr & Powell, 2009).

Industry insight: Let the travel writer experience the *real thing*

A friend of mine, John Wright, who loves his life as travel writer, has one pet hate when being hosted at a destination. He likes to write about authentic experiences that appeal to travellers, but sometimes it is difficult for him to see the *real thing*. His visits are relatively short, and he has limited time to explore the destination on his own, which is what he prefers to be able to do. However, he understands that as these trips are sponsored there are certain obligations in terms of what he visits, and so there is a balancing act when constructing a story. The difficulty occurs when the DMO has arranged to meet him at the airport with a chauffeured limousine, and then whisked him off to see local government officials who sing praises about the destination, and then have him escorted every moment of his stay. His message to DMOs and local businesses is to offer some balance between catering to the needs of the hosted/sponsored aspects of the visit, and allowing him some time during his stay to explore by himself to enable him to discover interesting story angles that are not scripted by the hosts. After all, the travel writer, whether for a newspaper, a blog or a TV show, knows more about what interests their audience, and sometimes the gems are aspects of a destination or business or slice of local life that the marketers are either unaware or take for granted.

Publicity stunts

Undertaking publicity stunts is similar to experiential (events) marketing, which were discussed in *9: Promoting Tourism Services to Consumers*, in that they involve staging a promotional event in a public place to attract attention. As well as having the potential to gain media attention, effective stunts can get onlookers telling their friends virally. Effective stunts need to be newsworthy, fascinating and/or entertaining. Hughes (2008) promoted six *buttons of buzz*, to start conversations and get people to tell their friends about the brand: taboo issues, the unusual, the outrageous, the hilarious, the remarkable, and the secret. The key is however that there must be a link between the type of buzz button and the brand.

Industry insight: Flashing downtown commuters

An example of a stunt that was unusual and outrageous was an initiative of tourism marketers from the state of Queensland, Australia, which was used in the southern Australian city of Melbourne in the middle of winter. Melbourne has a temperate winter climate where commuters usually wear coats and scarves, whereas Queensland is an all year beach destination with regions offering tropical or sub-tropical weather. Models were hired to parade in the Melbourne CBD, with instructions to flash passers-by, by opening their coat to reveal they were only wearing a bikini or swim shorts. The onlookers were told this is what they would be wearing in they were in sunny Queensland that winter's day. The unique stunt attracted coverage in traditional media as well in Australia's advertising industry media. As an aside, the brand positioning theme has consistently been based on Queensland's warm weather and outdoor/beach lifestyle. For example, during the 1980s the slogan was *Beautiful one day, perfect the next*, with the DMO's tour packages offering a money back guarantee if the weather wasn't perfect during a the visit! At the time of writing in 2017 the DMO's slogan is *Queensland – Where Australia shines*.

Activity 11.2: Evaluate the stunt

PR agency director James Herring (2016) promoted eight tips for successful stunts:

1. Stunts need to be entertaining but must link to the narrative of the brand's marketing.
2. Resist the urge to kill the photo/video opportunity for the audience and media by bombarding them with business logos. Great campaigns stimulate people to want to know *who did this, and why*?
3. Sometimes its easier to join an existing conversation, by tapping into the media news cycle for topical events.
4. Be audacious, original and brave. The greater the risk the bigger the return.
5. Look for ways to involve the audience with interactivity.
6. Interrogate the idea – what could go wrong?
7. Deliver something smart and entertaining that the media can be sure will delight their readers.
8. Hire a specialist agency (Maybe not an option for most small business, but Herring runs a PR agency after all!).

Use these criteria to rate the potential effectiveness of the *Industry insight: Flashing the commuters*. In your assessment, how many criteria were met in this publicity stunt?

11

There has been little published in the tourism literature about the use of publicity stunts. However, stunts have become so prevalent in marketing, including tourism where Richard Branson has been a standout, that there are many online commentaries about which ones have been most memorable. For example, check out the following links for standout creative stunts:

- National Geographic's *Best tourism gimmicks of all time*
  www.nationalgeographic.com/travel/features/the-best-tourism-board-gimmicks -of-all-time/
- Smoking Gun PR's *Great and not so great travel PR stunts*
  smokinggunpr.co.uk/2014/09/great-great-travel-pr-stunts-campaigns/
- Taylor Herring's *Top 50 PR stunts of all time*
  www.taylorherring.com/blog/index.php/tag/top-50-pr-stunts/

Lean marketing: Food challenges

A popular source of word of mouth publicity for small hospitality businesses is to offer a food eating challenge. The central idea is customers are invited to eat a huge and/or extremely spicy dish within a certain time frame for a reward such as a free meal or souvenir memento. These challenges lend themselves well to word-of-mouth, with thousands of hilarious video clips uploaded to social media and YouTube. Google the term *food challenges* or check out the following URLs for listings of food challenges around the world:

- www.foodchallenges.com
- thenewdaily.com.au/life/eat-drink/2014/03/20/man-vs-food-eating-challenges-will-bust-gut/
- www.stagweb.co.uk/blog/2016/10/fork-yeah-man-food/

Negative publicity

Not all publicity is good publicity, particularly for those in the restaurant business. Celebrity chef Gordon Ramsay has had his fair share of negative press, particularly from food critics. His response? Every negative restaurant review is made into newspaper for his Las Vegas fish and chip shop! Today's news is tomorrow's fish and chip wrapping paper! Ramsay also acknowledges that the rise of social media bloggers and feedback review sites has challenges and opportunities (Heaf, 2017). On one hand "It's hard for chefs to be judged by people who know less about food than they do – that's the kick in the bollocks". On the positive side: "The whole blog thing has only improved chefs. We get the feedback earlier."

More serious is when accidents occur at tourism facilities and visitors are injured or killed. Regardless of the nature of the crisis, handling negative publicity necessitates being patient, acknowledging constructive criticism, sticking to the facts, and learning from the experience. Remember the media aren't stupid, so when a business is faced with negative publicity they should be open and truthful and avoid the temptation to only offer *positive spin*. It's also a good idea to never offer *no comment*, if you want a future positive reciprocal relationship with the media. A journalist is unlikely to be interested in a future media release from a business that previously refused to cooperate. There has been a lack of attention in the tourism literature about negative publicity and small businesses. However, there is a growing resource of research about how destinations have responded to negative media following disasters, and disaster response planning (for example Faulkner & Vikulov, 2001; Frisby, 2002; Hopper 2002, Granville et al., 2016).

Key points

1: The distinction between the roles of *public relations* and *publicity seeking*

The chapter focussed on opportunities for small tourism businesses to gain free media publicity. Public relations (PR) is however more than just publicity seeking, which is a common misconception. PR is a strategic process of managing an organisation's relationships with its various publics (stakeholders). This is a planned effort to evaluate public attitudes, and develop two-way communications that foster mutually beneficial understanding and acceptance. Seeking media publicity is one component of strategic PR, but for small tourism businesses will be the main PR activity.

2: The key advantages of media publicity

The key appealing factors of media editorial coverage, relative to other types of promotion, are greater cost-efficiency (potentially free) and higher public credibility (more believable than advertising). These make publicity attractive to small businesses with limited resources, and therefore a key component in the marketing plan.

3: Publicity seeking opportunities for small tourism businesses

The three main publicity seeking approaches for small tourism businesses presented in the chapter were: media releases; the DMO's visiting media programme; and, publicity stunts. Is any publicity good publicity? What is critical is developing interesting story angles that both capture the attention of the target media, as being of appeal to their audience, and support the desired brand image, so that the ensuing editorial content provides the *right message for the right audience*.

11

Discussion questions

1. What is a story angle, and why is it critical in publicity seeking?

2. Is any publicity good publicity? Explain your answer. What is good publicity?

3. Summarise the ways in which a small tourism business could take advantage of the DMO's *Visiting Media Programme*.

References

Belch, G., Belch, M., Kerr, G. & Powell, I. (2009). *Advertising and IMC*. McGaw-Hill: Sydney.

Broom, G. (2009). *Effective Public Relations*. (10th Edition). Upper Saddle River, NJ: Pearson Prentice Hall.

Faulkner, B. & Vikulov, S. (2001). Katherine, washed out one day, back on track the next: A post-mortem of a tourism disaster. *Tourism Management*, **22**(4): 331-344.

Frisby, E. (2002). Communicating in a crisis: The British Tourist Authority's responses to the foot-and-mouth crisis outbreak and 11 September, 2001. *Journal of Vacation Marketing*, **9**(1): 89-100.

Gentile, D. (2013). 5 restaurants that pride themselves on being total d*cks to their customers. *Thrillist.com*. 21 October. Accessed at: https://www.thrillist.com/eat/nation/restaurants-who-are-dicks-wieners-circle-dicks-last-resort

Granville, F., Mehta, A. & Pike, S. (2016). Destinations, disasters and public relations: Stakeholder engagement in multi-phase disaster management. *Journal of Hospitality and Tourism Management,* **28** (September): 73-79.

Harlow, R.F. (1976). Building a definition of public relations. *Public Relations Review*, **2**(4): 34–42.

Heaf, J. (2017). Out to lunch!...with Gordon Ramsay. *GQ*. January: pp. 252.

Herring, J. (2016). The 25 greatest publicity stunts of our time. *The Drum*. 16 June. Accessed at: www.thedrum.com/opinion/2016/06/16/25-greatest-publicity-stunts-our-time

Hopper, P. (2002). Marketing London in a difficult climate. *Journal of Vacation Marketing*, **9**(1): 81-88.

Hughes, M. (2008). *Buzzmarketing – Get People Talking about your Stuff*. New York: Penguin Group.

L'Etang, J., Falkheimer, J. & Lugo, J. (2007). Public relations and tourism : Critical reflections and a research agenda. *Public Relations Review*, **33**(1): 68-76.

Pike, S. (2004). *Destination Marketing Organisations*. Oxford: Elsevier Science.

Pike, S. (2016). *Destination Marketing Essentials*. (2nd Ed). Abingdon, Oxon: Routledge.

Tench, R. & Yeomans, L. (2014). *Exploring Public Relations*. (3rd Edition). Harlow, UK: Pearson Education Limited.

Trout, J. & Rivkin, S. (1995). *The New Positioning*. New York: McGraw-Hill.

12 Customer Relationship Management in Tourism

Chapter outline

A lot of effort is required by small tourism businesses to attract new customers. It makes sense then to consider the potential for stimulating repeat visits and/or referrals from them, because it can a more efficient use of scarce resources to stay in touch with previous customers than to spend on advertising to attract a continual stream of new ones. Customer relationship management (CRM) emerged from the IT sector during the mid-1990s as a means to enhance customer loyalty. CRM loyalty programmes that provide economic incentives have a positive effect on customer retention and market share. A small increase in the number of loyal customers can result in reduced marketing costs, increased sales, and higher profits. While traditional promotional activities are necessary to attract new customers, there are opportunities for small tourism businesses to supplement these with initiatives to increase loyalty. Five fundamentals of effective CRM are discussed: develop a philosophy of nurturing long term mutually beneficial customer relationships that foster a sense of community or belonging; develop a customer database; select customers who offer maximum yield; provide added value to selected customers; communicate with loyal customers via direct media in a *meaningful* way. Even if a loyalty programme to attract repeat business is not practical or feasible, there will still be opportunities to encourage customers to create conversations about the brand with others through word-of-mouth referrals. Online customer reviews and ratings, along with the advice of friends, play a major role in consumers' tourism purchase decisions.

Learning aims

To enhance your understanding of:

- The rationale for customer relationship management (CRM)
- The fundamentals of an effective customer loyalty programme
- Opportunities to stimulate word-of-mouth (WoM) referrals.

Key terms

Loyalty
The commitment by a customer to return to the business to make further purchases, and/or to recommend the business to others.

Customer relationship management (CRM)
A philosophy, technology, strategy and tactics, making use of customer information to stimulate increased customer loyalty.

Word-of-mouth (WOM and eWOM) referrals
A powerful organic source of brand image development that occurs naturally, and where a firm can actively encourage satisfied customers to create conversations about the brand with others in their network. Also known as *influencer* marketing.

Customer loyalty

The ultimate aim of any promotion is to generate customers (sales). The greater the amount of sales that are in the form of repeat purchases, the greater the benefits for the business. Small tourism businesses put in a lot of effort to attract new customers, who should then be regarded as a resource for the firm to capitalise on for mutual benefit. As discussed in *4: Tourism Marketing Planning*, a resource is something within the firm's control that could represent a potential competitive strength. A customer relationship management (CRM) programme that increases customer loyalty is valuable to the business because it reduces marketing costs and increases yield. An effective CRM programme is not only a potential source of competitive advantage, but is also an intangible asset on the balance sheet that adds to the financial value of the brand. Importantly, effective CRM is also valued by customers when they are suitably rewarded for their repeat business. Loyalty programmes offering economic incentives can have a positive effect on customer satisfaction, customer retention and market share (Verhoef, 2003).

Critical point: Customer loyalty shouldn't be confused with customer satisfaction

Customer satisfaction does not denote loyalty. While loyalty is built on customer satisfaction, a business could have high levels of satisfaction but have little loyalty. Satisfaction is a perception about how needs were met during a past service transaction, whereas loyalty is future behavioural intention/action. A customer could be very satisfied with a service, and yet quite easily switch to another brand offering a cheaper deal, or not be in a position to visit the business again.

For businesses operating in markets where there is potential for repeat visitation, the starting point is to set up a customer database, as a basis for developing a loyalty programme. It can be more efficient use of scarce promotional resources to stay in touch with previous customers, than only attempt to attract the attention of consumers with costly mass media advertising. It makes sense then to supplement the promotional plan objectives to increase new customers, with a customer relationship management (CRM) programme to foster increased loyalty. The key aims of CRM are to increase customer retention and stimulate repeat purchases (Chang et al., 2002; Marchand, 2006; Ozgener & Iraz, 2006). CRM can be used to boost capacity, increase the contribution towards fixed costs of the business, and save on marketing costs. A 5% increase in customer retention levels can result in an increase in profitability of 25% - 100% (Reichheld, 1996). Therefore it can be at least five times more cost-effective to retain existing customers, rather than continually acquire new ones (Ozgener & Iraz, 2006). For small accommodation businesses, effective CRM can also help to counter the competition from online travel agents (e.g. Hotels.com), search engines, and other third party information and transaction channels (Tian & Wang, 2017).

Industry insight: 50% of revenue from 3% of customers

A marketing representative of one of Australia's most recognised travel agency chains, during a guest speaking role in one of my classes, told us that 50% of the company's revenue that year came from only 3% of their customers. A further 45% of revenue came from another 27% of customers, while 5% of revenue came from a staggering 70% of customers. Speaks volumes about the value of retaining high yield repeat customers doesn't it?

Tourism businesses were among the early adopters of CRM technology, particularly hotel chains such as the Ritz Carlton (Vogt, 2011), and Harrah's (Lee et. al., 2003). The cruise ship industry has also been a leader in tourism CRM. A cruise ship will rarely depart with any empty suites, because the marketing team stays in touch with the company's frequent customers. It is not uncommon in the US for example for travellers to have undertaken over 20 cruises with the same company. The most frequent customers are offered a cruise at short notice, where capacity needs to be filled quickly, with a heavily discounted, or even free, offer. Cruise companies know these customers will spend enough on board (e.g. bar packages, casino, shore excursions, souvenir photos) to make a contribution towards the fixed costs of the business, which are incurred regardless of whether the cabin is occupied or empty. So, the marketing plan for any tourism business should consider developing initiatives to retain selected customers, in addition to attracting new customers. However, even though there is a growing body of CRM research in the tourism literature, little has been published about CRM activities of small tourism businesses (Vogt, 2011; Rahimi & Kozak, 2017), and the long

12

term impact of CRM on the bottom line for hotels (Josiassen et al., 2014). For reviews of the literature on CRM in tourism see Maggon and Chaudry (2015) and Rahimi et al. (2017).

There are two types of loyalty of interest to tourism businesses. *Behavioural loyalty* represents action, in the form of repeat purchases and word-of-mouth referrals to their social network. *Attitudinal loyalty* represents the extent to which an individual intends to make a repeat purchase as well as the likelihood they will recommend the business to others. Both forms of loyalty are regarded as assets to the firm. Therefore the pursuit of customer loyalty is not only of benefit in increasing tomorrow's cash flow, but also for the longer term valuation of the business' brand. Strong repeat purchase data can be used by accountants to calculate an intangible asset value on the firm's balance sheet, contributing to the *goodwill* value that a prospective buyer of the business would need to pay over and above the value of tangible buildings, fixtures and fittings. This goodwill is representative of consumer-based brand equity (CBBE) and underpins the brand equity valuation, which is an estimate of future earnings potential. Therefore, initiatives such as loyalty programmes to enhance customer loyalty levels are an important consideration for every business. Measurement of CBBE is discussed in *14: Tourism Marketing Performance Measurement.*

Activity 12.1: Discounting to attract new customers?

It is common for businesses to offer a discount to attract new business. Often the promotional material will include an addendum, such as *This offer is only available to new customers.* Why is this tactic potentially counterproductive?

Loyalty rewards programmes

The first contemporary loyalty rewards programme was launched by American Airlines in 1981 (McCall & Voorhees, 2010). Loyalty programmes have since become a mainstay in travel and hospitality sectors (Hoffman & Lowett, 2008). However, despite the proliferation of loyalty programs it has been suggested there has been little empirical evidence indicating *how* such programs influence customer loyalty and business profitability (McCall & Voorhees, 2010). This comment from the manager of a Millennium hotel (p. 36):

> *You know, I have this customer reward programme. Its kind of expensive but, I feel like I have to have a program because everyone else has one. Honestly, I don't know what, if anything it does for me.*

The problem is not that loyalty programmes don't work, because many do. The challenge is in directly quantifying the relationship between the costs of CRM and firm performance. This is similar to the difficulty in measuring the effectiveness of outdoor media advertising, which we know can be a powerful promotional tool, but is difficult to quantify the effect on sales. In a study of hotels, Josiassen et al. (2014) found that while CRM has the potential to benefit hotels, adoption in the latest technology may not increase profitability unless the firm's staff develop CRM capabilities around information collection and dissemination. Clearly there are costs associated with developing loyalty programmes, and these will depend on the size of the database, the sophistication of the technology and the amount of data being processed. For large retailers, for example, the programme will cost between 2% and 10% of the customers total spending (Oracle, 2005). Many sophisticated CRM programmes implemented by large businesses have failed due to the high cost of the technology and/or an incorrect strategy that fails to recognise customers' true value levels. For an exploratory study investigating reasons for CRM success and failure in the hotel industry see Luck and Lancaster (2013).

Not having a loyalty program, when just about every other hospitality business has one, is akin to not advertising. This could therefore put the business at a competitive disadvantage since customers will probably switch to a competitor that does offer incentives for repeat purchases. McCall and Voorhees' (2010) review on the literature relating to loyalty programme effectiveness across different sectors identified the following indicators of effectiveness:

- Increased purchase frequency
- Decreased customer price sensitivity
- Customer advocacy
- Extended relationship lengths
- Increased share of wallet
- Development of consumer community and connectedness
- Increased firm performance

Typically, a loyalty programme records a member's purchases, allocates points in accordance with the rules, categorises the customer in tiers based on their value to the organisation, and allows them to collect rewards for their purchasing points (Oracle, 2006). Rewards can include discounts, added value, free gifts, and advance access to new product developments. As discussed in *5: Tourism Marketing Research*, the CRM programme therefore forms part of the business' marketing research, because over time more is knowledge is gained about individual customers' preferences, responses to promotional offers and purchase behaviour.

The key for small tourism businesses is to keep the programme relatively simple, in terms of both the technology requirements and the level of understanding required by customers, and to maintain a focus on customers' needs. A loyalty programme might not suit every business, and an assessment must be made on the extent to which any investment will lead to increased switching costs for customers. In other words, the extent to which the business will be able develop a programme that differentiates the service from competitors. A programme that simply mimics a key competitor will at best be a source of competitive parity. Key

12

questions to be asked when considering the feasibility of a loyalty programme include (Oracle, 2005:16):

- Are purchasers willing to identify themselves?
- Can rewards be offered at a reasonable cost?
- Will customers make enough purchases to receive benefits from the programme?

There are five fundamentals of an effective loyalty programme:

- Develop a philosophy of nurturing long term mutually beneficial customer relationships that foster a sense of community and belonging
- Develop a customer database
- Select customers who offer maximum yield
- Provide added value to loyal customers
- Communicate with loyal customers via direct media in a *meaningful* way

Develop a philosophy of nurturing long term mutually beneficial customer relationships

An understanding of the value of customer loyalty through relationship-building should be ingrained in the business culture. While rewards are a feature of a loyalty programme, remember the focus is on relationships. Staff should be aware that the benefits of individual relationships for the business must outweigh the costs, because it is not possible for all customers to be loyal. However, initially each new customer should be regarded as a potential repeat purchaser, and one deserving service value. A key aim of CRM is to make the cost of switching brands expensive or require more effort by the customer. Most tourism services are substitutable in the minds of consumers, who can easily switch providers if a better offer becomes available at the time of purchase decision making. For example, you probably wouldn't switch from your favourite local coffee shop or gym, to a competitor offering cheaper prices, if it was part of your social routine, and where you feel a sense of community and belonging.

This principle represents an opportunity where small family owned operations have a potential advantage over the large corporate businesses. It is critical that frontline staff are empowered to deal with customer requests, using their best judgement on how to delight them, and also encourage interaction between guests who might not ordinarily speak to each other. We all like to feel special when spending our hard earned money, and yet how often do we perceive we are taken for granted as customers? Welcoming someone by name as they enter the space (e.g. a long stay guest or frequent customer) and encouraging banter with other guests (e.g. new arrivals) are common practices by some smaller accommodation businesses, such as luxury lodges and bed-and-breakfast homes. For example, as discussed in 4: *Designing Tourism Services and Experiences*, a small family run motel in the regional city of Mackay became the highest rating accommodation in Australia in 2017 on the online booking site Hotels.com, on the basis of the personal touch: "We go the extra mile for our guests and show an interest in who they are and where they come from". Instilling a sense of community or belonging will go a long way to making the visit memorable for guests, which in turn can lead to increased customer loyalty. Make this a business mantra. Greet customers by name, be attentive to their individual needs, and remember their likes and dislikes.

Lean marketing: Employ someone like Mags

Mags is a friendly Irish woman who runs the bar at the historic Star Hotel in the main street of Southampton, England. I have stayed at this hotel more than once, and one of the reasons I am a repeat visitor there, aside from the location and price, is because of Mags' *genuine* hospitality. Mags makes a friendly effort to make every guest feel at home, to the extent that she often introduces people to other guests, which is particularly appreciated by solo travellers. To create a welcoming sense of belonging, employ someone like Mags who genuinely enjoys a friendly chat with visitors while providing a great service. (Oh, and this is of course a simple example of customer loyalty from me to you, through this word-of-mouth referral).

Develop a customer database

Effective loyalty programmes are reliant on the development of customer information on a database, where members have a unique identifier. Databases range in sophistication from simply using the customer's name on a card kept by the cash register at a café, which is clipped and counts towards a free coffee after x number of purchases, to a membership card or key tag containing a barcode or magstrip that can be scanned at the time of purchase and automatically recorded in the CRM system. Recorded transactions provide the business with information on purchases and effectiveness of rewards initiatives such as a short term coupon offer. This is a repository of customers' information that can be accessed by sales staff and service staff. Simple database software is inexpensive and not difficult to set up by anyone used to working with spreadsheets. The database is set up with different fields of customer data that will depend on the objectives (e.g. a customer email list for a newsletter) and types of reports to be generated (e.g. level of uptake on a promotional coupon). Typically, data includes individual customers' contact details, demographic characteristics, birthday, anniversary, purchases, preferences, along with any personal idiosyncrasies they mention in conversations with staff. For more sophisticated dimensions of customer insight data collated by large businesses in an ideal CRM system see Bligh and Turk (2004).

12

Lean marketing: Collecting customer email contacts in return for free Wi-Fi

Leon de Bruxelles is a Belgian themed restaurant on the edge of the Place de la République square in Paris, France. The square celebrates the 18th century French revolution, has a main metro station, and is popular with international visitors and local Parisians. Like many eateries, Leon de Bruxelles offers free Wi-Fi as added value to customers. Instead of using a password to obtain access to the Wi-Fi, customers need to enter their name and email address. This forms a database of customers, many of whom are potential repeat visitors, which is used by the business for promotional offers and marketing research. The first offer provided to new customers is to sign up for membership to Club Leon, the main benefits of which are: guaranteed reservation at any time, exclusive email offers, a discount off the next meal, and a bottle of champagne on the membership anniversary.

An investigation into the relationship between CRM and hotel profitability found the key to successful implementation was the firm's ability to generate important customer information and disseminate this to staff (see Josiassen et al., 2014). Importantly for small businesses, they suggested a firm's personal relationships with customers, and staff skills in managing customer relationships were more likely to be effective than investing in expensive CRM technology. One important implication of this is that small tourism businesses need to be very clear about setting a few realistic customer relationship objectives. The customer database can then be designed to meet the needs of these objectives, by dictating the type of customer information required and the type of reporting that will be helpful to staff in developing incentives for customers.

Critical point: It's not all about technology

Small tourism businesses are able get closer to their customers than the big brands can. While case studies of CRM programmes for large chains focus on the development of complex technology systems to handle the information gathered from a huge database of customers, it must be remembered that at the core of CRM is building meaningful relationships with selected customers. The key for small businesses is not a complex IT system but a simple database of information collected from customers during personal interactions. Think of a small hairdressing business for example. Hairdressers typically have a card for each customer, on which they write details of product preferences, hair colouring chemical balances, and snippets of information about their personal life. Prior to each appointment, the hairdresser digs out the individual customer's card to refresh their memory, to be able to start conversing from where they left off at the last visit. A simple system that could be digitalised in a software programme, but doesn't need to be. A simple but single minded focus on the customer's unique needs.

Select customers who offer maximum yield

A key objective is to identify customers who offer the best yield, since it is not possible or feasible to develop an ongoing relationship with every customer. The key is to identify those loyal customers who will be less price sensitive and therefore less likely to switch to other brands offering special deals, since a small increase in the number of loyal customers can lead to a major increase in profitability (see for example Reichheld & Sasser 1990, Reichheld 1996). Selection criteria includes frequency and volume of purchase, spending patterns and probability of future visitation. A tier system can be developed to differentiate members by their value level. Importantly, select those profitable customers whose needs the business is best able to cater to.

Provide added value to loyal customers

Financial rewards are essential in a loyalty programme, and can be short term (e.g. make a purchase and receive a reward) and long term (e.g. purchase points accrue towards a prize target). A tier system provides the customer with added incentive to commit to the firm, and can provide an enhanced sense of their status. It is important that long term targets are realistic, to ensure customers maintain interest. As well as discounts and free offers, there is a range of ways to provide added-value to loyal customers, which will enhance satisfaction. Depending on the type of business, options include:

- Exclusive offers
- Service upgrades
- Priority seating
- Exclusive opportunities to preview new service and product offerings
- A preferential reservation contact number
- Guaranteed reservations at any time
- Members only events
- Special dedicated amenities such as a members' lounge

Case 12.1: Friends of Laphroaig

Laphroaig is a brand of Scotch whisky, dating back to 1815, from the island of Islay (pronounced eye-la) off Scotland's rugged west coast (www.laphroaig.com). On Islay there is a saying: "We don't make friends easily but the ones we do are for life". This spirit underpins the distillery's customer relationship management approach. Every bottle of Lahproaig, purchased anywhere in the world comes with the opportunity to register as a Friend of Laphroaig (FOL). While Lafroaig was formerly a small family business, it is now part of a larger corporate brand. However, the FOL programme is one that could be adapted by small businesses that make spirits, craft beers, wines, cheeses, gourmet foods or artisan

12

products. The FOL club was established in 1994, and all members are given a lifetime lease over a one square foot (930 centimetres) plot of land on Islay. When a FOL visits the distillery they given a free dram of Laphroaig as rent for their land, and are encouraged to visit their plot and mark their territory with their national flag. On the FOL website, members are able to message their plot's neighbours, join the chat forum, post photos, enter competitions and charity auctions, receive email updates, and purchase products from the distillery including opportunities to buy special bottlings.

Discussion question

What other initiatives could a similar business (e.g. a winery) develop to reward loyal customers?

Communicate with loyal customers via direct media in a *meaningful* way

While mass distribution of company newsletters to all members of a customer database is a useful public relations tool, effective CRM involves personalised messages that will be meaningful to an individual customer. Think like a customer…what would attract your attention? Individual customer information is at the core of CRM, and so there is little point collecting such data if it is not going to be used in a way that will delight the customer. Among the leaders in this area are supermarket chains, which are able to generate emails to members to alert them of special offers related to their recent purchases and other incentives. These are often targeted as previously frequent customers who are overdue for another purchase, since this is more effective than trying to win back a customer who has defected. Other personalised messages representing *meaningful* messages include:

- Special offers to customers on the database who have reported a negative service experience. Complaints are an opportunity to learn from the customer experience, and therefore a chance to improve the relationship, by thanking them, letting them know the feedback is appreciated.

- Competitions that acknowledge customers' tier status

- An off-peak offer of added value that recognises the customer's personal preferences

- An email seeking feedback on the recent service

- Birthday and anniversary special offers

Activity 12.2: Think like a customer

Have any hospitality or retail businesses collected your contact details in the past year? For example, have you stayed in accommodation at a nearby destination you have visited before and/or might visit again in the future? Have you made a reservation at a local restaurant by email? Have you made an in-store retail purchase where they have entered your contact details into their system? If so, has the business made any effort to keep in touch with you? If yes, was the message meaningful to you? If no, have they missed an opportunity for a repeat purchase from you? Would you have appreciated receiving a special offer? Think like a customer, to understand what the customer might appreciate.

Repeat visitation to destinations

For many destinations there are strong levels of potential repeat visitation from different markets. For example, in Australia the Victorian state tourism organisation found up to 90% of visitors to the state from New Zealand had previously visited Australia, along with 60% of visitors from Singapore and 10% of visitors from Japan (Harris et al., 2005). Similarly, Tourism Queensland (2006) found 93% of visitors to the state from New Zealand were repeat visitors. For research about repeat visitation to destinations see Gitelson and Crompton (1984), Gyte and Phelps (1989), Fakeye and Crompton (1991), Milman and Pizam (1995), and Um et al. (2006). The diversity of potential repeat visitation segments includes:

- University students on their spring breaks during the course of their studies.
- Daytrips and short breaks by car for residents of large cities to nearby beaches, rural areas or ski fields.
- People with second homes in a holiday area.
- End of season sports team celebration trips.
- Retirees in cold climates who head to warmer climes for the winter season.
- The annual family ski trip or summer beach holiday.
- Travel to festivals, and sporting and cultural events.
- Supporters tours for fans of major sports teams.
- Low cost airline short breaks.
- Travel to visit friends and/or relatives.
- Travel for health reasons such as visits to medical specialists or spiritual retreats.
- Travel for business, such as territory sales calls, trade shows, seminars and conferences.

Just as it makes sense for individual tourism businesses to stay in touch with previous customers, so to it does for destination marketers to try and stimulate repeat

12

visitation. However, destination stakeholders need to understand that engaging in CRM is problematic for DMOs (Fyall et al., 2003; Pike, 2007; Pike et al., 2011; Murdy & Pike, 2012. Pike & Page, 2014). The central problem is that destination marketers rarely get to meet any of the visitors they have helped to attract, unless at a local visitor information centre, and therefore have no way of collecting their contact details. Therefore, the DMO is usually reliant on individual accommodation businesses to use their customer registration databases to engage in CRM, and developing followers through social media and the destination website. One of the earliest adopters was Travel Michigan, a state tourism office in the US, which invested millions in a web-based CRM (Oguntoyinbo, 2007). The STO was able to demonstrate massive increases in market exposure and conversion rates to the system. Individual businesses can help the DMO by adding a link to the destination newsletter URL on their own website. While destination websites have links to local businesses, it is rare that these businesses reciprocate with a link back to the destination site.

Stimulating word-of-mouth referrals

One major advantage that small tourism businesses have over the large corporate brands is the ability to get close to the customer and have a more intimate understanding of their individual experience. Small businesses should use this advantage to really focus on their service delivery to increase satisfaction and perceived value. Truly delighted customers can be an asset to the firm, even if there is little likelihood they will return in the near future. For example, a honeymoon couple from Tokyo staying at a small hotel in Brighton, England for a couple of nights will be unlikely to return in the near future, and so wouldn't be considered as potential high yield loyal customers on the database. However, honeymoons are memorable, and something the couple will reminisce about over time. If the small hotel exceeds the couple's expectations with outstanding personal service, there is a likelihood they will share the experience with their social network via word-of-mouth (WoM) and social media (eWoM – electronic word-of-mouth). This is also referred to as *influencer marketing*. The power of WoM referrals lies in the extent to which we as consumers use online customer reviews and ratings, along with advice from friends, in our tourism purchase decision making.

WOM referrals can be a potentially powerful organic image building agent. As discussed in *3: Tourism Consumer Behaviour*, there are two sources of stimuli that lead to image formation (Gunn, 1988), and the level of influence of the marketer varies between the two. Organic (natural) image formation occurs through an individual's everyday assimilation of sensory information, such as media editorial content, movies, school history lessons, and word of mouth. Induced (forced) image formation on the other hand is stimulated through the efforts of marketers through advertising. Organic images are considered more influential in consumer decision making. WoM referrals helps to counter the problem of intangibility that is characteristic of so many tourism services, and therefore lessen perceived risk in purchase decision making.

Lean marketing: Ask for feedback and referrals

Most small businesses don't ask customers for feedback or referrals. Where possible try to make a point of asking guests to leave a comment. This could be in a guest comments book or on a company tablet opened on the Facebook or TripAdvisor page. Offer a discount on their next purchase if they make a review on TripAdvisor. For example, Sydney Backpackers hostel offers guests a $5 discount off their next stay. Consider asking your favourite customers to speak briefly in a short fun video clip, recorded on the spot with a portable device, which can then be used in marketing communications and the website.

Critical point: Exceeding a customer's expectations gets harder and harder

Remember with any value-added initiative you can only exceed that customer's expectations once, because next time (hopefully there is a next time) that will be their new expectation. So continually delighting a repeat customer becomes harder and harder in terms of finding new and different ways to exceed their expectations.

While delighting customers with great service might result in WoM, the chances are greater when proactive tactics are used, particularly when incentivised. In this regard, the two main opportunities are to encourage customers to 1) share their positive experience with others, and 2) recruit their friends as customers.

Encourage customers to share their positive experience with others

It doesn't take much effort to ask customers to spread the message about great service experiences. There are a range of tactics used to encourage customers to create conversations about the brand with others. These include:

- Creating a social media photo opportunity (e.g. a unique architectural feature), Facebook 'check in', and Twitter hashtag.
- Offering payment or free product samples to popular influencers, such as professional Instagrammers and bloggers, to post pics or comments in their feed.
- Providing a link for an online testimonial site such as Tripadvisor, and ensuring any comment made receives acknowledgement. Some businesses offer rewards for positive online comments.
- Providing a unique aspect to service delivery (see *6: Designing Tourism Services and Experiences*).

12

- Running an online competition, such as on Facebook, where entry requires the participant to share the post.
- Using a celebrity's endorsement in advertising and PR initiatives.
- Producing a viral advertisement or social media post.
- Selling mementos such as souvenir photo/video of the experience, or souvenir apparel.
- Asking for customer reviews, and/or using a guest satisfaction survey to elicit testimonials for use in promotional material.
- Doing something thoughtful for a guest, such as a surprise birthday cake with a personalised message.
- Providing some component of the service for free, not available at competitors (a small offering can be a lot cheaper than the cost of advertising).

See also 10: *Digital and Social Media in Tourism*.

Lean marketing: Let the customer start the conversation

It's important to let the customer start any conversation about the brand with their friends. So, don't include the *buzz* element in your advertising. If you promise something in an advertisement, it won't be a surprise to customers, won't exceed their expectations, and is less likely to be shared with others.

Encourage customers to recruit other customers

As discussed, one of the indicators of a loyal customer is the extent to which they are likely to recommend the business to others in their network. Most of us do this naturally, as we like to help friends with useful advice. We do this without expecting a reward from the business. Many businesses do incentivise this tactic by offering a reward to customers for recruiting their contacts as new customers. These are commonly in the form of a discount or prize. However, if the customer service experience is not great, such referral initiatives will be wasted. So, building a relationship with individual customers is more important than the nature of the reward, because delighted customers won't need an incentive to refer the business to others. Nevertheless some people will be motivated by rewards and so an incentivised referral scheme can increase overall referrals.

An incentivised referral scheme requires a balance between what the business can afford to pay to acquire a new customer, and offering rewards that will be of value to the referring customer and to the new customer. For example, customer A gets one type of reward for referring customer B, while customer B gets another type of reward when they make their first purchase. Customer B then knows the referral programme works and can then be recruited as a referrer. Get feedback from customers on what type of reward they value.

Customers need to be made aware there is a referral programme that will be to their benefit. Opportunities to communicate this, in ways that let them know it is about offering *them* something and not just advertising the business, include:

- Advertise the referral programme on the website, social media, on-site, and in the business newsletter, in a way that details are easy to find and easy to understand.

- Incorporate a *Refer us* tab on the business website.

- Personalise the communication to frequent customers by mailing a postcard or sending a text message, which are less likely to be treated as spam as an email would.

- Remind those customers who have previously been rewarded for referring a new customer, to refer again.

- Have a leaflet on the programme at the checkout and ask customers to join when they are paying. Let them know what the best reward would be next time.

Lean marketing: Discounts for locals

For some tourism businesses, particularly attractions and theme parks, offering a discount for locals can be an effective generator of referrals. The host community provides accommodation for visiting friends and relatives (VFR). VFR visitors usually rely on their hosts for advice on what to see and do at the destination. Offering an incentive to local residents can lead to increased awareness of what the business offers, and hosts are more likely to recommend something they are familiar with. Another form of incentive is to offer the local resident free or heavily discounted admission when they are accompanied by a paying visitor who can show ID from out of town.

Critical point: Be aware of local laws and ethics relating to WoM marketing

In some countries there are disclosure laws for influencer marketing. Laws require paid WoM referrers to disclose their relationship with the business and/or their compensation. Marketing industry associations in many countries now also provide a code of ethical behaviour for WoM initiatives. See for example the code of ethics promoted by the Word of Mouth Marketing Association (www.WOMMA.com).

12

Key points

1: The rationale for customer relationship management

Customer relationship management (CRM) is used to enhance long term customer loyalty. A small increase in the number of loyal customers will be more profitable than striving for a continual stream of new customer transactions through paid media advertising. Effective CRM can result in reduced marketing costs, increased sales, and higher profits.

2: The fundamentals of an effective customer loyalty programme

There are five fundamentals of an effective loyalty programme: develop a philosophy of nurturing long term mutually beneficial customer relationships that create a sense of community or belonging; develop a customer database; select customers who offer maximum yield; provide added value to selected (e.g. repeat) customers; communicate with loyal customers via direct media in a *meaningful* way.

3: Opportunities to stimulate word-of-mouth referrals

Even if a loyalty programme to attract repeat business is not practical or feasible, there will still be opportunities to encourage customers to create conversations about the brand with others through word-of-mouth (WoM) referrals. Online customer reviews and ratings, along with the advice of friends, play a major role in consumers' tourism purchase decisions.

Discussion questions

1. What are the potential financial benefits for a business investing in CRM?

2. Why is it difficult to continually delight a repeat customer?

3. Why are customer referrals important in the development of the brand image?

References

Bligh, P. & Turk, D. (2004). *CRM Unplugged: Releasing CRM's Strategic Value*. Hoboken, NJ: Wiley.

Chang, J., Yen, D., Ku, C.-Y. & Young, D. (2002). Critical issues in CRM adoption and implementation. *International Journal of Services and Technology Management*, **3**(3), 311-324.

Fakeye, P. C. & Crompton, J. L. (1991). Image differences between prospective, first time, and repeat visitors to the Lower Rio Grande Valley. *Journal of Travel Research*, **30**: 10-16.

Fyall, A., Callod, C. & Edwards, B. (2003). Relationship marketing: The challenge for destinations. *Annals of Tourism Research,* **30**(3) 644-659.

Gitelson, R.J. & Crompton, J.L. (1984) Insights into the repeat vacation phenomenon. *Annals of Tourism Research,* **11**: 199-217.

Gunn, C. (1988). *Vacationscape: Designing Tourist Regions,* (2nd Ed). Austin: Bureau of Business Research, University of Texas.

Gyte, D.M & Phelps, A. (1989). Patterns of destination repeat business. British tourists to Mallorca, Spain. *Journal of Travel Research,* **28**(1): 24-28.

Harris, R., Jago, L. & King, B. (2005). *Case Studies in Tourism & Hospitality Marketing.* Pearson Education Australia: Sydney.

Hoffman, J.L. & Lowitt, R.M. (2008). A better way to design loyalty programs. *Strategy and Leadership,* **36**: 44-49.

Josiassen, A., Assaf, A.G. & Cvelbar, L.K. (2014). CRM and the bottom line: Do all CRM dimensions affect firm performance? *International Journal of Hospitality Management,* **36**: 130-136.

Lee, H,S., Whang, K., Ahsan, K., Bordon, A., Faragalla, A., Jain, A., Mohsin, A. & Shi, G. (2003). *Harra's Entertainment Inc. – Real time CRM in a Service Supply Chain. A Harvard Case.* Boston: Harvard Publishing.

Luck, D. & Lancaster, G. (2013). The significance of CRM to the strategies of hotel companies. *Worldwide Hospitality and Tourism Themes,* **5**(1): 55-66.

Maggon, M. & Chaudry, H. (2015). Revisiting relationship marketing and customer relationship management in leading tourism and hospitality journals: Research trends from 2001 to 2013. *Journal of Relationship Marketing,* **14**: 53-77.

Marchand, D. (2006). Customer relationship management challenging the myth: focus on people not the technology. *Perspectives for Managers,* **131**(1), 1-4.

McCall, M., & Voorhees, C. (2010). The drivers of loyalty program success: An organizing framework and research agenda. *Cornell Hospitality Quarterly,* **51**(1): 35-52.

Milman, A. & Pizam, A. (1995). The role of awareness and familiarity with a destination: The central Florida case. *Journal of Travel Research,* **33**(3): 21-27.

Murdy, S. & Pike, S. (2012). Perceptions of visitor relationship marketing opportunities by destination marketers: An importance-performance analysis. *Tourism Management,* **33**(5): 1281-1285.

Pike, S., Murdy, S. & Lings, I. (2011). Visitor relationship orientation of destination marketing organisations. *Journal of Travel Research,* **50**(4): 443-453.

Oguntoyinbo, L. (2007). With help, tourism makes virtual splash. *The Detroit News.* October 5. Pp. 2c.

Oracle. (2005). *Ensuring Customer Loyalty: Designing Next-Generation Loyalty Programs.* Redwood Shores, CA: Oracle Corporation. February.

Ozgener, S. & Iraz, R. (2006). Customer relationship management in small-medium enterprises: The case of Turkish tourism industry. *Tourism Management,* **27**(6), 1356-1363.

12

Pike, S. (2007). Repeat visitors – an exploratory investigation of RTO responses. *Journal of Travel & Tourism Research*, Spring: 1-13.

Pike, S. & Page, S. (2014). Destination Marketing Organizations and destination marketing: A narrative analysis of the literature. *Tourism Management*, **41**:202-227.

Rahimi, R., Koseoglu, M.A., Ersoy, A.B. & Okumus, F. (2017). Customer relationship management research in tourism and hospitality: A state-of-the-art. *Tourism Review*, **72**(2): 209-220.

Rahimi, R. & Kozak, M. (2017). Impact of customer relationship management on customer satisfaction: The case of a budget hotel chain. *Journal of Travel & Tourism Marketing*, **34**: 40-51.

Reichheld, F. (1996). *The Loyalty Effect*. Boston: Harvard Business School Press.

Reichheld, F. F., & Sasser, W. E. (1990). Zero defections – Quality comes to services. *Harvard Business Review*, **68** (Oct/Nov): 105-111.

Tian, J., & Wang, S. (2017). Signaling service quality via website e-CRM features: More gains for smaller and lesser known hotels. *Journal of Hospitality & Tourism Research*, **41**(2): 211-245.

Tourism Queensland. (2006). Why do kiwis come to Queensland? *T.Q. News*, **7**: 45-47.

Um, S., Chon, K. & Ro, Y. (2006). Antecedents of revisit intention. *Annals of Tourism Research*, **33**(4): 1141-1158.

Verhoef, P.C. (2003). Understanding the effect of customer relationship management efforts on customer retention and customer share development. *Journal of Marketing*, **67** (Oct.): 30-45.

Vogt, C.A. (2011). Customer relationship management in tourism: Management needs and research applications. *Journal of Travel Research*, **50**(4): 356-364.

13 Tourism Distribution

Chapter outline

For intangible tourism services, *distribution* represents the point of sale, as well as a cost of getting a sale through travel trade intermediaries. Fundamentally, distribution is based on a tourism service provider paying a commission to an intermediary who supplies a customer, and for many tourism businesses this can have a major impact on pricing, competitiveness and profits. Intermediaries act as agents by providing tourism businesses with access to consumers, often in markets they would otherwise not be able to realistically reach. As many intermediaries have a powerful influence in travellers' itineraries, distribution is an important aspect of tourism marketing planning. The chapter discusses opportunities for distributing tourism services through a range of intermediaries, such as concierge services, visitor information centres, retail and online travel agents, inbound tour operators, and overseas wholesalers. It also summarises distribution challenges faced by small tourism businesses, such as attracting the attention and interest of important intermediaries, understanding the different commission arrangements, securing preferred supplier agreements, and ethical contractual obligations.

Learning aims

To enhance your understanding of:

- Tourism distribution opportunities and challenges
- Commission as a cost of getting a sale through an intermediary
- The range of travel trade intermediaries.

Key terms

Tourism distribution (place)
The point of sale (*place* is the 4th P in the traditional marketing mix) for intangible tourism services, as well as a cost of getting a sale through travel trade intermediaries.

Travel trade intermediaries
Agents in the distribution chain, in between a business and their target consumers, such as concierge services, visitor information centres, retail and online travel agents, airlines, inbound tour operators, and overseas wholesalers.

Commission
The cost of getting a sale through an intermediary, on behalf of the business, typically as a percentage of the advertised retail selling price. Commission levels vary between different types of intermediaries, and can include an override payment to secure *preferred supplier* status for the tourism business.

Distribution of tourism services

Distribution of an intangible tourism service represents the point of sale. This can be in the form of a direct sale to a customer at the business site, or a sale made at another location through a third party intermediary such as a travel agent. Therefore, *distribution* is regarded as the *place* of sale in the 4 Ps of the traditional marketing mix, along with *product*, *price* and *promotion* (Borden, 1964). Also, as discussed in *8: Pricing Tourism Services*, distribution also represents a cost of getting a sale through travel trade intermediaries, and can therefore be an important consideration in costing a tourism service. This cost of a sale is in the form of a commission payment.

Commission

The concept of paying a commission to a third party for a sale on behalf of a business is neither new nor complex, and yet can be easily misunderstood by new entrants in the tourism industry. A common complaint is about how high the rate of commission is. Think of this as akin to someone groaning about having to pay too much income tax. The positive is they are only paying that level of tax because they have received a certain level of income, whereas no income tax means low or no income. Much in the same way, a commission is only paid when a sale is made, and a perceived high commission is a market reality if a business wants access to a major intermediary's customers. Trying to reach those same consumers independent of an intermediary would cost a lot more, even if it were possible to reach them. Intermediaries have access to a customer database the individual small tourism business would never achieve, and the intermediary is undertaking promotion on their behalf. So commission should be acknowledged as a cost of getting a sale through a distributor, just as advertising is a cost incurred to get direct sales.

Another misunderstanding is where a tourism supplier attempts to undercut the intermediary's price by offering a cheaper rate if a consumer books direct. In this case the supplier avoids paying commission but will likely lose the goodwill and business of the intermediary. This commonly occurs where online travel agents (OTA) advertise accommodation suppliers, with which they have a commission arrangement. Some consumers will see the listings and contact the hotels direct to try to negotiate a lower rate. In some parts of the world this issue is being debated in legal circles with a view to establishing the legal rights of the intermediary and the suppliers. While the legality of undercutting an intermediary's advertised price might be in question, ethically it is not good business practice and therefore not sustainable in the long term.

Activity 13.1 – Offering a discount for direct bookings

When customers have made their booking via an intermediary, for which the business has paid a commission, it can be tempting to offer guests a discount for their next visit if they book direct with your business. Also, your business website could openly advertise a discount for direct bookings. While this would save the business the cost of future commissions, what is the potential downside of this approach?

Commission levels vary around the world, and have traditionally been costed as a percentage of the advertised retail price. In general, traditional commission levels could be expected to be in the range of the following percentage of the retail price:

- Visitor information centres (10%)
- Retail travel agents (10% – 20%)
- Concierge service (10% – 20%+)
- Inbound tour operators (25% – 30%)
- Tour wholesalers (25% – 30%)
- Airlines (25% – 30%)

In the current deregulated global economy, remembering there is no overall coordinator of the *tourism system*, there are many variations to the traditional commission levels above. Digital disruptor Airbnb changed the traditional accommodation commission structure, by levying a *service fee* of 3% – 5% to the hosts and 5% – 15% to guests. Some specialised niche operators, such as personal homestay wholesalers charge a 100% mark up on what the host charges, which equates to 50% commission. Major online retailers can also charge as much as 50%

13

commission. For decades airlines around the world provided a base commission to travel agents of 9% for international flights, under an international agreement. However, since 2000 this has gradually been reduced to as low as 1%. Without any formal industry agreement in a given sector, the commission level will be whatever is agreed to between the tourism service supplier and the intermediary. In other words, what the cost of the sale is worth to each party.

Other terms related to commissions include:

- **Kickbacks**. This is a form of unethical commission where someone is paid an under-the-counter payment (e.g. cash in a brown paper bag that is not declared for tax purposes) for bringing in customers. This has been common in the development of new international markets, particularly where the early visitors don't speak the local language, travel in organised groups, and are reliant on their tour guide who determines almost all of their movements at the destination. This has been particularly rife in competition between souvenir shops, which can make thousands from each tour group. In this situation, the group doesn't know they are paying higher prices (e.g. +40% the usual retail) as a captive audience, in order for the shop pay for the kickback to the tour guide.

- **Spotter's fee.** Similar to a kickback, where an intermediary such as a hotel concierge service might arrange a reservation at a local restaurant or show but doesn't take the payment from the guest. Instead, there will be an arrangement between the service supplier and the concierge desk for a spotter's fee to be paid for each booking made, to be settled weekly or monthly for example.

- **Preferred supplier agreements**. In this arrangement, a tourism service supplier is recommended by an intermediary (e.g. travel agent, cruise ship) to their customers first, over their competitors, as their preferred product for a given service category. In return the supplier pays the intermediary a higher than normal rate of commission, often referred to as an *override* payment. Many travel agents, for example, have a tiered system of different preferred status levels and varying override commission levels.

Activity 13.2: Observe a nearby travel agency

Stand outside a nearby travel agency and observe how they display product information. To what extent is it obvious which are the preferred brands. Is there a feature display window? Do they explicitly list their preferred suppliers? How many different brands' brochures are displayed in various categories (e.g. cruises, coach tours) on the racks. What is your overall impression of how important the *preferred* agreements must be?

Lean marketing: Trial an offer of a little more commission

If your product is one of many on offer at a particular agency (e.g. a visitor information centre or hotel concierge), where competitors offer similar services at the standard rate of commission, why not trial an offer of a little more commission? Meet with management and offer an extra 2% – 3% for a trial period. Even if the agency has no official *preferred agreements* with suppliers, the extra commission might help differentiate against the competition. Confidentially of course.

The power of travel trade intermediaries

In many travel markets, a small number of intermediaries have enormous influence over travellers' buyer behaviour and itineraries. This can be a blessing, as discussed in Case 13.1 below, for a tourism service supplier who gains access to key intermediaries such as inbound tour operators. However, in the case of Alanya, Turkey, discussed in the *Industry insight* below, the rector of the local university lamented how his destination had gone from "Heaven to Hell" due to the excessive influence of European tour wholesalers see (Pike, 2008: 11):

> *In terms of economy, productivity is decreasing not increasing. The competition of the foreign tour monopolists is kept on by decreasing the price and marketing all-inclusive packets, which causes the best hotels to be marketed at very low prices. Only about 25% of this income stays in Antalya and 75 % of it goes out of the city.*

Industry insight: Welcome to Alanya, we have gone from Heaven to Hell!

During the opening session of the 2006 International Tourism Conference, held in Alanya, Turkey, the rector of the host university opened the event with these words: "Welcome to Alanya, we have gone from Heaven to Hell!" Clearly passionate about his destination, he was lamenting how the local tourism industry and wider community was suffering as a result of losing control of visitor flows to powerful travel trade intermediaries. Alanya is a picturesque beach destination on the Mediterranean, in Turkey's south west, and has a warm climate with over 300 days of sunshine each year. However, due to the influence of European tour wholesalers at this time, the city's hotels were forced to close for the three months of the winter each year. During this winter season the tour wholesalers stopped *distributing* package tours to Alanya, and instead directed their substantial customer base to warmer destinations. Alayna had unfortunately developed into an all-inclusive summer commodity resort destination that travel intermediaries could easily substitute for other destinations in the off-season. At the time Alanya lacked an off-season strategy to counter the massive loss of visitors. The negative economic impact affected the wider

13

community of 500,000 residents, with so many businesses struggling for survival during the three months of winter. This not only included the staff at local hotels, sightseeing tours, taxis, cafes, and shops in the bazaar, but also the plethora of small businesses supplying products and services to the tourism industry.

Source: Adapted from Pike (2008, 2016).

Case 13.1: It's just a sheep show isn't it?

The Agrodome is New Zealand's best known sheep-based visitor attraction. In a country famous for the quality of its wool and lamb exports around the world, it is not surprising that visitor attractions have been developed to take advantage of the sheep association many people have with New Zealand. As an aside, it is interesting this perception is so strong, because it is Australia that produces 75% of the world's wool. However, while there are more sheep in Australia, the sheep to people ratio in New Zealand is about 10:1. Also, the small predominantly rural nature of the New Zealand countryside means that the sight of sheep is commonplace while driving between towns.

In 1971, the Agrodome became the first visitor attraction in the tourist resort area of Rotorua to not be based on a natural landscape feature, and the first in New Zealand to showcase sheep. The initial idea came from the success of New Zealand's sheep shearing show at World Expo 1970 in Osaka, Japan. The founders were Godfrey Bowen, from one of New Zealand's pioneering sheep shearing families, and entrepreneur George Harford. Harford achieved a high profile in the New Zealand tourism industry during the 1970s and 1980s, and a key to the business' success was the relationship he established with influential inbound tour operators (ITO). During this period in New Zealand's tourism history, coach tours operated by these ITOs were the dominant travel mode for overseas visitors. The relationship between the Agrodome and the ITOs became the source of competitive advantage for the attraction, even though many imitators entered the market and competed on price.

While the level of coach touring has declined dramatically in New Zealand since the late 1980s, relative to the rise of independent self-drive options, the power of the Agrodome brand had been established as a dominant tourism icon. The Agrodome's sheep show format is easily imitated, but the attraction's success is an example of how a brand name can create effectively differentiate in the minds of travellers and travel intermediaries. To the extent that for many years one question on the Australian government's incoming passenger card asked international visitors: *Have you visited a farm in the last 30 days (not including New Zealand's Agrodome)?* A big part of the business' success was George's strong relationship he had developed with the key ITOs who controlled the majority of coach tour visitors to Rotorua. George's strategy was simple. Each Friday he would make the 240 kilometre road trip to Auckland where most of the ITOs were based, and buy drinks all night for these key travel trade intermediaries. When his son Warren joined the business, and started accompanying his father on the Friday missions to Auckland he was given one simple instruction from George: "For the first five years you accompany me you keep your mouth shut and just buy the drinks". By the time Warren eventually took over the business on his father's retirement he had learned everything he needed to know about ITO relationships from those Friday sessions, and had himself become part of an influential business network.

Discussion question

What are the Agrodome's key strengths? Aside from attracting tour groups, how would the strong relationship with travel intermediaries have enhanced the Agrodome brand?

The range of travel trade intermediaries

The diverse range of travel trade intermediaries at various levels in the distribution system between the small tourism business and consumer markets include:

- Visitor information centres (VIC)
- Concierge services
- DMOs as information brokers and convention & visitors bureaus (CVB)
- Retail travel agents
- Corporate travel offices
- Online travel agents (OTA)
- Online daily deal sites
- General sales agents (GSA)
- Inbound tour operators (ITO or IBO)
- Tour wholesalers
- Professional conference organisers (PCO)
- Incentive travel planners
- Airlines

Visitor information centres

Most communities operate a visitor information centre (VIC), and in many countries the VICs collaborate in a network that is officially branded so as to make it easier for travellers to find information during their travels. Even in the digital age, VICs can be effective in *distributing* information about local services to visitors, particularly when they are located next to a major traveller transport hub such as bus depot or central railway station. Providing information is costly,

13

and few VICs will ever make a profit. Costs are often offset by using volunteer labour (meaning levels of professionalism can vary between VICs) and by selling local tourism services and packages for a commission. Opportunities for small tourism businesses include having their brochure in a display rack (usually free of charge), a listing in the computer database and self-service kiosk, and having a commissionable ticket item for sale.

Concierge services

Most cruise ships and major hotels offer a concierge service, providing information and bookings for local sightseeing, transport and entertainment. On cruise ships the only tourism information provided will be for the preferred shore excursions, which must be purchased on board ship. These shore excursions often have the highest level of commission mark-up in the tourism industry, and are a lot more expensive than a guest buying direct on arrival at the port of call. However, as guests have to pay extra if they want to access Wi-Fi at sea, many are not able to search online for alternative shore excursions, and so are a kind of captive audience for the cruise ship travel desk. In the case of hotels, concierge desks usually have a limited space brochure rack for preferred local attractions. There might be a fee for having a brochure in the display rack, and the concierge can make bookings for guests in return for a spotter's fee.

Lean marketing: Electric bike on display in hotel foyer

Alhao is a beautiful fishing village near Faro in Portugal's Algarve region. An easy way for visitors to get around the area is by bicycle and there are many businesses offering road bikes, mountain bikes and electric bikes for hire. Visitors staying at the largest hotel in Alhao, the 5 Star Real Marina Hotel and Spa Resort, are an obvious target for local tourism operators, and private tour operators are able to lease a travel desk in the large reception area to sell their services. One of the local bicycle hire businesses has direct access to the guests. They have secured space at the main entrance to display one of their new electric bikes. Through the hotel reception, guests are able to arrange to have such a bike delivered to them. In return the bike operator pays a commission to the hotel.

DMOs as information brokers, and convention & visitors bureaus

While most DMOs these days don't sell wholesale packages or retail products, they serve as information brokers in the tourism distribution system. The DMO provides information to intermediaries on local tourism services, and updates the local industry on intermediaries needs. As well as opportunities to feature tourism services on the DMO website, many coordinate a digital database of local tourism information, enabling businesses to list their services. For example, the Australian Tourism Data Warehouse (www.atdw.au) has over 40,000 product listings, which are freely accessible for travel trade intermediaries around the world. Most DMOs regularly organise and participate in travel trade promotional events, such as tourism exchanges, travel exhibitions, and trade educations programmes to showcase the destination's businesses. For more discussion on these see Pike (2016: 302-310). Also, some DMOs, at a local level, operate a convention & visitors bureau (CVB). The key role of the CVB is to attract conferences, conventions, exhibitions and other types of business meetings to the destination.

Retail travel agents

Travel agencies have traditionally been the most visible element in tourism distribution, with a presence in every city's CBD and suburban shopping centres. In the digital age there is always much discussion about the potential demise of travel agents through disintermediation. However, while online sources are accounting for increasing volumes of some tourism sales, the traditional retail agent does still have a role to play in major travel purchase decisions, where trust is a major factor in overcoming the risks inherent with intangible services. While official statistics in different countries show a decline in the number of registered travel agencies, the figures often don't take into account the increasing number of independent home-based travel agents.

Corporate travel offices

While many large corporate organisations and government departments outsource staff business travel to a preferred travel management company, some handle this with in-house travel staff. As an example, almost all travel by employees of the Northern Territory Government in Australia must be booked through the in-house corporate travel office (Travelandtourworld.com, 2015).

Online travel agents

Online travel agents (OTA), such as Expedia.com, have emerged in earnest in recent years as a convenient booking mechanism for consumers, and therefore an integral part of the distribution system for some tourism businesses such as hotels. A report by online travel agent Expedia suggested that 2017 would witness half of all travel bookings in Europe (52%) being made online, following by 45% in the USA and 37% in Asia (Rokou, 2016).

Online daily deal sites

These deal sites, such as Groupon and LivingSocial, emerged during the 2008/09 global financial crisis, providing heavily discounted deals for consumers and high exposure for businesses. These sites can be useful for small tourism businesses using a discount strategy (see *8: Pricing Tourism Services*), and are particularly popular for restaurants, accommodation, and adventure activities.

13

General sales agents

A general sales agent (GSA) represents the interests of a group of independent tourism businesses in a particular market. This is based on the premise that it is more economical for a small business to be represented by a GSA, rather than employ their own sales and reservations staff in that market. In turn, the GSA needs to secure representation of a certain number of clients to operate feasibly in that market. Think of a sales representative who is responsible for selling a portfolio of 10 businesses, rather than employed by one brand.

Inbound tour operators

Inbound tour operators (ITO or IBO) act as a conduit between local tourism businesses and international wholesalers. ITOs specialise in international inbound tourism, provide local businesses with international market access and offering international wholesalers local product knowledge. Typically, an ITO bundles a package of local tourism services and offers this to the international wholesalers who then on sell the packages through retail travel agents.

Professional conference organisers

Professional conference organisers (PCO) are contracted by large organisations and business associations to handle the logistical arrangements for staging conferences or conventions. The PCO can negotiate travel discounts and take care of accommodation for delegates, meeting venues and equipment hire, social functions, and pre- and post-conference tours.

Incentive travel planners

An incentive travel programme is often used by a large corporate organisation to motivate staff to achieve ambitious targets, such as sales. The incentive is the reward of a travel package for those staff who achieve the target. Rewards travel packages are tailor made for the organisation by an incentive travel planner, rather than an off the shelf product, and tend to involve creative activities and venues. Since the outcome is a unique trip to a destination that has brag value for the winning staff, incentive travel planners are always looking for innovative service ideas. The global peak body for the incentive travel industry is www.siteglobal.com.

Airlines

In recent years airlines have slashed commissions to travel agents and at the same time created inducements for consumers to book flights online. Once a consumer is in the airline booking system they have access to range of other third party services such as rental cars and hotels.

Promoting to travel intermediaries

Gaining access to these power brokers is a key aspect of marketing planning for many tourism suppliers. Simply being prepared to pay commission for access to their customers is not usually enough. Attracting the attention and interest of travel trade intermediaries is a key challenge in markets teeming with competitors offering similar features and benefits.

Sales calls

Sales calls are an expensive promotional cost, but necessary in getting noticed by travel trade intermediaries. While dropping in unannounced at a VIC or hotel concierge desk might be practical, an appointment will be needed to get time with most intermediaries such as travel agents, ITOs, PCOs, wholesalers and airlines. They will be most interested in new innovative services not being offered by their competitors, so there should be a clear selling proposition to them.

Brochure distribution

There are professional brochure distribution companies that can arrange for your brochure to be displayed at various visitor information centres and hotel foyers and other locations within your target market catchment areas.

Lean marketing: Do it yourself brochure distribution?

There is often a good cause to distribute your brochures personally to key outlets, such as the local visitor information centre and major hotels. If you have an arrangement allowing you to display your brochure, make a regular scheduled visit to ensure the brochures don't run out. Without making a nuisance of yourself with busy information centre staff, becoming a regular visitor to the office can help you establish more personal contact with them and help keep your offering in their minds. Ask how your brochure can get prime placement, but never ever move another supplier's brochures to your advantage.

Familiarisations/educationals

Other than recommending their preferred agreement suppliers, intermediaries are more likely to favour those they have personally experienced. Familiarisations, also known as educationals, involve hosting intermediaries on a visit to the business to experience what's on offer first hand. For a small tourism business this could be an informal invitation to an individual VIC staff member or hotel concierge, or a more formal group event targeting a variety of different intermediaries and media. Also, as discussed in *2: Destination Marketing Organisations*, there are opportunities for many businesses to work with the local DMO on destination familiarisations and educational programmes.

13

Travel trade events

As discussed in *9: Promoting Tourism Services to Consumers*, participation in consumer travel expos can be a viable tactic for small tourism businesses. While there are many similar events around the world aimed at reaching travel trade intermediaries, most are not feasible for an individual small business. Other than familiarisations there are two types of travel trade events: travel trade expos and travel industry exchanges. Travel trade expos are similar to consumer expos where visitors explore rows of product displays. For example, the world's two largest are ITB in Berlin (http://www.itb-berlin.de/en), which attracts over 10,000 exhibitors from 180 countries who vie for the attention of 115,000 travel trade visitors, and World Travel Mart in London (http://london.wtm.com), which attracts over 50,000 intermediaries. Travel exchanges involve a DMO inviting key international intermediaries to a 2-3 day expo where they typically have a series of up to 50 fifteen minute meetings with tourism businesses who have paid for display space. Examples from around the world include:

- America's IPW travel trade exchange (www.ipw.com/)
- Australian Tourism Exchange (www.tradeevents.australia.com)
- British Travel Trade Fair (www.britishtraveltradefair.com)
- China Outbound Travel & Tourism Market (see www.cottm.com)
- Pacific Asia Travel Association Travel Mart (see www.PATA.org)
- South Pacific Tourism Exchange (see www.spto.org)
- Tourism Rendezvous New Zealand (TRENZ) (see www.trenz.co.nz),

For small tourism businesses, participation at these events becomes more viable when using a GSA, pooling resources with other businesses, or assisting the local DMO's participation.

Industry insight: Working with the NTO

Tourism Australia provides a free downloadable guide that outlines how local tourism businesses and overseas travel trade intermediaries can work with the NTO. The guide summarises Tourism Australia's strategy, target markets, campaigns and partnership approach. It also provides links to other related resources such as the *Planning for Inbound Success Toolkit* and *Making a Splash Guide* on how to work with the media. Available at:

www.tourism.australia.com/content/dam/assets/document/1/6/y/t/a/2004670.pdf

Horizontal integration

Horizontal integration is where a business forms an alliance with other businesses that are at the same level in the supply chain. This alliance doesn't take the businesses any closer to consumers, as occurs in a vertical alliance. Vertical integration is where a company purchases other businesses at different levels in the supply chain. For example, if an airline purchases a hotel chain and travel agency chain, the combined business takes the hotel services closer to consumers. Horizontal integration is more viable for most small tourism businesses, as it is about cooperating to compete; pooling resources to create a bigger impact in the market. Examples of horizontal alliances include:

- **Branded road trips**, where small communities work together with other communities to create a *must-do* touring route. These include Route 66 in the USA, Ireland's Wild Atlantic Way, and Australia's Great Ocean Road. Variations include wine trails, such as the Margaret River in Western Australia, and literary trails such as Jane Austin's Hampshire in England.

Industry insight: The world's longest golf course

The Nullarbor Links claims to be the world's longest golf course, stretching 1365 kms across two states in Australia. The par 73 course has 18 holes starting at the goldmining town of Kalgoorlie, Western Australia, and continues on the Eyre Highway across the Nullarbor Desert, to finish at Ceduna, South Australia. Visitors can also cross in the reverse direction. The course is a cooperative initiative of the Eyre Highway Operators Association, comprising small businesses situated in mostly remote locations across the route. Golfers purchase a scorecard at the first hole, get stamps at each individually operated hole, and on completion receive a certificate for playing the World's longest golf course.

- **Branded collectives**, where small businesses form an umbrella brand, for marketing purposes. This is particularly useful for independent accommodation operators to promote what appears to be a national or regional chain. See for example Big 4 Holiday Parks, which is a collective of 180 holiday parks (https://www.big4.com.au/about). Pooling resources this way creates more opportunities to participate in travel trade events, develop a reservations system and customer loyalty programme, and develop a saleable product of interest to intermediaries.

Key points

1: Tourism distribution opportunities and challenges

Distribution is based on a tourism service provider paying a commission to an intermediary who supplies a customer, and for many tourism businesses this can have a major impact on pricing, competitiveness and yield. Intermediaries act as agents by providing tourism businesses with access to consumers, often in markets they would otherwise not be able to realistically reach. Key challenges for new entrants are understanding commission structures, gaining access to influential travel trade intermediaries, securing preferred supplier agreements, and ethical contractual obligations.

13

2: Commission as the cost of getting a sale through an intermediary

Commission represents the cost of getting a sale through an intermediary, typically as a percentage of the advertised retail selling price. Commission levels vary between different types of intermediaries, and can include an override payment to secure *preferred supplier* status for the tourism business.

3: The range of travel trade intermediaries

Travel trade intermediaries act as agents in the distribution chain, in between a business and their target consumers, such as concierge services, visitor information centres, retail and online travel agents, inbound tour operators, airlines, and overseas wholesalers.

Discussion questions

1. Why is paying commission to an intermediary a positive outcome?

2. Describe what is meant by the role of the local DMO being an information broker.

3. How could a small group of local tourism businesses work together to improve their access to travel trade intermediaries.

References

Borden, N. (1964). The concept of the marketing mix. *Journal of Advertising Research*, **4**: 2-7.

Pike, S. (2008). *Destination Marketing*. Burlington, MA: Butterworth-Heinemann.

Pike, S. (2016). *Destination Marketing Essentials*. (2nd Ed). Abingdon, Oxon: Routledge.

Rokou, T. (2016). *How can online travel agents help connect you with today's digitally savvy travelers*. 7 December, www.traveldailynews.asia/news/article/63581/how-can-online-travel-agents .

Travelandtourworld.com. (2015). *Travel companies to compare quotes for NT government travel management.* 16 June. http://www.travelandtourworld.com/news/article/travel-companies-compare-quotes-government-travel-management/

14 Tourism Marketing Performance Measurement

Chapter outline

Effective marketing performance measurement is essential for small tourism businesses, which have to compete using relatively small promotional budgets. Promotional spending must be monitored for effectiveness to ensure efficient and best use of resources. Evaluating marketing performance necessitates having measurable objectives, benchmarking of the current performance, and clear performance indicators. While the ultimate marketing performance indicator is sales, there is a range of other quantitative and qualitative markers used to measure the outcomes of promotions, relative to the objectives. Performance measurement can be quite complex, with the greatest challenge being to quantify the direct impact of different promotions on sales. A range of practical options for small tourism businesses to evaluate the effectiveness of different promotional tactics is presented. The chapter then concludes with an introduction to consumer-based brand equity (CBBE), a model for evaluating brand performance over time. CBBE enables the evaluation of past marketing effectiveness, and provides indicators of possible future performance, through the analysis of brand salience, brand image, and brand loyalty. This then informs the next situation analysis, and new objective setting, in the continuous cycle of marketing planning, implementation and evaluation.

Learning aims

To enhance your understanding of:

- The need for clear marketing performance indicators

- Approaches for evaluating the effectiveness of promotions

- Consumer-based brand equity as an indicator of branding performance over time.

Performance measurement
Evaluation of the extent to which an objective has been achieved.

Marketing performance indicators
Measurable markers used to evaluate effectiveness in achieving marketing objectives.

Consumer-based brand equity
A model for measuring the strength of a brand in consumers' minds, over time, which analyses brand salience, brand image and brand loyalty.

Marketing performance indicators

Good management starts with good measurement (Aaker, 1996: 316). Measuring the effectiveness of marketing activities is critical in the management of small tourism businesses. Operating with scarce resources requires careful decision making about budget allocation, and therefore a need to monitor the effectiveness of promotional spend. As performance measurement is the evaluation of the extent to which an objective has been achieved, three questions underpin the process:

1   What is the marketing objective aligned with the promotion?

2   What is the current level of performance, in relation to the marketing objective?

3   What performance indicator(s) will be used to evaluate success?

As mentioned in *4: Tourism Marketing Planning*, performance indicators are measurable markers used to evaluate effectiveness in achieving objectives. The ultimate performance indicator, and the goal of all promotional activity, is level of sales. Sales level indicators are typically the number of paying customers or units sold (e.g. beds, seats), often as a ratio of capacity, and the amount of sales revenue.

Case 14.1: Getting sales in an old fashioned way

Owen Eagles recently retired from his position as Managing Director of ANZCRO (www. anzcro.com.au), Australia's most successful wholesaler of travel packages to New Zealand. While ANZCRO is no longer considered a small tourism business, with over 100 staff, overseas offices in the UK and USA, and annual sales over $75 million, Eagles helped the founder start the business, working from his kitchen table with no staff. This case outlines the effectiveness of what Eagles describes as "getting sales the old fashioned way", which ultimately cemented the success of what was then a start-up small business.

During the 1990s, the travel pattern for Australians visiting New Zealand was shifting from predominantly coach touring holidays towards self-driving rental cars and campervans. ANZCRO aimed to capitalise on this opportunity and become a leading wholesaler of self-drive products for Australian travel agents. A key strategy of the New Zealand NTO at this time was a joint venture marketing fund to stimulate cooperative promotions in overseas markets. The NTO offered to match private sector contributions dollar for dollar, in marketing initiatives that could produce measurable sales of travel to New Zealand. ANZCRO's plan was to target Australia's rural population, an important sector of the Australian market that Eagles argued had been generally ignored by the New Zealand tourism industry. Australia is such a vast country, larger in size than Europe for example, that international tourism marketers concentrated on the city markets. ANZCRO's decision to target rural Australia was based on the following research findings:

- Postcode analysis of Australian arrivals at New Zealand's international airports showed a sizeable proportion were from rural areas.

- Rural farming communities had a strong awareness of New Zealand, through agricultural associations.

- New Zealand's travel industry sales representatives rarely visited travel agents in rural areas.

- Travel agents in rural areas indicated loyalty to travel companies that made an effort to service them.

ANZCRO's promotional idea was to organise an old fashioned sales mission, to talk to rural people face to face. The company renovated an old coach to serve as a mobile showroom, which was also was fitted with a kitchen to prepare breakfasts for travel agents. The travelling road show toured rural towns in four Australian states, in a series of two-week bursts. Group members, who included a small Maori entertainment group, as well as ANCRO's travel product suppliers, travelled long distances, and had to assemble and disassemble displays at each town. To save costs the group stayed in camping grounds. In advance of each stop, ANZCRO contacted the town council for permission to set up shop in the main street, and advised local agents and media what was going to happen. At each stop the team would park the coach in the highest profile main street location by 5am. A breakfast presentation for travel agents was held at 7am. During the rest of the day the team put on Maori cultural entertainment and 'spruiked' New Zealand to passers-by.

A simple method was designed to track the effectiveness of the campaign. In the mobile showroom, ANZCRO provided interested consumers with a personalised travel itinerary and a fully costed quote. A copy of the quote was sent to the consumer's preferred travel agent, who was advised to call to the consumer to follow up. ANZCRO was able to track the number of bookings made from the quotes, and these exceeded expectations. This is an example of a clever but simple promotion, designed to take advantage of several opportunities, and was results oriented with measurable indicators such as sales leads for agents, and actual sales.

Source: Adapted from Pike (2008)

Discussion question

What key marketing principles do you take from this old fashioned promotion, which remain relevant today?

14

Not all promotional activities result in sales, however. The goal of achieving sales, is often broken down into different objectives and performance indicators. For example, in *9: Promoting Tourism Services to Consumers*, the concept of AIDA was discussed as a process of guiding a consumer through the stages of **A**wareness, **I**nterest, **D**esire, and **A**ction. Each of the four stages represents a different marketing objective. Different promotional methods and messages are chosen purposefully for each stage, with different performance indicators used to evaluate effectiveness. Depending on the marketing objectives, performance indicators will either be in the form of objective quantitative numbers, or subjective qualitative comments, and are tracked through the business' data and marketing research. Examples of types of performance indicators that are relevant to small tourism businesses are shown in Table 14.1.

Table 14.1: Examples of key marketing performance indicators

	Quantitative	Qualitative
Tracked through the business' data	Sales volume Sales value Yield Cost per enquiry Visitor numbers Length of stay Repeat visitation levels Occupancy rates Revenue per room Customer satisfaction scores Coupon/special code conversions Numbers of consumer enquiries Number of complaints Website metrics Social media metrics Email signups	Customer feedback comments Digital and social media comments
Tracked through marketing research	Equivalent advertising value (EAV) of media publicity Advertising recall Brand awareness Brand image Brand loyalty	Consumer perceptions Travel trade perceptions Customer satisfaction Media editorial content Digital and social media comments

Even with clear performance indicators, evaluating the success of promotions can be challenging, and subjective to different interpretations. This complexity was acknowledged by tourism industry representatives and academics attending the 2011 Tourism and Travel Research Association conference in Massachusetts, USA. A survey of participants, along with roundtable discussions, was undertaken to prioritise research issues for the next decade. The most important issue identified was *validating marketing programmes and standardising return-on-investment (ROI) performance measures* (Williams et al., 2012). This is a wider marketing issue, rather than just a problem facing the tourism industry. For example, leading advertising agency CEO David Fox highlighted the problem following his role on the jury of the Cannes Lion creative awards in France (Fox, 2017). The awards attracted 42,000 global entries, of which only 160 were for the *Creative Effectiveness* category. That's 0.38% of all entries attempted to demonstrate how much product was sold, or perceptions changed, as a result of their promotional campaign. Similarly, at the Spikes Asia awards, Fox found only 0.44% of entries were for the *effectiveness* category. This highlights what is a global challenge in quantifying the direct impact of different promotions on sales.

Activity 14.1: Who was responsible for attracting the visitors?

Pick any successful major city destination (e.g. Vancouver, Paris, Rio de Janeiro, Budapest etc.) and think about the tens of thousands of visitors who are there today. It would be useful for the tourism businesses to understand who or what was responsible for attracting these visitors to the destination. However, the city's DMO would find it extremely difficult to identify who was responsible . Why is it impossible to quantify the extent to which the DMO's promotional activities were responsible for attracting today's visitors to the city?

Longer term residual value of promotions

It is important to recognise that even when there are clearly quantifiable performance indicators that can be used to measure the short term success of a promotion, there will be long term effects that will be unknown. That is, a promotion can have an impact on a consumer, such as making them aware of the business or creating an interest in a service, but they might not act on their desire until a long time afterwards. A customer today, might be the result of a promotion from months ago, but the business will probably never know this. Thus, there will be a longer term residual value, over and above the short term impacts of a promotion, which is difficult to measure.

Lean marketing: Ask the customers

One of the simplest and efficient means of understanding how customers were attracted to the business is to ask them. Where possible, a simple question asked at the point-of-sale (on site or online) asking the customer how they found out about the business can be insightful about promotional effectiveness.

14

Benchmarking current performance

One of the essential activities in measuring the effectiveness of the marketing plan is to benchmark the current performance of the business related to the marketing objectives. To recap from *4: Tourism Marketing Planning*, marketing planning, implementation and evaluation is a cycle of four stages:

- Where are we now? (Situation analysis)
- Where do we want to go? (Objective setting)
- How do we get there? (Implementation of tactics)
- How will be know we got there? (Performance measurement)

Data gathered during the situation analysis stage provides benchmarks, against which performance can be tracked and compared over time. As an example, when a new brand campaign was launched for an emerging destination in Queensland, Australia in 2003, I undertook marketing research to benchmark existing perceptions in the most important market. The 2003 data provides benchmarks enabling comparative evaluations of the effectiveness of the branding over time. To date I have repeated the brand perceptions study, which analyses brand awareness, brand image, and intent to visit, in 2007, 2012, and 2015 (Pike 2006, 2007, 2009, 2015; Pike & Mason, 2012; Pike et al., 2017). A small business' data can also be benchmarked against local industry averages in some cases. For example, at many destinations, RTOs produce regular updates on average accommodation occupancy levels. This type of data enables accommodation businesses to compare their own performance with the industry average. Other sources of benchmarking data include industry associations such as the Chamber of Commerce, Restaurant Association etc.

Critical point: Marketing is an ongoing cycle

As shown in Figure 4.1 (p. 55) the process of marketing doesn't stop with performance measurement. The evaluation of performance then informs the next situation analysis and new objective setting, and so forth, in what is a continuous cycle of planning and implementation and evaluation.

Evaluating advertising

The topic of evaluating advertising effectiveness has not been widely reported in the tourism literature, in spite of the historical popularity of the medium (Pike, 2016a). This is a major gap in the literature, particularly given the advertising adage *we know half of our advertising is working…we just don't know which half*. It has even been claimed that the link between advertising and sales has never been proven in the wider marketing literature (Schultz & Schultz, 2004). The most practical means of evaluating advertising effectiveness for small tourism businesses are:

- Tracking the number of enquiries within a given time period
- Estimating the cost per enquiry
- Conversion studies
- Surveying the level of advertising recall and purchase intent.

There are two types of conversion study. One approach is to estimate the level of enquiries generated from advertising that were converted to sales. This can be undertaken by surveying a sample of consumers who responded to an advertisement with an enquiry. The other approach is to run an experiment comparing the sales results from advertising in two locations (e.g. nearby suburbs), compared to a *control* location where no advertising is undertaken (see *5: Tourism Marketing Research*). A survey can also be undertaken in the three areas to measure variables such as brand awareness, advertising recall, and intent to purchase/visit.

Outdoor media

In spite of the high profile of outdoor advertising, traditionally it has been very difficult to evaluate effectiveness. Simply counting vehicles or foot traffic passing a billboard, for example, gives no insights into how many people noticed the advertisement, comprehended it, retained it in memory, or acted on it. However new technologies enabling consumers to use their smart phones to engage with electronic outdoor media do provide emerging metrics.

Evaluating public relations and publicity

The most common means of evaluating the effectiveness of publicity initiatives is estimating the equivalent advertising value (EAV). EAV is a measure of what the published media editorial space would cost if purchased as an advertisement. This technique can be applied to all traditional forms of media, such as newspapers, television and radio. Clearly there is value in gaining free media editorial. However, while EAV is easy to measure, and can be an impressive metric to share with stakeholders, there are limitations. For example, EAV does not indicate:

- the content of the editorial
- the extent to which the editorial was positive
- how many of the audience noticed and paid attention to the story
- the extent to which the audience who did pay attention to the editorial represent the target market
- any resultant consumer action as a result of the editorial.

14

While probably beyond the resources of a small tourism business, a more accurate evaluation requires a survey in the target market, to identify (Witt & Moutinho, 1994):

- who has been reached by the publicity
- what was communicated to the target audience
- what has happened as a result.

Evaluating digital and social media

Key performance indicators used in digital and social media measurement, which relate to categories of interaction, content redistribution and influence, include:

- counts
- completions
- page visits
- shares
- tweets
- posts
- time spent
- viewable impressions
- cost per mile (CPM)
- cost per click (CPC)
- click through rate (CTR)

Bear in mind, however, just like EAV for editorial publicity, while these metrics can be easy to measure, and are impressive to share with stakeholders, they aren't necessarily related to sales and so care must be taken in examining which marketing objectives they relate to. These are referred to a *vanity* metrics, because they don't address a specific objective. Increased numbers of followers is an indication the social strategy is working, but doesn't show any financial impact for the business. For example, most social media metrics won't convince the jury at the Cannes Lion creative effectiveness awards (Fox, 2017):

> *Quite simply for us - likes, tweets, shares were all cast aside. Who cares how many likes it got. Donald Trump gets likes and he's not effective. It was quite simply – what was the clear objective you set out to achieve and how did you go against that objective? Did you sell more stuff after the work ran or not? If yes, then by how much and what else could have influenced the positive result?*

As well as understanding which marketing objective a digital or social media performance indicator is aligned with, two further issues should be considered (Hootsuite, 2017:13):

- **Does it help decision making?** The social media metrics should enable the business to make informed decisions. When you look at the metric, does it help you to understand what you need to do next?

- **Does the business have the capacity to measure it effectively?** Without the right social media listening *platform* and the right skill set, tracking effectiveness such as the conversion rate of traffic pushed to the website via social media won't be possible.

Social media listening platforms

At the time of writing, popular social media listening platforms of practical relevance to small tourism businesses include Facebook Analytics, Google Analytics, and YouTube audience reports.

Facebook Analytics

Facebook Analytics enables organisations to undertake real-time social media analyses for their page and to track effectiveness of paid and owned content (https://analytics.facebook.com/).

Google Analytics

Google provides this product as a freemium service for tracking and evaluating website traffic. The free online Google Analytics for Beginners course takes 4-6 hours to complete, and shows how to set up an account, implement tracking code, set up metrics dashboards, and generate reports on basic audience reports and campaign tracking (https://analytics.google.com/analytics/academy/course/6).

YouTube audience reports

YouTube offers various analytics for individual video uploads as well as channels. Reports can be generated on: watch times, audience retention, playback locations, devices used, and audience demographics (see https://support.google.com/youtube/answer/1715160).

Getting help

Small tourism businesses don't have the luxury of doing as the large corporates do in the social space, such as employing specialist staff and setting up a social media listening lab. Not having a clear social strategy, listening platform and analysis skills means any investment of time and resources in running promotions will be largely wasted. Instead, it is highly recommended outsourcing the initial setup of the platform and analysis to a specialist consultancy. Investing in good advice at the outset won't guarantee more business, but it does mean effective evaluation is much more likely, much in the way a business outsources accounting services. Given the pace of digital change, evaluating the return from social media is an iterative process, and so it makes sense for small businesses without the expertise to seek advice from specialist firms that live and breathe in the social space and have access to real time third party research.

14

Lean marketing: Trial a social media marketing consultant

Start with a low risk pilot programme, with a clear objective (e.g. to increase traffic to the website). For example, targeted advertising on Facebook can be trialled inexpensively through a social media marketing firm, who monitor and report impact, and then provide ideas about what to do next. As a guide, in the US, Facebook advertisements by the travel industry cost $7.94 per 1000 impressions (CPM), achieve a click though rate (CTR) of 2.52%, with a cost per click (CPC) of 32 cents per click to your website (https:// fitsmallbusiness.com/how-much-does-facebook-advertising-cost/).

Evaluating sales promotions

Sales promotions are essentially sales incentives, which are used when there is a short term need for a quick increase in sales. Since this is a short term tactic, the immediate impact is relatively easy to monitor, particularly when discount codes must be used by the customer to redeem the offer. Practical performance indicators include:

■ The number of enquiries during the promotion period

■ The number of sales coupons redeemed

■ The cost per redeemed coupon

■ Ratio of total costs relative to total redeemed coupon sales

Evaluating trade and consumer expos

Little has been reported in the tourism literature about evaluating effectiveness of participation in consumer expos and travel trade expos, exchanges, and familiarisation tours (Pike, 2016a). Evaluations of travel trade events are relatively more manageable and quantifiable than for consumer events. The trade can be contacted for feedback and sales pitches for business are easy to track by analysing the levels of sales from different distribution channels and from specific trade intermediaries.

At consumer expos, where crowds are usually larger than trade events, it can be difficult to screen the genuine potential customers from the tyre kickers and brochure collectors. The most realistic means of evaluating effectiveness are:

■ The number of sales leads generated

■ The number of promotional coupons with discount codes redeemed

■ The ratio of total costs relative to total redeemed coupon sales

■ The use of a competition can generate consumer contact details, for follow up contact, and for inclusion in a direct mail database.

Monitoring visitor satisfaction

It is a no brainer to state that increased customer satisfaction leads to better financial performance. Therefore small tourism businesses need to continually monitor customer satisfaction. As discussed in *5: Tourism Marketing Research*, guest satisfaction can be measured on site using a short paper-based questionnaire or electronic tablet, or online via a follow up survey. Also, many businesses monitor unsolicited customer reviews posted online to third party sites such as TripAdvisor. Now, more than ever before, it is important to keep guests satisfied, since any performance below their expectations is potentially just a click of a button away from being shared online as a bad experience. The availability of customers' online reviews about tourism services is enabling increasing research into the complexities of what makes a guest satisfied. See for example a study by Radojevic et al. (2017), which analysed reviews relating to 13,410 hotels in 80 global destinations.

Expectancy-disconfirmation theory holds that satisfaction is achieved when a customer's perceptions of performance exceeds their expectations (Oliver 1977, 1980). A readily available instrument for measuring this theory is SERVQUAL (Parasuraman et al., 1991). SERVQUAL is a ready-made 22 item questionnaire that divides service quality into the five dimensions of tangibles, reliability, responsiveness, assurance, and empathy. In the academic literature there are thousands of published studies that have used the SERVQUAL model of service quality measurement. Small tourism businesses can see how the questionnaire has been used in so many service sectors in the literature, and adapt to suit their local situation. Simply go to Google Scholar and enter SERVQUAL and the type of business of interest (e.g. 'SERVQUAL' and 'hotel').

Identifying sources of customer satisfaction/dissatisfaction

Any survey of customer satisfaction must include those service features that are important to them. Typically, guest satisfaction surveys at hotels ask participants to rate the performance of the hotel, on attributes such as the check-in service, room service, bed comfort etc, without asking how important these are to the guest. Therefore high performance attributes are not so relevant if the guests don't consider them important. There are three main approaches to identifying important determinants of customer satisfaction for any given type of business. First, a search of the literature can be undertaken to see what attributes have been used in studies using SERVQUAL in the context of the business type. Second, by asking guests what is important to them. Third, conducting qualitative interviews or focus groups with consumers, which might include a mix of customers and non-customers. Attributes identified from these approaches can then be tested over time in guest surveys.

14

Industry insight: Crying as a visitor satisfaction indicator

Visitors' eyes welling with tears really is an important, albeit informal and subjective, visitor satisfaction indicator at a historic visitor attraction at Whakatane, in New Zealand's North Island. Built in the 1870s, *Mataatua, the house that came home* is a tribal Maori meeting house that was so impressive the British colonial government dismantled it and shipped to the 1879 Sydney International Exhibition in Australia. By this time the British had already confiscated 90% the local tribe's lands. The meeting house was dismantled again in 1880 and shipped to the Melbourne International Exhibition, before being shipped to London for the South Kensington Colonial Exhibition, and then the 1924 British Empire Exhibition. Sadly, when the building was shipped back to New Zealand in 1925, it was sent to the Otago Museum in the South Island rather than returned to its original owners. *Mataatua* was eventually returned home to Whakatane in 1996, and after 15 years restoration work was opened to visitors in 2011 on the original site it had been removed from 136 years previously. The name *Mataatua* was one of the seven great voyaging *waka* (canoe) in the 1300AD migration of the Maori people to New Zealand. Each of these waka found home in a different part of New Zealand, and the people of the Mataatua formed three tribes in the Whakatane region. The attraction now provides an authentic Maori cultural experience, which through storytelling by the descendants of the original waka, can be a very moving experience, bringing many visitors to tears.

Source: Coventry (2017)

Measuring branding performance

In the past decade the model of consumer-based brand equity (CBBE) has attracted the interest of tourism researchers, as a way to measure branding performance. Underpinned by the idea that "the power of a brand lies in the minds of consumers" (Keller, 2003: 59), CBBE enables evaluation of past marketing effectiveness as well as providing indicators of possible future performance. Developed by Aaker (1991, 1996), CBBE can be used as a long term measure of brand strength over time. For some small tourism businesses CBBE might not be practical, as it is based on conducting marketing research, for which the initial set up of the measurement survey can be time consuming. However, once the survey has been established it becomes more efficient to then use this each year to track how the business brand is performing over time in the target market. CBBE data can also be used by an accountant in estimating brand equity for the business. Brand equity is shown as a financial intangible asset value on the balance sheet, and is used to calculate the overall value of the business, in terms of future earnings potential. While there are now different variations of the model being used by researchers, CBBE essentially has three key dimensions, which address typical marketing objectives (Table 14.2).

Table 14.2: CBBE dimensions relative to marketing objectives

CBBE dimension	Marketing objective
Brand salience	To increase awareness of the brand
Brand image	To increase interest in the brand To educate the market about our offerings
Brand loyalty	To increase word of mouth referrals To increase visitation To increase revisitation

Brand salience

Fundamental to a brand's success is the strength of the brand's presence in the minds of consumers when they are considering a purchase/consumption situation. Since the small number of brands considered during decision making are top of mind, brand salience is more than just being aware a brand exists. Therefore, open ended questions are asked of the survey participant to list which brands/businesses first come to mind when thinking about a purchase situation, rather than simply ask if they are aware of the brand/business. This is an effective means of measuring a typical marketing objective: *To increase awareness of the brand/business.* Two questions can be used in a survey to identify the extent to which the business is top-of-mind for a given purchase situation. The brands elicited from consumers with these questions have a stronger likelihood of being selected for purchase (see the discussion on Decision Set Theory in *3: Tourism Consumer Behaviour*).

■ Of all the {insert business type, e.g. restaurants} available for your next {insert purchase situation, e.g. family dinner}, which one first comes to mind?

■ What other {insert business type} would you probably consider for your next {insert purchase situation}?

Brand image

As discussed in *7: Tourism Branding*, brand image represents the perceptions held of the business. Consumer perceptions play a major role in intangible service purchases and so are as important as a business' tangible features. In particular brand image relates to the extent to which the business is perceived to provide those features (attributes) of a purchase situation that are salient (top of mind) in decision making. Brand image is measured to address typical objectives such as: *To increase interest in the brand,* and *To educate the market about our offerings.* The most popular way of measuring brand image is to use Likert-type scales asking participants to rate the business on a list of attributes that are salient for a purchase situation.

14

- To what extent do you agree **Restaurant X** provides each of the following:

1 Strongly disagree	2	3	4	5	6	7 Strongly agree
Friendly staff	1	2	3	4	5	6	7
Good value for money	1	2	3	4	5	6	7
Good location	1	2	3	4	5	6	7
Great food	1	2	3	4	5	6	7

...etc

Brand loyalty

The link between customer loyalty and improved profitability of hospitality businesses has been demonstrated many times by research in the academic literature (see for example Assaf et al., 2015). Strong levels of behavioural and attitudinal loyalty lead to a higher brand equity value on the balance sheet and therefore a higher valuation of the business. Measuring behavioural loyalty involves monitoring the number of repeat purchases by recording in a database, as discussed in *12: Customer Relationship Management*. However, attitudinal loyalty can also be measured, as an indicator of possible future performance. Measuring brand loyalty addresses typical marketing objectives such as: *To increase word of mouth referrals*, *To increase visitation*, and *To increase revisitation*. Two questions can be asked to measure attitudinal loyalty:

- What is the likelihood of you visiting **Restaurant X** for a meal in the next three months?

Definitely not	Very unlikely	Unlikely	Neither likely nor unlikely	Likely	Very likely	Definitely

- To what extent would you recommend other people visit **Restaurant X** for a meal?

Definitely not	Very unlikely	Unlikely	Neither likely nor unlikely	Likely	Very likely	Definitely

For more detailed discussion of CBBE see Aaker (1996), Keller (2003), and for references to tourism applications and insights into how I have developed questions to measure CBBE, in a way that could be adapted by small tourism businesses see Pike & Ryan (2004); Pike (2007, 2016b, 2017).

Importance-performance analysis (IPA)

A useful tool for displaying SERVQUAL results, and the brand image component of CBBE, is importance-performance analysis (IPA), developed by Martilla and James (1977). IPA requires consumers to rate the importance of a set of attributes using a Likert-type scale, and then to indicate their perceived performance of the business across the same range of attributes. For a restaurant interested in customer satisfaction, examples of *attributes* would include friendly staff, value for money, meal quality etc. The IPA matrix graphical output (see Figure 14.1) is particularly useful in summarising key findings, particularly when shown to those with no research experience. The mean scores for a sample of consumers for each of the attributes are loaded on to a scatter plot. The mean for an attribute's importance is plotted on the vertical axis, while the mean for the business' performance is plotted on the horizontal axis. The two means for each attribute meet up in one of four quadrants in the IPA matrix. Attributes plotted in Quadrant 1 are considered important, but where the business performance needs to improve. The business should concentrate on improving perceptions of these attributes. In Quadrant 2 attributes are important and where the business is performing well. It is these attributes that should be emphasised in promotions, to reinforce already positive perceptions on attributes that are important to consumers. Since attributes in Quadrants 3 and 4 are considered relatively less important to consumers, they warrant a lower priority.

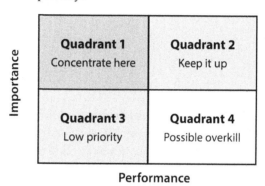

Figure 14.1: Importance-performance analysis matrix

Gap analysis

Gap analysis between SERVQUAL's expectations and performance, and IPA's importance and performance can also provide useful insights. For example, Figure 14.2 shows a gap analysis for 20 attributes related to a tourism brand. The top line shows the means for attribute importance, while the bottom line shows the mean performance. The figure provides a useful visual to indicate the size and importance of the gap between importance and performance for each of the 20 attributes, and in doing so highlight where management's attention is most warranted.

For more detailed explanation of the IPA technique, and references to applications in the tourism industry, see the following publications where I have applied IPA in destination image research (Pike, 2002a, 2002b, 2015, 2017; Pike & Ryan, 2004).

14

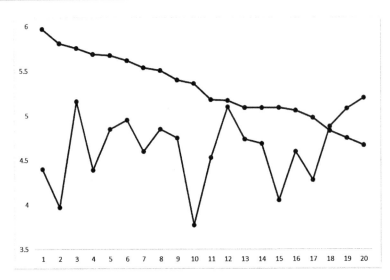

Figure 14.2: Gap analysis

Key points

1: The need for clear marketing performance indicators

Effective marketing performance measurement is essential for small tourism businesses, which have to compete using relatively small promotional budgets. Evaluating marketing performance necessitates having measurable objectives, benchmarking of the current performance, and clear performance indicators. While the ultimate marketing performance indicator is sales, there is a range of other quantitative and qualitative markers used to measure the outcomes of promotions, relative to the objectives.

2: Approaches for evaluating the effectiveness of promotions

Performance measurement can be quite complex, with the greatest challenge being to quantify the direct impact of different promotions on sales. A range of practical options for small tourism businesses to evaluate the effectiveness of different promotional tactics were presented.

3: Consumer-based brand equity as an indicator of branding performance over time

Consumer-based brand equity (CBBE) is a model for evaluating branding performance over time. CBBE enables the evaluation of past marketing effectiveness, and provides indicators of possible future performance, through the analysis of brand salience, brand image, and brand loyalty. This then informs the next situation analysis, and new objective setting, in the continuous cycle of marketing planning, implementation and evaluation.

Discussion questions

1. The chapter shared an old marketing adage: *We know half of our advertising is working…we just don't know which half.* Why is it so challenging to quantify the direct contribution of the entire promotion mix to sales?

2. Why is performance measurement part of a cycle rather than the end point of marketing planning?

3. Why is CBBE considered to provide an indicator of future performance?

References

Aaker, D. A. (1991). *Managing Brand Equity*. New York: Free Press.

Aaker, D. A. (1996). *Building Strong Brands*. New York: Free Press.

Assaf, A.G., Josiassen, A., Knezevic Cvelbar, L. & Woo, L. (2015). The effects of customer voice on hotel performance. *International Journal of Hospitality Management*, **44**: 77-83.

Coventry, N. (2017). Emotional experience, where crying is a KPI. *Inside Tourism*. Issue 1,131, 19 July, p. 9.

Fox, D. (2017). Where's the effing effectiveness entries? AdNews.com. 6 October. Accessed at: www.adnews.com.au/opinion/where-s-the-effing-effectiveness-entries

Hootsuite. (2017). *The Role of Social Media: How to measure and prove the value of your investment*. Hootsuite.com.

Keller, K.L. (2003). *Strategic Brand Management*. Upper Saddle River, NJ: Prentice Hall.

Martilla, J. A. & James, J. C. (1977). Importance-performance analysis. *Journal of Marketing*, **41**: 77-79.

Oliver, R.L. (1977). Effect of expectation and disconfirmation on postexposure product evaluations: An alternative interpretation. *Journal of Applied Psychology*, **62**: 480-86.

Parasuraman, A., Zeithaml, V.A. & Berry, L. (1991). Refinement and reassessment of the SERVQUAL scale. *Journal of Retailing*, **67**(4): 421-450.

Pike, S. (2002a). *Positioning as a Source of Competitive Advantage – Benchmarking Rotorua's Position as a Domestic Short Break Holiday Destination*. PhD Thesis. University of Waikato. November.

Pike, S. (2002b). The use of importance-performance analysis to identify determinant short break destination attributes in New Zealand. *Pacific Tourism Review.(Tourism Review International)*, **6**(2): 23-33.

Pike, S. (2006). Destination decision sets: A longitudinal comparison of stated destination preferences and actual travel. *Journal of Vacation Marketing*, **12**(4): 319-328.

Pike, S. (2007). Consumer-based brand equity for destinations: Practical DMO performance measures. *Journal of Travel & Tourism Marketing*, **22**(1): 51-61.

Pike, S. (2008). *Destination Marketing*. Burlington, MA: Butterworth-Heinemann.

14

Pike, S. (2009). Destination brand positions of a competitive set of near-home destinations. *Tourism Management,* **30**(6): 857-866.

Pike, S. (2015). Destination brand performance measurement over time: Tracking consumer perceptions of a competitive set of destinations over a 10 year period. *Acta Turistica,* **27**(2): 135-164.

Pike, S. (2016a). *Destination Marketing Essentials.* (2nd Ed). Abingdon, Oxon: Routledge.

Pike, S. (2016b). Destination image: identifying baseline perceptions of Brazil, Argentina and Chile in the nascent Australian long haul travel market. *Journal of Destination Marketing & Management,* **5**(2): 164-170.

Pike, S. (2017). Destination image temporality – Tracking perceived strengths and weaknesses over time. *Journal of Hospitality & Tourism Management,* **31**: 126-133.

Pike, S., Gentle, J., Kelly, L. & Beatson, A. (2017). Tracking brand positioning for an emerging destination during the advent of the social media era: 2003 to 2015. *Tourism and Hospitality Research.* (In press).

Pike, S. & Mason, R. (2011). Destination competitiveness through the lens of brand positioning. *Current Issues in Tourism,* **14**(2): 169-182.

Pike, S. & Ryan, C. (2004). Destination positioning analysis through a comparison of cognitive, affective and conative perceptions. *Journal of Travel Research,* **42**(4): 333-342.

Radojevic, T., Stanisic, N. & Stanic, N. (2017). Inside the rating scores: A multilevel analysis of the factors influencing customer satisfaction in the hotel industry. *Cornell Hospitality Quarterly,* **58**(2): 134-164.

Schultz, D. & Schultz, H. (2004). *Brand Babble: Sense and Nonsense about Branding.* Mason, Ohio: South-Western.

Williams, P.W., Stewart, K. & Larsen, D. (2012). Toward an agenda of high-priority tourism research. *Journal of Travel Research,* **51**(1): 3-11.

Witt, S.F. & Moutinho, L. (1994). *Tourism Marketing and Management Handbook.* (2nd ed). London: Prentice Hall.

Index